FOREIGN POLICY
and
Maritime Security of India

FOREIGN POLICY
and
Maritime Security of India

Edited by

K.S. Pavithran
Professor of Political Science and Head,
K.M. Centre for West Asian Studies and Indian Ocean Studies,
University of Calicut, Kerala

New Century Publications
New Delhi, India

NEW CENTURY PUBLICATIONS
4800/24, Bharat Ram Road,
Ansari Road, Daryaganj,
New Delhi – 110 002 (India)

Tel.: 011-2324 7798, 4358 7398, 6539 6605
Fax: 011-4101 7798
E-mail: indiatax@vsnl.com • info@newcenturypublications.com
www.newcenturypublications.com

Editorial office:
LG–7, Aakarshan Bhawan,
4754-57/23, Ansari Road, Daryaganj,
New Delhi – 110 002

Tel.: 011-4356 0919

First Published: **July 2013**

ISBN: **978-81-7708-351-4**

Published by New Century Publications and printed at Salasar Imaging Systems, New Delhi.

Designs: Patch Creative Unit, New Delhi.

PRINTED IN INDIA

About the Book

Since Independence in 1947, foreign policy experts and maritime strategists have been assessing the nature of threat to India's maritime security. After the 26/11 sea-borne terrorist attack on Mumbai, the maritime threat perception of policy makers, especially at strategic and foreign policy level, has undergone a fundamental change.

With a coastline of over 7,500 kilometres, India is naturally a maritime nation. The maritime dimension is vital for coastal security, energy security, geo-strategic and geo-political developments, and trade with other countries.

This book contains 13 research papers which provide in-depth analysis of various dimensions of India's foreign policy and maritime security in a broad-based multi-disciplinary perspective. Authored by experts in the field, the papers are sure to interest scholars and students involved in the study/research of these vital areas of national importance.

About the Editor

Dr. K.S. Pavithran is presently Professor of Political Science and Head, K.M. Centre for West Asian Studies and Indian Ocean Studies, University of Calicut, Kerala. Specialising in India's foreign policy, he has contributed numerous articles to reputed journals and edited volumes. He is the General Editor of ISDA Journal *Studies in Development and Administration*, Thiruvananthapuram. He is also on the editorial board of *Puthuvazhy*, a bi-annual publication of the Pratheeksha Trust.

Dr. Pavithran is also a member of the Advisory Committee of C. Achutha Menon Centre for Study and Research, Thrissur and advisory committee member of Maulana Abul Kalam Azad Chair, University of Calicut. He was a member of Kerala State Higher Education Council from 2008 to 2012.

Contents

About the Book .... *v*
About the Editor .... *vi*
Contributors .... *ix-x*
Preface .... *xi-xiii*

1. India's Redefined Maritime Interests: Navy as the Foreign Policy Instrument **1-14**
P.V. Rao

2. India's Maritime Security and Foreign Policy **15-40**
G. Ram Reddy

3. Coastal Security of India **41-66**
K.R. Singh

4. India, US and the Indian Ocean: The Strategic Interest and Convergence **67-88**
S.Y. Surendra Kumar

5. India's Maritime Interests and the Growing Influence of China in the Indian Ocean **89-104**
Chandrakant Yatanoor

6. Maritime Dimensions of Energy Security: China and South China Sea **105-126**
C. Vinodan

7. Growing Convergence between India, Australia and the United States in the Asia-Pacific **127-151**
Josukutty C.A.

8. India's Two Decades of Naval Engagement with ASEAN — 152-175
S. Utham Kumar Jamadhagni

9. Security Dimensions of Andaman and Nicobar Islands — 176-186
Gopalji Malviya and K. Udhaya Kumar

10. India's Energy Security Policy: A Review — 187-206
Dharitri Parija and Mohanan B. Pillai

11. Euro-Asian Maritime, Trade and Security Issues and the West Asian/Gulf Factor — 207-254
A.K. Pasha

12. Indo-US Nuclear Deal: Implications for India's Foreign Policy and National Security — 255-268
K.S. Pavithran

13. India's Foreign Policy: Need for Democratization — 269-308
Biju B.L.

Index — 309-318

Contributors

A.K. Pasha Professor and Director, Gulf Studies Programme, Centre for West Asian and African Studies, School of International Studies, Jawaharlal Nehru University (JNU), New Delhi.

Biju B.L. Assistant Professor, Department of Political Science, Hyderabad (Central) University, Hyderabad.

Chandrakant Yatanoor Professor and Head, Department of Political Science, Gulbarga University, Karnataka.

C. Vinodan Assistant Professor and Chair, Centre for Strategic and Security Studies, School of International Relations and Politics, Mahatma Gandhi University, Kerala.

Dharitri Parija Research Scholar, Department of Politics and International Studies, Pondicherry (Central) University, Puducherry.

Gopalji Malviya Professor and Head, Department of Defence and Strategic Studies, University of Madras, Chennai.

G. Ram Reddy Professor, Department of Political Science, Osmania University, Hyderabad.

Josukutty C.A. Assistant Professor, Department of Political Science, University of Kerala, Trivandrum.

K.R. Singh Formerly Director of National Security Programme, Senior Professor at the Centre for West Asian and African Studies, School of International Studies, Jawaharlal Nehru University (JNU), New Delhi.

K.S. Pavithran Professor of Political Science and Head, K.M. Centre for West Asian Studies and Indian Ocean Studies, University of Calicut, Kerala.

K. Udhaya Kumar Research Scholar, Department of Defence and Strategic Studies, University of Madras, Chennai.

Mohanan B. Pillai Professor and Director, UNESCO, Madanjeet Singh Institute of South Asia Regional Cooperation, Pondicherry (Central) University, Puducherry.

P.V. Rao Formerly Professor and Director, Centre for Indian Ocean Studies, Osmania University and Presently Visiting Professor, NALSAR Law University, Hyderabad.

S. Utham Kumar Jamadhagni Senior Lecturer, Department of Defence and Strategic Studies, University of Madras, Chennai.

S.Y. Surendra Kumar Assistant Professor, Department of Political Science, Bangalore University, Karnataka.

Preface

The contemporary theoretical debate over the security studies in international politics and the development of the sub-field of maritime security can be traced to at least as far back as the last quarter of the 20th century. The end of Cold War hastened the trend towards refashioning the agenda of international security analysis towards new and expanding emphasis upon terrorism at the regional and global levels. The post-Cold War era has witnessed a shift from strategic to security studies, having both transnational and international ramifications. Consequently, security studies are promoted as new sub-field within the study of international relations. This shift has now reversed the priorities of security studies away from the earlier central strategic questions to be emerging security predicament of the Third world. The regional character of global security has opened up a new agenda of substantive security issues based on each region's unique features.

The term *security* has become ubiquitous for contemporary policy making. This has been a growing trend beginning with the early 1980s, a period of heightened Cold War tensions. To the old idea of *collective security* were added concepts of comprehensive and co-operative security. Although these various concepts have often been applied to the maritime sphere, somctimes explicitly and at others only implied, there have been few extended attempts to explore the idea of maritime security itself. This is important, as maritime security increasingly is a commonly used term in policy circles, yet it seems clear that those who use the term often are doing so from different scripts. The questions posed are: What exactly is maritime security? What are the different ways in which to conceive of maritime security? What are the maritime dimensions of India's foreign policy?

It is pertinent to note that any policy that has an outward orientation, as does foreign policy, the overlap with security, land and maritime frontier dimensions, is difficult to ignore. For Peninsular India, the lure of the sea around it has moulded and set the course of the history of the people who inhabit it. That was why Jawaharlal Nehru succinctly remarked that "we cannot afford to be weak at sea. History has shown that whoever controls the Indian Ocean has, in the first instance, India's re-borne trade at her mercy and in the second, India's very independence itself."

India is naturally a maritime nation—a coast line of over 7,500 kilometres. The maritime dimension is vital for energy security. The 26/11 sea-borne terrorist attack on Mumbai focused the need for strengthening maritime and coastal security against threats from sea. It follows that foreign policy has to focus on these critical aspects for national development and security. As a mature responsible nation, one of our foreign policy interests is to evolve a regional architecture based on the twin principles of shared security and shared prosperity.

Since India's Independence in 1947, maritime strategists and foreign policy makers have been trying to assess the nature of threat to India's maritime security. Keeping in view the Mumbai terrorist attacks, the maritime threat perception of policy makers, especially at strategic and foreign policy level has also undergone fundamental changes. This is so because most theorizing about security studies was not focused on maritime security.

The essays in this volume give a variety of perspectives on maritime security and foreign policy of India. The inter-disciplinary perspective sheds light on the security studies and foreign policy perspective of India in the 21st century. Thus, the book offers a fascinating area of academic discourse which needs to be examined for a clear understanding of the elements of maritime security.

Acknowledgements

I wish to express my gratitude to all the contributors to this volume for their scholarly contributions. I specially thank Professor K.R. Singh, Professor P.V. Rao and Professor A.K. Pasha for their co-operation and academic support. Thanks are also due to Dr. J. Prabhash, University of Kerala and Dr. Mohanan B. Pillai of Pondicherry University for their moral support for this endeavour. Sincere gratitude is expressed to Professor C. Jayan, Professor Asokan Mundon, Dr. P. Sivadasan, Sri. Sunilkumar. K and Sri. Saharudheen.

The support received from Sri. Balakrishnan. M, Smt. Bindu. K, and Sri. Sreejith. K, is also appreciated. Finally I would like to express my gratitude to New Century Publications, New Delhi for bringing out this book in its present form.

June 2013 **K.S. Pavithran**
Calicut

1

India's Redefined Maritime Interests: Navy as the Foreign Policy Instrument

P.V. Rao

India's 'extended neighbourhood', a post-Cold War strategic concept, devised the comprehensive framework of engaging the regions to her east and west. Regions which hitherto figured least in the country's external priorities such as Central Asia, Southeast and East Asia had assumed greater and even urgent priority in the larger canvass of India's foreign policy. Extended neighbourhood is not just an operational concept of enlarged involvement of India in new areas, but this concept had rather superseded the foreign policy values of the Nehruvian and post-Nehruvian era. A new set of values, ambitions, power equations, regions and countries became integral to the extended neighbourhood. It carved out a vision of power play and projection for the 21st century India in her external relations.

To accommodate foreign policy to the above objectives, India is upgrading her military capabilities and projecting power in the Indian Ocean Region (IOR) and even beyond. She is adopting a dual strategy which aims at bolstering the hard military power and at the same time cultivating close political and economic synergies with the Asian countries. A number of bilateral and multilateral agreements are signed with the Asian countries so much so today there is hardly an Asian regional group in which India is not represented. The Indian Navy (IN) has come to be regarded as an important instrument of enforcing India's interests and influence in the extended neighbourhood. It is a highly visible and vibrant military force around the Indian Ocean, a role hitherto was denied to her given the limited involvement of the country in regional affairs. In fact, Indian Navy today is the symbol of India's power and prestige abroad, the sentinel of her maritime security interests and emissary of goodwill missions. To play such combined roles the navy's military capabilities are heavily augmented.

What follows is an examination of the different roles assigned to the Indian Navy and the strategies adopted by it in pursuit of India's foreign and security objectives mentioned above in the Indian Ocean Region. What needs to be noted is that maritime security is not understood in the conventional military sense alone but as a multidimensional strategy aimed at ensuring the country's peacetime economic, energy, trade and safety of sea lines of communications (SLOCs).

India's Maritime Objectives

India's geographical location astride the east-west highway in the Indian Ocean–maritime Asia-Pacific linkage with the Europe-Atlantic–imposes greater security burdens on her. Large number of military, cargo and oil vessels criss-cross the sea lanes of the Indian Ocean and its choke points. Several regional and extra-regional powers who depend on oil and other resources of the Indian Ocean Region maintain regular military presence in this third largest ocean of the world. Hence India has reason to be concerned with such military developments and regional conflicts like the Iraq and Afghan wars on her security.

In consonance with India's newly defined and expanding interests in the IOR, the Ministry of Defence (MOD), through successive doctrines, chartered the maritime dimensions of India's security and the necessary strategies for the purpose. Three major policy documents which elaborately defined and updated the role, rationale, strategies and employment of maritime power by the Indian Navy are: *Indian Maritime Doctrine* (2004); *Freedom to Use the Seas: India's Maritime Military Strategy* (2007); *Indian Maritime Doctrine (2009).*

These public documents draw the vision and policy-framework for IN's growth, maritime political and diplomatic role, strategic plans and the challenges which the naval forces should be prepared to encounter. Explaining the IN's role, Admiral Suresh Mehta, former chief of the IN would say:

"The Indian Navy is the primary maritime means by which the state ensures the use of sea for its own purposes, while at the same time ensuring that others do not use it in a manner prejudicial to its interests. The Indian Navy by virtue of its capability, strategic presence and robust presence in the Indian Ocean Region (IOR), can be the catalyst for peace, tranquillity and stability in the IOR. It can be used to engage other maritime nations and extend our hand of friendship and co-operation. Also it can act as a strong deterrent to prevent conflict, or to respond, should it become inevitable." (Freedom to Use Seas, 2007: iv).

What is obvious from the above statement is that the IN is envisaged to undertake several responsibilities in defence of the country's overall maritime objectives. Primarily, it has to act as the instrument of India's foreign policy interests overseas, deter hostile countries and forces threatening the country's security by projecting its naval military power, play a pro-active role in ensuring the freedom of navigation or what the naval people would like to call good order at sea. Further, the IN is mandated to promote friendly relations with other littoral powers of the Indian Ocean and develop maritime confidence building. 'Bridging bridges across the seas' has become a familiar catchphrase in the IN's recent lexicon. This kind of functional approach is a departure from the conventional responsibilities which meant that the IN like any other navy is concerned with ensuring the country's maritime security from military threat or attack from an adversary.

Considering the fact that the IOR is encountering today a complex set of issues such as maritime terrorism, piracy, drug-trafficking, arms trade, poaching and illegal migration, naval functions of a littoral state like India have too grown multifariously. No single coastal and its naval forces can effectively counter these non-conventional threats to their maritime order and peace. In other words, contemporary maritime security is hinged on friendly cooperation and multilateral strategies to meet the new challenges from the violent and unlawful agents mentioned above.

Recognising such combat and non-combat security scenarios, the IN's missions of activity are broadly enumerated as follows. *Military missions* which include conventional and strategic nuclear deterrence against regional states; deter extra-regional powers against India's security interests; exercise sea control in Arabian Sea and Bay of Bengal as well as at the entry/exit points of the IOR; provide security to country's coastlines and offshore assets. *Diplomatic missions*: using navy as an effective instrument of India's foreign policy; develop maritime partnerships to gain confidence of IOR littorals; contribute to UN peacekeeping forces. *Constabulary* such as regular surveillance of the country's maritime zones and extended neighbourhood; and lastly, *Benign missions: which* include providing humanitarian aid, disaster relief and hydrographic services to littoral states. (Indian Maritime Doctrine 2004: 100-103)

In pursuit of the above objectives, Indian Navy today is gas drawn strategies in advancing the country's political objectives, sea power projection and naval partnerships. The geo-political rationale for employing the national naval forces is explained in terms of "the shift in global maritime focus from the Atlantic-Pacific combine to the Pacific-Indian Ocean region," and, geo-economically too the centre of gravity "is shifting from the North America-Western Europe axis to the North America-Asia Pacific rim, with Japan, China and the Asian Tigers looming large in global economic deliberations."

Maritime Non-conventional Threats

India is, like any other maritime power, is very concerned about the growing maritime threats to freedom of seas from non-state actors in the IOR. Since all the major sea-based threats are located in the Indian Ocean—terrorism, piracy, WMD proliferation, etc.—the region has become the obvious foci of naval military deployments by the concerned states, in particular by the extra-regional powers, to ensure the safety of SLOCs. Such maritime presence in the Indian Ocean has far surpassed the deployment of foreign naval forces during the cold war years. The series of threats to peace beginning with the first gulf war, their growth in frequency and violence ever since and western strategic responses to counter these threats, had drawn in the maritime combat forces of highest sophistication into the region which had given "extra regional navies an unparalleled situational awareness and an ability to influence operations in the IOR." (*Freedom to Use the Seas*, 2007: 41) India therefore has strong reason to be worried about interests.

Unlike in the past decades, IN has declared that the county's "maritime vision for the 21st century must look at the arc from the Persian gulf to the straits of Malacca as a legitimate area of interest." (Indian Maritime Doctrine, 2004) Accordingly, IN has brought under its strategic penumbra, the IOR west encompassing the Persian Gulf, Arabian Sea, Red Sea; eastern and southern African rim; central Indian Ocean basin including its islands and the Southern Ocean skirting the Antarctica; to the east areas beyond the Malacca straits stretching up to the Philippines and South China Sea. Plainly speaking, IN's pervasive presence across the Indian Ocean Region symbolizes India's new strategic vision and ambition. The pronouncement of extended strategic interests in Asia is meaningless unless supported by a matching and mobile instrument of state power.

Hence, the IN today is receiving unprecedented budgetary support to meet its force modernization programmes. IN's augmented military strength includes 140 war ships, 1 aircraft carrier, and 16 submarines. The proposed Ship Building Programme plans 185 ships for IN by 2017. Another aircraft carrier, in addition to the present *Vikrant* bought from Russia called *Adm. Gorshkov*, renamed as *Vikramaditya*, is being refitted to suit Indian requirements and is expected to enter the IN's formidable fleet soon. The navy's military doctrines have been substantially revised to bolster its sea power and reach in the Indian Ocean.

The IN was criticized during eighties for being one of the "few major navies which first acquire hardware and then thinks about how to use it." It meant that the country's naval force lacked a doctrine and strategy. (Prakash, From the Crow's Nest: 97)—hence, the current effort to provide it with a clear military vision and strategy. IN has redefined conventional and nuclear deterrence as the primary strategies of denial and punishment, capable of convincing a potential enemy of unbearable costs if a military or nuclear attack is contemplated against India.

The Indian Nuclear Doctrine, launched following the 1998 nuclear tests, is a composite doctrine designed to provide nuclear deterrent capacity to the country's three defence forces, Army, Air force and Navy. The "primary military objective for the IN is to deter any military adventurism against the country, including intervention in India's affairs and subversive strategies against our national interests...The ways and means of deterrence by the IN would include developing a sea-based second-strike capability." (Indian Military Doctrine, 2009: 92) The imperative need to equip the IN with a credible deterrent military capability to counter the other naval powers and maintain naval power balance in the Asia-Pacific is the recurring theme in the Indian naval military discourse today. Of course the Maritime Doctrine as spelt out in 2004 also did not fail to invite a few dissenting reflections like the one from a formal admiral who thinks that the Doctrine "would have made better sense if its formulation had flowed from an overarching national or defence perspectives," and moreover, "it does not specify how specific operations will be conducted but rather, what operational activities will be necessary and must be catered for." (Premvir Das: 87)

In augmenting its military capabilities, IN has been procuring naval combat vessels and equipment from conventional sources like Russia which had been the largest supplier during cold war years and continues to be so, the United States whose strategic partnership with India mandates as the second largest provider of naval armoury, and other countries including France and United Kingdom. While outsourcing its requirements from foreign countries, IN has also greatly increased the domestic base to produce military capabilities to attain self-reliance so much so that it is "one of the largest and most significant indigenous production capabilities in the developing world." Thus the IN's major modernisation and upgradation programmes which have enormously increased its fire and fleet strength have ranked it as the fifth largest navy in the world and, "barring a war against a major power, India appears capable of securing its national interests and responding to its traditional threats through its blue water strategy." (Hiranandani)

Naval Diplomacy

In consonance with India's new range of strategic ambitions, country's naval forces are actively engaged in peacetime diplomacy. It involves projecting India's sea power by showing her flag around the IOR, gaining littoral friendship and confidence through naval goodwill missions, offering disaster relief and sharing the country's naval expertise with the other coastal states. Naval diplomacy, simply speaking, is "concerned with the management of foreign policy short of the actual employment of forces." (Booth: 1979:142) Naval diplomacy is a combined display of the country's hard and soft power endowments overseas in national interest. While hard power accounts for the navy's military capabilities including its deterrent capacity, nuclear power, warship mobility, submarine arm and naval military exercises, soft power is the use and sharing of naval skills and technologies with willing littorals to build friendly bridges.

Major Asian powers today are actively encouraging their soft power skills to gain regional confidence and friendship. China has excelled in invoking this skill in the Asia-Pacific and Africa by offering soft loans, credit lines, trade concessions, technical know-how and many such. Though India has realised the importance of soft power in her diplomacy, she is lagging much despite sufficient potentialities in this regard. In maritime parlour, soft power means offering military training to the naval personnel of other maritime powers, giving naval aid, sharing naval military technologies, building maritime infrastructure, helping in hydrographic surveys, rescue and relief assistance to countries and ships in distress, etc. Indian Navy today is offering all these peacetime services to the IOR littorals. Geoffery Till has captured rightly the IN's current strategy of building synergies with other navies in the following language: "(This) maritime consensus-building can be developed by ship visits, fleet reviews, joint procurement and combined exercises. India is well along this track in this 'age of engagement' and its 'look east policy'... has conducted a series of important exercises with locals and outsiders and has also participated in patrols in the waters off Southeast Asia." (Geoffery Till, p. 208)

IN has been undertaking peacetime goodwill missions to the Southeast Asian countries immediately after the end of the cold war. Primarily the IN carried the strategic message of engaging itself in the void left by the withdrawing Soviet Union, and also counter the growing Chinese involvement in the region. In fact, India's Look East policy which aimed at closely engaging the country strategically and economically with the dynamic Asia-Pacific region chose the navy as its instrument. Beginning with early nineties, defence and naval cooperation agreements were signed with Malaysia, Thailand, Singapore, Vietnam and others in the region. Cold War suspicions by South-eastern neighbours about an 'expansionist Indian navy' were relaxed and a demonstrated willingness to accord the IN a positive role in the region was displayed by them. A well-informed Southeast Asian scholar GVC Naidu would claim that the IN was responsible for opening the initial channels of communication with the Southeast Asian countries and that its' CBMs formed the basis of India's Look East policy. (Naidu, 2007: p. 7)

The IN had also initiated the multinational naval exercises, beginning with the *Milan* in 1995. This biennial naval conclave in the Andaman and Nicobar islands (AN) was a true naval initiative, without a precedent. *Milan* is not just an Indian initiative, but it is the first Indian Ocean attempt to assemble the regional navies on a common platform. For India it is a notable diplomatic success in the sense that the participating countries, increasing in their number, had displayed confidence in Indian regional maritime role and leadership. India's strategic objective of expanding her influence into the Asia-Pacific cherished by the Look East policy has borne results. And the Indian Navy can rightfully take the credit for this positive diplomatic outcome. The *Milan* tradition was extended to gather a wider fora of international naval forces. Thus the International Fleet Review (IFR) hosted by the IN in 2001, off the Bombay coast included almost all the navies of the IOR.

A maritime power possessing strong naval and oceanic capabilities can employ them for diplomatic purposes by lending relevant maritime services to other littorals. IN has been lending maritime services such as conducting hydrographic surveys to Indonesia and Oman; disaster relief to the 2004 tsunami victims of Sri Lanka, Indonesia and Maldives; and naval training programmes to personnel from Singapore, Maldives, and some African countries. IN has also deployed its forces to offer security to the US high value cargo in the Malacca Straits and offered security to the OUA summit in Mozambique in 2004. These peacetime services are the currency of gaining influence and prestige overseas and the IN is exploiting its soft power tactics to the till. Justifying the diplomatic motives behind IN's immediate response to the tsunami-affected countries, unnamed Indian naval officials were heard saying that "we have proved the navy can be used as a diplomatic instrument in support of our political and geo-strategic objectives." (Scott, 2006:15)

The China Factor

While maritime strategy is to provide a broader framework of a country's naval engagement in a given maritime region and environment, naval strategies are the more specific plans of defining the navy's activities, its operational doctrines, nature of building relationships with foreign navies to advance the country's overall foreign policy interests. Naval strategies lay down patterns of relationships the country's naval forces should build with others to serve the specified strategic interests. As mentioned above the IN since the nineties has been actively building strategic relations with several Asian maritime powers both in the east and west. Such partnerships have extended into the eastern hemisphere with countries like Japan and South Korea. But the most significant of the IN's strategic relationship is with the United States Navy (USN) which is part of the broader Indo-US cooperation in Asia. In fact, Indo-US maritime strategic partnership has added a newer dimension to the Asian security framework and both have been working together to draw more Asian powers like Australia, Japan, Singapore and Vietnam to give a multilateral basis to such framework.

China is at the core of the Indo-US naval partnership as both share the common perception that rising China and her increasing presence in the Indian Ocean is a challenge to the Indian and American interests in the region. The Chinese People's Liberation Army-Navy (PLAN) has been actively moving around the Indian Ocean littoral countries ranging from Southeast Asia to the gulf region and Africa in west Indian Ocean. A series of naval facilities, though not bases like the USN, have been obtained by the PLAN from some of the

IOR countries. In other words China is allegedly building a 'string of pearls,' a strategic euphemism for the Chinese drive to encircle India through closer political and military ties with India's neighbours.

Such Chinese strategic behaviour of active involvement in the IOR is offered as the chief justification for closer Indo-US strategic comraderi to counter the rising Asian giant. The need to balance Chinese power is the major narrative in the Indian strategic discourse. Working with the US is seen as a compelling reason which serves the interests of both in any case. *The US Maritime Strategy*, 2007 postures combined role for the IN and USN not only in the Indian Ocean but western Pacific too. (USN, 2007) Both navies have been regularly conducting war games nicknamed *Malabar exercises* around the Indian peninsula in the Arabian Sea and Bay of Bengal.

Conclusion

The Indian Navy has emerged as an important interlocutor of India's foreign policy objectives in the Indian Ocean. It has succeeded in sending clear message to the regional and extra-regional powers that the country should no more be seen as reactive to the regional geo-political developments as was its practice during Cold War years, but that it had chartered a definite political agenda of playing active role in Asia's security. India's Look East policy unveiled almost soon after the advent of the post-Soviet era testifies such doctrinaire approach to India's blueprint of active engagement with the Asia-Pacific region. As the maritime representative of India's enlarged role in Asia the IN to a larger extent had so far fulfilled satisfactorily the country's expectations out of its role. "Its confident, competent and visible maritime presence has served to build stronger relations and demonstrate an 'abundance of empathy' to the many nations which it has come into contact. Its emphasis on international cooperation has significantly contributed to its overall political objectives..." (Rahn, 2006: 39)

Among the IN's major diplomatic achievements since the waning years of the previous century are its commendable job in shedding the fears of Southeast Asian countries of Indian 'naval expansionism,' entertained by them in Cold War years. Countries like Malaysia, Indonesia and even far off Pacific power Australia shared the apprehension about a rising Indian Navy capable of threatening the Asian regional security order. Fortunately, such misperception dissipated out of the Asian mind not long after the cold war break.

Thus as early as in the first years of nineties Malaysian Prime Minister Mahathir could confidently assert that the region had no reason to be worried about the Indian Navy. Further, gradually the regional powers represented by the ASEAN and its security forum ARF (ASEAN Regional Forum) which included the Pacific powers also preferred the IN's regional presence as they saw it as a balancing force against the Chinese in the South China Sea. Hence, all these powers along with the Australian, Japanese and even the South Korean maritime forces are regularly interacting with the Indian naval forces. In other words, in the contemporary Asia-Pacific regional security environment IN is well regarded as a consensual maritime force worth its role and presence.

India's maritime strategy in this period had also departed from the cold war tradition. That bygone era marked by super power competition in the Indian Ocean, India's foreign policy emphasised opposition to extra-regional presence and building naval bases in the region as the US did at Diego Garcia. The country's naval forces, operating in a limited geo-political framework, were not involved in working with any other regional or extra-regional navy.

Of course such a non-participatory naval policy did not prevent the IN involving on lease basis the Russian nuclear-powered submarine *Charlie* though returned later to Moscow. Nor the IN exercised with as many foreign naval forces as it is involved today as part of a broader strategy. Implicitly, through her public pronouncements against extra-regional involvement in Indian Ocean affairs, India preferred the region to be left to her own naval influence and management. Hence, one could notice the Indian naval involvement in regional crises such as Maldives, Sri Lanka and Seychelles.

IN's initiatives in bringing the Indian Ocean navies on a common platform under its 'foreign cooperation' banner are well received. The IN sponsored *Milan* regional naval exercises in the Bay of Bengal, International Fleet Reviews off the Mumbai and Vishakapatnam coasts and the IONS—all these multilateral exercises, along with the many bilateral exercises, are symbolic of cooperative diplomacy, a strategy gaining wider regional attraction for its peace dividend. No other regional maritime power in the Indian Ocean in the past had managed to assemble regional naval leaders and their forces into a common assembly as the IN did. Such naval diplomatic initiatives have certainly served to convey the message that the IN is a major as well as a responsible naval force in the region.

References

Admiral Arun Prakash, *From the Crow's Nest*, Lancers, New Delhi, 2007.

Admiral Premvir Das, "India's Maritime Doctrine: The Good News and the Bad News," *Indian Ocean Survey*, Vol. 2, No. 1, 2006.

C. Raja Mohan, *Crossing the Rubicon-The Shaping of India's New Foreign Policy*, Viking, New Delhi, 2003.

Daniel Rahn, *Unlocking Indian Maritime Strategy*, Naval Postgraduate College, California, 2006.

David Scott, "Indian 'footprints' in the Indian Ocean: Power Projection for the 21st Century," *Indian Ocean Survey*, Vol. 2, No. 2, July-December 2006.

Freedom to Use the Seas: India's Maritime Military Strategy, Integrated Headquarters, Ministry of Defence (Navy), New Delhi, 2007.

G.V.C. Naidu, "India and Southeast Asia," *World Focus*, Vol. 25, No. 9, September 2007.

Indian Maritime Doctrine (2004), Integrated Headquarters, Ministry of Defence (Navy), New Delhi.

Indian Maritime Doctrine (2009), Integrated Headquarters, Ministry of Defence (Navy), New Delhi.

"International Maritime Trends and Indian Ocean in 21st Century," *Journal of Indian Ocean Studies*, August 2001.

Ken Booth, *Navies and Foreign Policy,* Holmes and MEIER Publishers, New York, 1979.

P.V. Rao, "India's Naval Diplomacy", *CNW Annual Journal*, College of Naval Warfare, Mumbai, 2008.

Vice Admiral G.M. Hiranandani, *Transition to Eminence, the Indian Navy 1976-90*, Lancers, 2004.

2

India's Maritime Security and Foreign Policy

G. Ram Reddy

Maritime security is a subset of national security and therefore nations would view it in direct correlation to their national interests. Therefore, the definition could vary from nation to nation and a generic definition would be more appropriate. Maritime Security is a term that encompasses the aspects and issues arising from the oceans surrounding the nation that impinge on its national interests.

The division of conventional and non-conventional threats again varies from nation to nation. Conventional threats traditionally would be the military threats faced by a nation from another nation that impinge on its sovereign integrity, trade, maritime area under its jurisdiction as per international law in which the various laws, both international and national, apply.

Non-conventional threats would cover a host of other aspects. The major ones being terrorism, piracy, natural disasters, drug trafficking, smuggling, illegal immigrants, changes in the climate and ecology to name a few. India's maritime policies will be one of the major determinants of success or failure in our attempt to transform India into a modern, plural, open, advanced country that is both secure and prosperous.

History shows that India was most prosperous and secure when she was most connected to the world, and that this connection was mainly by sea. It is well known that we are an ancient sea-faring nation, as the four thousand year old port at Lothal and other Indus Valley finds show. What is less well documented or taught is the extent to which the sea was the major means of our links with the world to the west and the east. While Buddhism's spread overland in the second half of the first millennium is known, the earliest travel and trade with China was by the sea route, and this was how Buddhism first came to China and East Asia. Satavahana, Chola, Pallava, and Pandyan prosperity and security were based on a maritime strategy that included South East Asia.

Jawaharlal Nehru's conclusion from our history was that: "We cannot afford to be weak at sea. History has shown that whoever controls the Indian Ocean has, in the first instance, India's sea-borne trade at her mercy and, in the second, India's very independence itself."

India's perception of maritime security stems from the "Freedom to use the Seas". This is an important aspect that is the focus of any maritime nation's outlook. There are some issues that require to be viewed and assessed when correlating maritime security to the Indian Ocean Region as they form the basis of India's perception.

1. The IOR is a region of diverse economies and systems of governance. One third of the world's populace resides here in a quarter of the world's land mass. It consists of 56 littoral and land bound nations.
2. It accounts for 65 percent of strategic raw material reserves, 31 percent gas and more than half of the world's oil exports.
3. The region is the largest producer of rubber, tea, spices, and jute. Some other important minerals found are manganese, cobalt, tungsten, coal and iron ore.
4. This region has seen the maximum number of conflicts post the Cold War and is considered the hub of global terrorism.
5. Piracy, gun running, human and drug trafficking are issues that are also affecting the maritime security environment.
6. Around 70 percent of the worlds natural disasters occur in the IOR.

7. The region has the presence of extra regional powers.

Therefore, the perception of India vis-à-vis the IOR is based on ensuring a safe and stable maritime environment that will firstly ensure security of India's national integrity and sovereignty; secondly, protection of our national interests; thirdly, ensure safe passage of maritime trade both national and international; fourthly, ensure cooperation amongst nations to combat and reduce the impact of non-traditional threats like terrorism, piracy and natural disasters.

These aspects require certain mechanisms that exist in the form of engagement with India's maritime neighbours. India also engages the extra regional maritime players who have a stake in the IOR. This has led to bilateral and multilateral understandings at the diplomatic, economic and military levels.

The Imperatives

What I would like to do here is to dwell on what our maritime imperatives are, and how they are reflected in our foreign policy. In the process, we might look at some relevant issues and developments, suggest elements for a strategy, and attempt a brief prognosis for the immediate future.

But whatever the mindset, the facts of India's geography and history are inescapable. What was true in history is equally or even more true today. In the midst of the third largest ocean in the world, India's location is in many ways her destiny. The seas, especially the Indian Ocean, are vital to India's interests. Transport by water remains the cheapest form available. And even when we speak of cyberspace, 95 percent of internet traffic is at some stage carried under the sea by underwater cables. Maritime trade and energy supplies are critical to India's transformation. Consider some statistics. Today, 90 percent of global commerce and 65 percent of all oil travels by sea. Of this half the world's container traffic and 70 percent of the total traffic of petroleum products is accounted for by the Indian Ocean. Energy—India depends on oil for over 33 percent of her energy needs, and imports almost 70 percent of that. We import coal from ten countries, (including Mozambique, South Africa, Indonesia and Australia), many of which are Indian Ocean littorals. This is also true of our LNG imports (from Qatar, Malaysia, Indonesia and South Africa).

The IEA estimates that global energy demand will grow by at least 45 percent between 2006 and 2030, and that half that increase will come from India and China. We are both at an energy intensive phase of our development. Between 1990 and 2003, oil consumption in India and China grew by 7 percent on average, against 0.8 percent in the rest of the world. By 2050 India could be the largest importer of oil in the world. Thus both India and China face a "Hormuz dilemma". For China this is compounded by a "Malacca dilemma" as well. Given the need for energy security, it is therefore natural that Indian companies would operate oil tank farms in Trincomalee and seek a role in oilfields from Sakhalin to Myanmar to Central Asia to Egypt, Sudan, Angola and elsewhere.

Add to this our other maritime interests: almost 5 million Indians work in the Gulf and West Asia and the significance of the remittances they send home cannot be underestimated. Populations of Indian origin are scattered through the littoral states of the Indian Ocean. India also has a mineral rich EEZ which is well over 2 million square km in area.

And then there is security, even in the limited classical military sense of the word. As the events in Mumbai last November 26 showed, the same Indian Ocean that carries our energy and goods is also used by our enemies to attack us. The threats from terrorism, smuggling, piracy, transnational crimes, and proliferation that the Indian Navy's 2004 Maritime Doctrine warned about have all come true in the last few years. The geo-strategic significance of the Indian Ocean is clear from the fact that about 60,000 ships transit through it each year.

Let us look a little more closely at the phenomenon of piracy off the Horn of Africa from the Somali coast. Through ad hoc arrangements, the navies of several Indian Ocean countries, NATO and China and Japan are cooperating in fighting this menace. This experience shows what international cooperation can do to keep the sea lanes open, but also suggests the limitations of military responses to such complex threat phenomena. There are about 20,000 ship transits through the affected area every year. As against this so far this year there have been about 135 pirate attacks from the Somali coast and 28 vessels have been successfully commandeered. My point is simple. One must re-examine the cost effectiveness of conventional military force in dealing with these new threats. This is no longer just a case of dealing with the pirates on the Spanish Main or off the Barbary Coast. Given the stakes involved, and the nature of piracy today, a broader set of comprehensive measures with much wider international participation is essential to deal with this problem. I will return to this aspect later.

Maritime Dimensions of Foreign Policy

With any policy that has an outward orientation, as does foreign policy, the overlap with security, land, and maritime frontier dimensions is difficult to ignore. For Peninsular India, the lure of the sea around it, has moulded and set the course of the history of the people who inhabit it. The ocean also brought traders and colonizers. Our vantage location with the Indian Ocean literally at our feet, became in those early times, also a source of vulnerability, laying bare our unpreparedness to face external threat. Learning lessons from the broad.

India is naturally a maritime nation—a coast line of over 7500 km.; the Lakshwadweep and the Andaman and Nicobar chains stretch over 600 islands, with southernmost tip just 90 nautical miles from Indonesia and the northern most tip less than 10 nautical miles from Myanmar. Our EEZ is more than 2.5 million square Kms. The mining areas of over 150,000 sq. km. allotted to India under UNCLOS are about 2000 km. from our southernmost tip. We have significant interests in Antarctica as well. Our inseparable bonds with the Indian

Ocean region are not merely geographical but of deeper civilizational significance. Historical, cultural, economic and political linkages have been forged between India and the Indian Ocean over millennia.

India is almost an island as far as trade is concerned. In the absence of good regional land connectivity, the bulk of our trade is seaborne. India's global mercantile trade has grown phenomenally and now constitutes 41 percent of our GDP. 77 percent of our trade by value, and over 90 percent by volume is carried by sea. India is now projected to become the fourth largest economy in the world by 2020, after China, Japan and the US. Our dependence on sea borne trade is expected to expand exponentially. The maritime dimension is also vital for our energy security. India's oil consumption is expected to rise to 245 million tons annually by 2020, with the country likely to be the world's single largest importer of oil by 2050.

Our economic growth would continue to be critically depended upon unhindered flow of oil. The sea borne terrorist attacks on Mumbai (26/11), focused the need for strengthening maritime and coastal security against threats from sea. Clandestine proliferation networks also use seaways for proliferation activities. It follows that our foreign policy has to focus on these critical aspects for our national development and security.

India has a vision of the Indian Ocean region unshackled from historical divisions and bound together in collective pursuit of peace, and prosperity. As a mature and responsible nation, one of our foreign policy interests is to evolve a regional architecture based on the twin principles of shared security and shared prosperity. India is well poised to play a substantive and formative role in this regard.

India has friendly and productive bilateral relations with almost all the states in the Indian Ocean region. Our bilateral relations with Sri Lanka, Bangladesh, Indonesia, Mauritius, Maldives, Myanmar, Seychelles, Oman, Mozambique, South Africa and others facilitate access to a wide swathe of the

Indian Ocean. Maritime Security is an important dimension of our relations with ASEAN countries, in particular Singapore and Vietnam. Many of these are territorial neighbours but all are our maritime neighbours. We have historical and civilizational ties with many of these countries. Some of these countries have large Indian communities. The broad spectrum of our ties with these countries has a strong economic and socio-cultural dimension. The Indian Navy has contributed towards expanding our diplomatic engagement in the region and beyond. An active Indian naval presence is welcomed in many waters, near and far from our shores. In cooperation with the Indian Navy, we are looking at ways of long term engagement with many of these countries in capacity building including training assistance, refit of ships joint exercises, coordinated patrols, supply of hardware and product support. We are also prepared to assist countries to conduct EEZ surveillance.

Maritime Security is emerging as an important element of our dialogue architecture with various countries, including with the United States. This includes periodic bilateral exercises, information exchanges through maritime domain awareness, sharing of best practices in areas such as search and rescue, maritime safety, pollution control, maritime law enforcement that could cover counter narcotics and counter piracy, training, exercises and humanitarian assistance and disaster relief and exchange of views on promoting a regional security architecture that enhances maritime security.

In addition to bilateral interactions, we are actively engaged with almost all regional bodies that are either based in or border the Indian Ocean region—ranging from SAARC, BIMSTEC, EAS, ARF, ASEAN, GCC, SADC to the AU. Prime Minister's participation in the second India-Africa Forum Summit held in Addis Ababa on May 25, 2011 was indeed a milestone. Our aim is to build a web of cooperative relations that brings together all the stakeholders based on mutual interest and benefit. India's soft power attributes give us an advantage that few countries have.

The scourge of piracy off the Somali coast poses a serious problem for safety of maritime traffic as well as the well-being of crew members. The Gulf of Aden is a major trading route for India. India, as a founder-member of the Contact Group on Piracy off the Coast of Somalia (CGPCS), established in January 2009, has been fully engaged in the efforts of the group to share information, coordinate actions of navies in combating piracy in the Gulf of Aden, raising public and merchant marine awareness and, examining legal and criminal justice issues with respect to apprehended pirates. Further, the Indian Navy has proactively cooperated with other navies through the SHADE (Shared Awareness and De-confliction) mechanism and otherwise.

The Indian Ocean Naval Symposium (IONS) was launched in February 2008 as a cooperative maritime security initiative following a meeting of Chiefs of Navy of nearly all littoral States of Indian Ocean in New Delhi. The Charter of Business of IONS is to provide a framework to promote shared understanding of maritime issues facing the littoral States of the Indian Ocean region; enhance regional maritime security and stability; establish and promote variety of cooperative mechanisms and develop inter-operability in terms of doctrines, procedures etc. IONS, an inclusive and consultative regional forum provides a platform for all IOR littoral navies to periodically and regularly discuss issues that bear upon regional maritime security. As per the charter the membership of IONS will be open to any country whose territory abuts or lies within Indian Ocean. Other countries can become Observers if they meet the agreed criterion.

The Regional Cooperation Agreement on Combating Piracy and Armed Robbery against Ships in Asia (ReCAAP) is the first regional Government to Government agreement to promote and enhance cooperation against piracy and armed robbery at sea in Asia. To date, 15 states have become Contracting Parties to ReCAAP. The ReCAAP initiatives have contributed significantly towards maritime security in the region. The ReCAAP has been recognized as a model organization by IMO for cooperation of regional governments to combat piracy and armed robbery. India is a founding member of ReCAAP and contributed financially towards the running of the Information Sharing Centre (ISC) of the ReCAAP ISC. India's contributions in ReCAAP have contributed towards enhancing our stature as responsible maritime state in the region. In addition, it has also helped our ongoing regional engagement initiatives.

The ASEAN+8 Defence Ministers Meeting (ADMM Plus) Plus is a significant milestone in the evolving security architecture in the Asia Pacific region. The ADMM Plus has identified five areas of cooperation—maritime security, humanitarian assistance and disaster relief (HADR), military medicine, counter-terrorism and peacekeeping operations. India is seen as an important stakeholder in the ADMM Plus activities. The evolution of the Asia-Pacific Security architecture will depend to a large measure how states are able to pull together interests and capabilities to address common threats and preserve and protect the Global Commons, including maritime security.

What is proposed here is different from what has been suggested elsewhere, for instance by Robert Kaplan, that the US act as "sea-based balancer" or "honest broker" between India and China in the Indian Ocean. Which major power would not like to play the role of balancer, given the chance? It is cheaper and easier and leaves the real work to the powers being balanced. For a superpower that is refocusing on Asia but finding the landscape considerably changed while she was preoccupied with Iraq and Afghanistan, this would naturally be an attractive option.

However, is it likely that two emerging states like India and China, with old traditions of state-craft, would allow themselves to remain the objects of someone else's policy, no matter how elegantly expressed? I think not. Instead, what is suggested is a real concert of Asian powers, including the USA which has a major maritime presence and interests in Asia, to deal with issues of maritime security in all of Asia's oceans. As Asia becomes more integrated from Suez to the Pacific, none of Asia's seas or oceans can be considered in isolation. This would be a major cooperative endeavour, and a test of Asian statesmanship.

It will be asked whether this quest is not utopian when the global and regional balance of power is shifting so rapidly, when there is a major build-up of naval strength taking place in Asia, and when each major Asian power is convinced that the future will be better for them, or at least that their relative position will improve rather than worsen in the years to come. It is precisely when uncertainty in the international system is higher than it has been for a long time, when the stakes are greatest, that the need for such an exercise is sharpest and it has the most chance of success.

Proliferation Security Initiative

The Proliferation Security Initiative (PSI) is a global effort that aims to stop trafficking of weapons of mass destruction (WMD), their delivery systems, and related materials to and from states and non-state actors of proliferation concern. Launched on May 31, 2003, U.S. involvement in the PSI stems from the U.S. National Strategy to Combat Weapons of Mass Destruction issued in December 2002. That strategy recognizes the need for more robust tools to stop proliferation of WMD around the world, and specifically identifies interdiction as an area where greater focus will be placed. President Obama strongly supports the PSI. In his April 2009 Prague speech, President Obama first called for the PSI to continue as an enduring international counter -proliferation effort. He has subsequently reinforced this as the formal U.S. Government position in significant U.S. policy documents, including the White House's National Security Strategy and the Pentagon's last Quadrennial Defense Review.

"The PSI is an important tool in our efforts to break up black markets, detect and intercept WMD materials in transit, and use financial tools to disrupt this dangerous trade. It is an innovative and proactive approach to preventing proliferation that relies on voluntary actions by states that are consistent with their national legal authorities and relevant international law and frameworks. PSI participants use existing authorities—national and international—to put an end to WMD-related trafficking".

When a country endorses PSI, it endorses the PSI Statement of Interdiction Principles, which commit participants to establish a more coordinated and effective basis through which to impede and stop WMD, their delivery systems, and related items. The countries commit to:

1. Interdict transfers to and from states and non-state actors of proliferation concern to the extent of their capabilities and legal authorities;
2. Develop procedures to facilitate exchange of information with other countries;
3. Strengthen national legal authorities to facilitate interdiction; and
4. Take specific actions in support of interdiction efforts.

The more than 90 countries that have endorsed the PSI so far share a deep concern that WMD, their delivery systems, and related materials could fall into the hands of terrorists. All of these countries have endorsed the effort to make PSI a flexible, voluntary initiative geared toward enhancing individual and collective partner nations' capabilities to take appropriate and timely actions to meet the fast-moving situations involving proliferation threats.

The United States seeks to strengthen and expand the PSI, ensuring that it remains an effective tool to stop WMD proliferation. We are playing an active role in the success of the PSI, by leveraging related counter proliferation efforts across the U.S. Government, by contributing military, customs, law enforcement, and other security experts and assets to interdiction exercises, by hosting PSI meetings, workshops, and exercises with other PSI-endorsing states, and by working with specific partner states to improve their capacity for combating the proliferation of WMD.

Interdiction Principles for Proliferation Security Initiative

PSI participants are committed to the following interdiction principles to establish a more coordinated and effective basis through which to impede and stop shipments of WMD, delivery systems, and related materials flowing to and from states and non-state actors of proliferation concern, consistent with national legal authorities and relevant international law and frameworks, including the UN Security Council. They call on all states concerned with this threat to international peace and security to join in similarly committing to:

1. Undertake effective measures, either alone or in concert with other states, for interdicting the transfer or transport of WMD, their delivery systems, and related materials to and from states and non-state actors of proliferation concern. "States or non-state actors of proliferation concern", generally refers to those countries or entities that the PSI participants involved establish should be subject to interdiction activities because they are engaged in proliferation through: (a) efforts to develop or acquire chemical, biological, or nuclear weapons and associated delivery systems; or (b) transfers (either selling, receiving, or facilitating) of WMD, their delivery systems, or related materials.
2. Adopt streamlined procedures for rapid exchange of relevant information concerning suspected proliferation activity, protecting the confidential character of classified information provided by other states as part of this initiative, dedicate appropriate resources and efforts to interdiction operations and capabilities, and maximize coordination among participants in interdiction efforts.

3. Review and work to strengthen their relevant national legal authorities where necessary to accomplish these objectives, and work to strengthen when necessary relevant international law and frameworks in appropriate ways to support these commitments.
4. Take specific actions in support of interdiction efforts regarding cargoes of WMD, their delivery systems, or related materials, to the extent their national legal authorities permit and consistent with their obligations under international law and frameworks.

Will participation in the PSI advance Indian national interests? At first glance, it would seem so. The *Indian Maritime Doctrine* statement that New Delhi published in 2004 represents the government's appraisal of the country's oceanic surroundings and how to meet challenges emanating from the sea. The 'strategic realities' Indian leaders see as they survey the Indian Ocean region include the large and growing volume of trade traversing regional waters; the nation's central location, geographic conformation and proximity to the sea lanes; and the abundance of natural resources in littoral nations. India, like other seafaring Asian nations, depends heavily on sea-borne trade and it imports the majority of the oil and natural gas needed to sustain its economic growth and development.

Finally, there is a pronounced military component to the strategic realities India confronts in its aquatic domain. China, like India, relies on shipping through the regional sea lines of communication and has set out to build up a powerful navy. Pakistan has acquired French diesel submarines with air independent propulsion and the capacity to fire missiles. Throwing its support behind the PSI will benefit India in several respects. First, New Delhi needs to put to sea a capable maritime force—a powerful navy, joined by an effective coast guard with which it interacts smoothly—if it hopes to meet the challenges identified in the *Indian Maritime Doctrine*.

Combined exercises and operations with the US Navy will

help Indian mariners to overcome the tactical, equipment and bureaucratic impediments to joint maritime operations that they have faced to date. Second, delousing commercial shipping of weapons-related items will reduce the likelihood of a catastrophic terror attack made possible by deficiencies in maritime security. Stringent security on the high seas and in regional seaports following such an attack will drive up the transaction costs associated with international trade, harming economic prosperity for India and its neighbours. Maritime security is an international public good New Delhi can help to furnish through ventures such as the PSI. And third, accession to the PSI will signal that India intends to assume a position of stewardship over international trade and security after years of being targeted by the international non-proliferation regime. Under the bilateral strategic relationship now taking shape, the United States seems to expect leadership from this emerging great power. In this context, putting in place the tactics and capabilities needed to foil traffic in weapons-related goods only makes sense for New Delhi.

A 'Global Prohibition Regime' in the Making

We can use international relations theory to help explain India's sceptical attitude toward the PSI. While the PSI's framers rarely speak in such theoretical terms, the initiative bears closer resemblance to what international-relations theorists call a 'regime'—namely a set of implicit or explicit principles, norms, rules and decision-making procedures around which actors' expectations converge in a given interest area—than it does to an international organisation. The PSI displays the characteristics of a subcategory of regimes known as 'global prohibition regimes'. In both domestic and international laws, such regimes enjoin state and non-state actors from taking part in particular activities—in the case of the PSI, transportation of items destined for WMD programmes. Older, better-known prohibition regimes oppose piracy, slavery and drug trafficking. UN Security Council

Resolution 1540, which instructed UN member states to impose effective oversight on the trade in weapons-related commodities, is evidence of a maturing international norm against the proliferation of mass-destruction weaponry and the ballistic missiles used to deliver unconventional payloads.

Ethan Nadelmann argues that such regimes arise only when national and bilateral law-enforcement measures prove themselves inadequate to defeat criminal activities spanning national borders. The international community's experience with WMD trafficking, exemplified by the cracking of the A.Q. Khan network, seems to have convinced the founders of the PSI that existing non- and counter-proliferation initiatives had failed. In itself, the PSI may not qualify as a global prohibition regime, but it may be part of an emerging one when considered alongside Security Council Resolution 1540; statements from the UN Secretary-General urging universal participation in the initiative; the amendments to the Convention for the Suppression of Unlawful Acts Against the Safety of Maritime Navigation, approved in late 2005; and earlier declarations of purpose from bodies such as the G-8 and the European Union. Nadelmann posits four stages through which prohibition regimes take shape.

1. **Legitimate:** In the initial stage, the activity subsequently targeted for prohibition is considered legitimate under certain conditions and within certain circumscribed groups. The five nuclear weapon states officially recognised under the Nuclear Non- Proliferation Treaty might qualify as such an exclusive club, since they maintain types of weaponry placed off-limits for others. (The NPT, of course, envisions eventual nuclear disarmament).
2. **Stigma:** The activity is next redefined as a problem. Discoveries about Iraq's WMD programmes from 1991 onward, for example, prompted the international community to take the problem of weapons-related transactions more seriously. The unravelling of the Khan

proliferation ring, a 'grey-market' network that abetted nuclear weapons programmes in multiple states, lent further credence to the notion that proliferation posed a common threat.

3. **Lobbying and Ad Hoc Action:** Proponents of forbidding the activity take to arguing publicly in favour of suppressing and outlawing it. Arguments for quashing proliferation, by forcible means, if necessary, have become commonplace in recent years. These arguments have found policy expression primarily through UN activities, but also through more active measures such as the PSI and multilateral supplier regimes, including the Nuclear Suppliers Group, the Australia Group (AG), and the Missile Technology Control Regime.
4. **Banned:** Once regarded as legitimate in some cases, the activity ends up as the subject of domestic criminal law and police enforcement activity throughout much of the world. The PSI Statement of Interdiction Principles calls on participating states to use existing law to support interdiction activity on their soil, in their territorial waters and in their territorial airspace, while also passing new legislation and working to bolster international law.

The PSI can become the vehicle by which a regime opposing shipments of WMD-related materiel reaches Nadelmann's fourth stage, becoming truly universal and embedded in national and international law. As noted before, some 80 countries have already endorsed the initiative's basic principles while Security Council Resolution 1540, passed under Chapter VII of the UN Charter, directs UN member states to enact robust laws banning WMD trafficking. The PSI represents a mechanism for international police activity, regardless of whether military or law-enforcement means are used to prosecute an interdiction operation.

The Measurement Dilemma

Using an approach like Nadelmann's is one way to

determine whether the PSI has made progress and whether it qualifies as 'effective multilateralism', as Bush Administration officials have advertised. While such an indirect analytical approach is less than satisfactory, certain characteristics of the WMD trade and the PSI render direct measurements of the initiative's efficacy problematic. PSI participants have been relatively forthcoming about military exercises undertaken under the initiative. At the same time, they have displayed a penchant for operational secrecy, disclosing little information about actual interdiction operations. This secretive mode of Operation makes a certain degree of sense, given the intelligence and policy sensitivity of such operations, but it complicates efforts to rally additional states behind PSI principles while frustrating efforts at independent analysis.

It is worth pointing out that the secretive approach is not confined to the PSI. Multilateral export control arrangements, such as the AG, transact business in similar fashion. How many export licenses AG members reject on proliferation grounds each year and how many known proliferators they thwart by sharing information among themselves on license requests and denials constitute privileged information.

But even if the precise number of interdictions considered, attempted and successful within a given time period is publicly known, this will still represent only a crude gauge of merit. Consider this, the number of interdictions attempted will represent a percentage of WMD-related shipments detected (a number of PSI participants will themselves resist making them public).

In turn, the figure for shipments detected will represent a percentage of all WMD-related shipments that take place—an unknown number, owing to proliferators' proficiency in their craft. In this sense, the problem of assessing the effectiveness of the PSI and other counter-proliferation and non-proliferation efforts resembles the measurement problem associated with counter-terrorist efforts.

Is PSI Truly Global? The Case of China

That the counter-proliferation norm underlying the PSI will take root is not foreordained. Just as a group of like-minded states can band together to generate new norms and perhaps international law, over time, steadfast opponents can register opposition to emerging norms; a critical mass of states can prove indifferent, depriving new norms of any force; or events can intercede to render existing rules or norms moot. This makes the process of creating customary and treaty law an intrinsically messy one. While the initiative has made important strides given its infancy—the Statement of Interdiction Principles was issued less than 4 years ago—the future of counter-proliferation activities of this sort remains uncertain.

Before moving on to India and the PSI, it is worth reviewing the case of China, a state whose central geographical position in East Asia, proximity to problem states, such as North Korea, and intelligence, law enforcement and military capabilities, not to mention its standing as a permanent member of the UN Security Council, make it an ideal contributor to the PSI. In certain respects, the cases of India and China resemble each other. Each is a rising Asian diplomatic, economic and military power, with considerable reserves of soft power; each is a traditional continental power turning its attention to the seas; each understands that the chief threats to its security in recent centuries have emanated from the sea; and, intent on economic development, each thinks in distinctly geo-strategic terms about its oceanic environs. And, Beijing and New Delhi have lodged similar complaints about the PSI.

Thus, China's outlook on counter-proliferation can help illuminate India's own outlook and options in this area. The United States and its PSI partners have been unable to push a resolution through the UN Security Council authorising this form of counter-proliferation. As noted previously, Security Council Resolution 1540 directed UN member states to take a range of measures to curtail proliferation, but it stopped short of explicitly endorsing the PSI, in large part because of Chinese objections. Beijing succeeded in having references to interdiction struck from the language of the resolution. Indeed, China's ambassador to the United Nations, openly boasted that 'this interdiction [language] has been kicked out' of the resolution. A Security Council resolution would have gone far toward alleviating China's ostensible legal concerns about the PSI and it was in Beijing's power to make such a resolution a reality. Its effort to keep UNSCR 1540 from granting the authority for interdiction operations suggested that other motives were at work in Chinese diplomacy.

As a result, Bush Administration spokesmen have been reduced to arguing that the 'PSI and 1540 are complementary', rather than citing the resolution as unambiguous legal authority for PSI activities. Chinese accession to the initiative will bring the last of the permanent five members of the Security Council into the PSI's core group—presumably, clearing the way for a resolution giving the initiative the legal sustenance it needs to attract more universal support from the international community. Beijing has endorsed the PSI's overarching goal of stemming weapons proliferation while remaining noncommittal about eventual Chinese membership in the initiative. Why? Chinese spokesmen have voiced a variety of objections and concerns.

The PSI is weakly anchored in international law, owing to the lack of a treaty or Security Council resolution; it would represent an 'intrusion and encroachment' on state sovereignty were a cargo to be intercepted in national waters or airspace; while the Bush Administration had seemingly conceded the need for a supporting UN Security Council resolution, it nonetheless wanted to leave the 'implementation and enforcement components' outside the world organisation's purview Beijing's criticisms of the PSI are explicable in terms of Chinese national interests and are probably sincerely held, if in some respects exaggerated. Like other PSI sceptics, Beijing seemingly objects less to what the PSI is today—an initiative under which participants agree to work together to intercept suspect shipments where national sovereignty is at its apex—than to what it could mutate into in the future. But the PSI *is* only tenuously moored in international law, as the Bush Administration tacitly admitted when it attempted to obtain the UN imprimatur by means of UNSCR 1540. And, additional legal authority *will* be necessary, especially in the rare case when PSI members want to interdict a cargo in international waters or airspace but lack a boarding agreement with the flag state.

Since China has expressed its protests against informal arrangements like the PSI in legal terms, observers have tended to interpret the challenge of wooing Beijing into the initiative solely as a matter of crafting legal arguments able to persuade Chinese leaders. Yet other, less obvious factors also help account for these leaders' ambivalent attitude toward the PSI. While Beijing has premised its critique of the PSI primarily on the initiative's legal shortcomings, geopolitical imperatives figure just as prominently, if not more so, in Chinese diplomacy toward the PSI—just as such imperatives have influenced ongoing efforts to bring China into elements of the international non-proliferation regime.

For China, clearly, acceding to the PSI is more than a simple matter of restating and acting on its fealty to the principle of non-proliferation. If the PSI participants hope to coax Beijing into their ranks, they need to fashion an outreach that factors in China's geopolitical needs and concerns while conceding China the leadership role it covets in East Asian waters. Whether even the most effective appeal would sway Beijing is unclear. It is possible, however, that China might work with the PSI on a low-key, ad hoc basis when mutual interests warrant. Over time, Beijing might come to view the initiative as an asset rather than as a threat to national aspirations, much as it has warmed to the multilateral export control regimes after years of denouncing them.

India

Like China, India would make a valuable contribution to the PSI. It possesses real and growing capacity to police the Indian Ocean basin, and its leaders have avowed their desire to do so. Indian leaders propound the ideal of non-proliferation with at least the same vigour as their Chinese counterparts, and they are not so averse to maritime counter-proliferation.

New Delhi has demurred from becoming a participant in the PSI, despite the initiative's mission of thwarting WMD proliferation in waters and skies of vital interest to India. Like Beijing, it has cited the PSI's shaky legal basis and its independence of Security Council oversight and control. Why is this so, given that Indian officials outspokenly oppose the proliferation of weapons-related material. First, the PSI has become a matter of contention in Indian domestic politics. This represents a marked difference from China, where the leadership can manage public opinion in the interests of the ruling Communist Party, and even from the United States, where the PSI enjoys broad bipartisan support.

In India, by contrast, the PSI has found its way into domestic politics, in large part because it was unveiled under the government of Atal Behari Vajpayee, head of the Bharatiya Janata Party (BJP). Vajpayee voiced guarded support for the PSI, and that was enough to alienate potential supporters of the initiative among the BJP's left-leaning adversaries in the Congress Party and its coalition partners. The government of Manmohan Singh, which depends on support from parties on the left, has studiously avoided aligning India with the PSI—especially following reports that the US side had attached a clause to the US-Indian nuclear deal mandating Indian participation in the initiative. No Indian prime minister would willingly be seen as carrying water for the United States, particularly in the George W. Bush years, and this apparent effort at arm-twisting inflamed sentiments against the PSI. Even Vajpayee never ran the risk of agreeing to PSI participation, and so a certain standoffishness on Dr. Singh's part is natural in light of domestic politics. Moreover, Indians strongly feel that they were not consulted on the initiative and have had no role in shaping its framework.

Second, discussions of Indian entry into the PSI conjure up memories of what Indians regard as maltreatment at the hands of individual governments and the international non-proliferation regime. History colours Indians' attitudes toward the initiative as much as partisan rancour does. Over the years—largely because it has remained clear of the Non-Proliferation Treaty and has maintained a distinctive, stand-alone export control system—India has been denied dual-use technology by the multilateral export control arrangements.

This despite good performance—perfect, say some officials—by the Indian export control system. Bad feelings linger despite the Bush Administration's decision to lift sanctions imposed following the 1998 nuclear tests, to engage in regular consultation with New Delhi on security affairs, and to negotiate a deal providing for partial UN supervision over the Indian nuclear complex in exchange for a US pledge to permit transfers of commercial nuclear technology. Acquiescence in the PSI, the de facto enforcement arm of a system that has unjustly targeted India in the past, may be a bridge too far for India's leadership.

Third, the PSI could impinge on Indo-Pakistan or Indo-China relations. Consider two scenarios. Pakistan could depict maritime interdiction—even of proliferation relevant material—as such an attempt on New Delhi's part. This understandably gives Indian officials pause. Similarly, were Indian military or law-enforcement services to intercept a Chinese vessel or aircraft, this is likely to prompt Beijing to step up its effort to amass 'hard power', manifest in forward-deployed naval forces, in India's nautical environs. India might see its overall geo-strategic position suffer for the sake of stopping a single—albeit lethal—cargo of hazardous substances or components. New Delhi, then, is understandably reluctant to see Indian mariners interfere with freedom of navigation in the Indian Ocean region.

Fourth, as in the case of China, geopolitical views and the nation's bid for regional and global stature figure into the question of PSI participation. At issue is not only whether illicit cargoes should be interrupted in the Indian Ocean region but who should do the interrupting. The elite consensus in New Delhi holds that India should take the lead in policing the Indian Ocean, with extra-regional powers such as the United States relegated to a supporting role at most.

Many Indian officials and pundits construe India's geographic environs, its natural sphere of influence very broadly indeed, holding that India should be pre-eminent from the Bab el-Mandeb Strait (or even the Suez Canal) in the west to the Strait of Malacca in the east. Ample evidence suggests that India has remained aloof from the PSI in large measure because it worries that PSI participation might seem to signify a formal alliance with the United States, something Indian governments have traditionally resisted. Worse, PSI participation might appear to show that New Delhi had accepted the junior role in this alliance, with the Indian Navy in effect reduced to an appendage of the US Navy—a South Asian equivalent to the Japan Maritime Self- Defence Force.

Accepting subordinate status in its own geographic neighbourhood, where successive governments have hewed to something resembling America's Monroe Doctrine, would vitiate India's claim to regional primacy. Despite its eagerness for closer defence ties with Washington, New Delhi may balk at such appearances.

And fifth, New Delhi probably fears the consequences should it gain a reputation for being a regional bully. The *Indian Maritime Doctrine* makes forward presence and naval diplomacy two of the primary functions of Indian maritime forces. If India were to accede to the PSI while maintaining its claim to regional predominance, it would find itself policing ships flying the flags of neighbouring Indian Ocean powers—not to mention East Asian powers such as China and Japan.

If the Indian Navy were seen as wantonly stopping and searching merchant vessels, and especially if it mishandled its visit-and-search efforts—of bullying could undercut regional goodwill and cooperation. This would affect not only India's neighbours in the Indian Ocean but also coastal nations in Southeast Asia, where India has courted good relations in hopes of extending its influence eastward of Malacca. Apparent highhandedness would threaten to sap the soft power New Delhi painstakingly earned through tsunami relief and other naval diplomatic enterprises. Perversely, then, policing the Indian Ocean basin in a good cause—halting proliferation—could leave India's neighbours hesitant about Indian-led training, exercises, and operations, impairing naval diplomacy and the forward-presence mission.

Sullen Indian Ocean governments would be less and less willing to follow India's lead in future security initiatives, to the detriment of Indian foreign policy. These intervening factors in New Delhi's strategic calculus help to explain its palpable ambivalence toward the initiative. PSI participation clearly carries implications for India far beyond the realm of WMD proliferation. The benefits of combined counter-proliferation may not justify the larger political costs.

Conclusion

So much then for the factors that might discourage India from participation in the PSI. What factors might encourage the Indian government to set aside its ambivalence, aligning itself with the initiative's purposes and activities? Vital security interests would clearly play a role. If Indian intelligence determined that multiple weapons shipments were bound for Pakistan, for example, indicating a determined arms build-up— that would engage vital Indian interests, nudging Indian leaders' inclinations in favour of forceful counter-proliferation measures Or, some event underscoring the potential of sea-borne proliferation to damage Indian energy security or economic development—say, a case in which maritime proliferation demonstrably contributed to a terrorist act involving WMD—could furnish the necessary political impetus. Such an event is likely to impel governments to shut down the maritime trade system until all shipping could be certified weapons-free; at a minimum they would impose cumbersome new inspections, raising costs and impeding trade worldwide. The PSI would represent a low-cost way to reduce the probability of such a catastrophic event.

If New Delhi came to see the PSI as a way to forge closer defence ties with Washington without forfeiting its claim to pre-eminence in the Indian Ocean region, its resistance to the PSI might abate. If US officials convincingly portrayed the PSI as a vehicle for combined training and exercises—activities that would bolster the capabilities of the Indian Navy and Coast Guard—this would tend to bias Indian decision-making toward PSI participation. This would be especially true if Washington clearly conveyed that it not only accepted but welcomed Indian leadership in the Indian Ocean basin, that it hoped to see a durable order emerge in the region under Indian stewardship, and that it was prepared to accord New Delhi the lead role in policing South Asian waters and skies. Savvy US officials could point to Operation Active Endeavour, NATO's maritime police operation in the Mediterranean, to show that they welcome help from foreign partners, if nothing else as a means of burden sharing for overtaxed US forces.

It is possible, of course, that India will never choose to openly become a PSI participant—particularly now that the initiative has made its roster of participants public, and in the process foreclosed a would-be participant's option of keeping its involvement confidential. And, India's legal objections to the PSI will be difficult to answer, as the Bush Administration seems ill-inclined to relinquish authority over counter-proliferation to the United Nations, while China, a veto-wielding member of the Security Council, will reject any resolution backing the PSI unless the measure grants the council some say over interdiction operations.

As in the case of China, however, India might collaborate with the initiative as its needs and interests warrant, while keeping its involvement in the US-led initiative out of public view. It might also agree to quietly expand Indo-US bilateral military-to-military endeavours to include tactics for combating the traffic in WMD-related materiel. An incremental, low key step of this sort would allow New Delhi to reap many of the benefits it could expect to gain from open participation in the PSI, while avoiding the semblance of subordinate status or of a formal Indo-US alliance. Such an outcome would leave the global prohibition regime against trafficking in WMD incomplete for the foreseeable future. If so, it would leave Washington cold—but US leaders should know better than to let the best become the enemy of the good.

3

Coastal Security of India

K.R. Singh

Maritime security is traditionally perceived in the context of the role, benign or hostile, of state actors. The navy is tasked to respond to it. Non-state actors (NSA) have also challenged national interest, be it by acts of piracy or that of smuggling. Piracy has once again raised its head and state actors are evolving means to combat that threat. Smuggling *via* adjacent sea space was and still is a major challenge to economic security of states including India. Indian Customs (Marine Organization) was strengthened since 1960s in that context. Subsequently, after the Coast Guard was formed in 1977-78, it was also tasked with anti-smuggling operations. Following the enactment of Maritime Zones of India Act, 1976, that delimited 200 n. miles from the coast as India's exclusive economic zone (EEZ), the Coast Guard was also entrusted with the responsibility of preventing poaching by unauthorized fishermen in India's EEZ.

For India, maritime terrorism emerged as a new threat since early eighties after the Liberation Tigers of Tamil Eelam (LTTE) of Sri Lanka began to use the waters adjacent to Tamil Nadu coast for acquiring material that helped it to confront forces of Sri Lanka. Assassination of Rajiv Gandhi was a glaring illustration of that linkage. Hostile elements in Pakistan also chose maritime route to target India. Attack on Mumbai on November 26, 2008, was a glaring example of maritime terrorism.

These developments have forced decision makers in India to evolve more effective means to meet the new challenge. It means framing appropriate legal regime as well as strengthening enforcement agencies. That will also mean that India will have to bring its maritime zones under a more effective order. At the moment, maritime affairs are managed, in their own ways, by multiple ministries and agencies of the Central Government as also State governments. They include fishery departments, shipping and port authorities, Customs, public and private sector firms that are involved in exploiting oil and gas in continental shelf of India, the Navy, the Coast Guard, the Marine Police etc. Some half-hearted steps have been suggested to coordinate their efforts. But it is not easy to replace old order and the old mindset.

India's efforts to strengthen its maritime security *vis-à-vis* the NSA and terrorists will also face the constraints of traditional international law and articles of the UNCLOS-III, especially those dealing with the freedom of the high seas. Under the terms of UNCLOS-III all waters, beyond the outer limit of territorial waters (maximum 12 n. miles from the coast), are open for navigation by all. That indirectly hampers efforts of the coastal state in sanitizing its adjacent waters. However, various steps are being taken at national and international level to meet the new challenge to homeland security directed *via* the adjacent sea space.

Though the term coastal security has become popular, it is grossly inadequate as the frame of reference to meet the new challenge. Though the coast (land adjacent to the sea) is the target of NSA and terrorists, the zone of operation of the concerned state does not begin nor does it end at the so-called coastal waters. In fact, there is no legal or political definition of coastal waters. Legal terms as defined in MZI Act of 1976, or UNCLOS-III are inland sea, territorial waters, contiguous zone, continental shelf and EEZ. UNCLOS-III does not recognize the term coastal waters.

Hence, there is the need first to define the term coastal security and to delimit coastal waters of a state so as to have a relook at the legal norms defining state's jurisdiction in that context. That will, in turn, define powers and functions of designated courts that are empowered to try these cases, as also those of various enforcement agencies like the Navy, the Coast Guard, the Customs (Marine Organization), the Marine Police etc. Thus, India will have to construct an effective maritime security framework *vis-à-vis* threats posed by NSA and terrorists, that are in consonance with national as also international norms.

Legitimizing Action under National Norms

India will have to confront the new challenge of maritime threats to homeland security in the years to come. Hence, its maritime enforcement agencies will need a clearly defined legal (and judicial) framework to enable them to intercept, apprehend and produce offenders before the court for trial.

On 'land', enforcement powers end where land border ends. By contrast, Indian legal system will need to take into account multiple layers of maritime security zones that spill over into what constitute coastal waters. Hence, it should have provisions for taking enforcement action even in that sea space against NSA and terrorists. To be effective, there should be provision for pre-emptive role.

As noted, there are no legally recognized norms for dealing with maritime terrorism on the high seas. Hence, India will need to evolve a comprehensive legal code by streamlining its own legal framework, as also through reinterpretation of available sources of international law, various conventions, international initiatives as also its own state practices.

One point that needs to be taken note of is that India's laws and practice on maritime affairs were framed under the sponsorship of various ministries and departments of the Central Government. These laws deal with various facets like shipping, ports, exploitation of living and non-living resources, environment, defence etc. The result was that there was absence of coordination among these agencies, especially in matters dealing with maritime security.

Another point that needs to be reiterated is the need to differentiate between 'defence' in the context of armed conflict with other states, and 'security' in the context of threat posed by NSA and terrorists. It is evident that legal norms to meet these two types of threat to homeland are going to be different.

Maritime Terrorism and India's Legal System

There are no Indian acts specific to maritime terrorism except the SUA Act of 2002. A Piracy Bill has been introduced in the Lok Sabha on March 21, 2012. It still has to be approved. There are, however, several acts whose contents can be interpreted to legitimise action against NSA and terrorists. These acts can be divided into two broad categories:

1. Those that target criminal elements in general, and
2. Those that target terrorists in general and whose provisions can be employed in containing threats of maritime terrorism as well.

Among the first category, the Indian Penal Code (IPC) provides a broad spectrum that gives legitimacy to enforcement action against maritime terrorism as well. Some of the sections of IPC that can be so invoked are Sections 121-126 that deal with offences against state like waging war, attempt to wage war, abetting insurgency etc., Sections 285 and 286 that can be read alongside Explosives Act as amended in 2002, Sections 299-304 that deal with various facets of homicide and wrongful confinement etc. These can be read along with SUA Act, 2002. Section 380 deals with theft on board vessels. IPC has no provision against piracy.

Beside IPC, other acts that also provide legitimacy to enforcement action include Passport Act as amended in 2002, Conservation of Foreign Exchange and Prevention of Smuggling Activities Act (COFEPSA) of 1974 which can be read alongside the Anti-Money Laundering Act of 2009, MZI (Regulation of Fishing by Foreign Vessels) Act of 1981 etc.

Acts Specific to Terrorism

Indian legal system has set of acts that are specific to

terrorism. They include UAPA, 1967 as amended in 2008, as also acts passed by the Parliament to give effect to various conventions/UN Security Council resolutions like the SUA Act, 2002, WMD Act, 2005, Anti-Money Laundering Act, 2009 etc. These acts give details of enforcement power of various maritime security agencies.

Unlawful Activities (Prevention) Act (UAPA) of 1967 is the basic act dealing with terrorism. Parliament had passed other acts dealing with terrorism like the National Security Act of 1980, Terrorist and Disruptive Activities Act (TADA) of 1987, Prevention of Terrorism Act (POTA), 2002 etc. They were repealed on ground of political misuse. UAPA was amended in 2008 and remains the basic act against terrorism though it does not use that term. Section 15 lists acts that can be classified as acts of terrorism. Section 16 prescribes punishment. Very often, Maharashtra Control of Organized Crime Act (MCOCA) is also invoked while dealing with acts of terrorism. Among other things, it accepts confession before police as part of evidence.

Parliament has passed acts to give legal effect to various international conventions as also resolutions of the Security Council. Suppression of Unlawful Acts Against Safety of Maritime Navigation and Fixed Platform on Continental-shelf (SUA) Act, 2002 is the most specific act dealing with some aspects of maritime terrorism. The act was passed to give legal effect to the SUA Convention and associated Protocol on Fixed Platform, 1988. India's SUA Act, like the SUA Convention, respects the constraints of UNCLOS-III regarding freedom of the high seas.

SUA Act, 2002 is a comprehensive act. Section 3 specifies what constitute acts of maritime terrorism. That section also lists punishment to be awarded for various offences. Section 5, provides for a special court to facilitate speedy trial. Section 9 provides for extradition. Section 13 provides for presumption of offence even though none was being committed while persons were being apprehended. In case arms, ammunition and explosives were recovered from their possession, or there was evidence of use or threat of use of force or intended threat to use bomb, fire etc "the designated court shall presume, unless the contrary is proved, that the accused had committed such offence." Section 14(1) is also significant since it protects members of the enforcement agencies from legal proceedings if they had acted in good faith in pursuance of the provisions of the act. This protects them from being charged under Article 106 of UNCLOS-III.

Section 1(2) of the SUA act says that it extends to the whole of India including the outer limit of maritime zones covered under MZI Act, 1976. Yet, under Section 1, sub-section 3 its enforcement operations are limited only to territorial waters of India and the fixed platforms on the continental-shelf. As noted, pre-emption is an important aspect of anti-terrorist operation, especially in multi-layered maritime security zones and needs to be provided for in these acts. As will be examined, Section 11, para 2a of the Customs Act, read along with Section 5, sub-section 4(a) of MZI Act provides for that in the part of high seas covered by the contiguous zone.

Acts Empowering Enforcement Agencies

Certain provisions of acts that empower enforcement agencies also contain sections that can legitimize their action *vis-à-vis* NSA and terrorists. These acts are Customs Act (as amended under the Finance Act, 2007), the Navy Act, 1957 and the Coast Guard Act, 1978.

Customs (Marine) is Central Government's enforcement agency and is duty bound to enforce provisions of the Customs Act. Section 11, sub-section 2(a) lists 'the maintenance of security of India' as one of its duties. Also, MZI Act, 1976, Section 5, subsection 4(a), dealing with contiguous zone, says that the Central Government is empowered to take action in respect to the 'security of India'. The Customs (Marine), as an enforcement agency of the Central Government empowered to take action in India's contiguous zone is, thus, duty bound to take action to maintain security of India in these waters. Thus, Customs (Marine), under at least these two acts, is directly involved in containing the threats posed not only by NSA but also by terrorists. This means that Customs (Marine) needs to be given a greater role in the context of coastal security.

The Navy Act, 1957, under Section 3, sub-section 7 of Chapter I, defines enemy as all armed rebels, armed mutineers, armed rioters and pirates and 'any person in arms against whom it is the duty of any person subject to naval law, to act'. That section needs to be read along with item 21 of List I of the VII Schedule of the Indian Constitution. It gives the Navy jurisdiction over piracy, and *crimes committed against the law of nation* committed on land, on the high seas or in the air. This empowers the Navy to act not only against pirates but also against hijackers and terrorists *even on the high seas* since terrorism is now accepted as a crime against humanity.

The Coast Guard Act of 1978 had no specific reference to piracy or terrorism. However, under Section 4 (Chapter II) it is tasked with ensuring the *security* of the maritime zones of India with a view to the *protection of maritime and other national interests in such zones.* Word security, however, does not figure in Chapter III that defines duties and functions of the Coast Guard. Chapter III, however, lists some sections that are significant in the context of maritime terrorism. Under Section 14 sub-section 2a, it is entrusted with safety and protection' of off-shore installations on the continental-shelf. Section 14, sub-section 2e is open ended and refers to duty to enforce the provisions of such enactments as are for the time being in force in maritime zones. That limits its zone of action to the outer limit of India's EEZ.

India: State Practices

Besides various conventions and acts listed above, India's state practice also needs to be taken into account while framing a comprehensive legal code legitimizing India's enforcement actions against criminal activities of NSA and terrorists on the high seas. Three specific examples can be quoted in that context. They are; actions against *MV Progress Light* (1988), *MV Ahat* (1993) and Thai fishing boats (so-called mothership) that were hijacked by pirates (2008 and 2011). Also, though India has not formally joined the PSI, its Navy holds periodic exercises with navies of powers that have subscribed to it like USA, UK, France and Singapore. These exercises include interoperability as also action against proliferation of WMD related material.

Action against *MV Progress Light* in November 1988 was significant because of two issues of international law. The one was hijacking of commercial vessel by Tamil mercenary group from Sri Lanka that had also taken hostages on board the vessel. They were trying to escape following an abortive attempt to overthrow the regime of President Gayoom in Maldives. Traditional international law as also UNCLOS-III have no provision against hijacking on high seas. Even SUA Convention, 1988 does not empower for enforcement action on the high seas.

Indian action, however, can be justified on two grounds. The one was the anti-hijacking resolution, October 7, 1987, of the General Assembly of the UN. That was in response to the hijacking of *Achille Laura* in 1985. The second was under Article 110(d) of UNCLOS-III which authorizes any warship to intercept on the high seas any vessel without nationality. As soon as the mercenaries had hijacked *MV Progress Light* that vessel had lost its nationality. Indian Navy was thus justified in intercepting it and even use force in that context.

The same logic also applies to action of the Indian warship in 2008 and 2011. In 2008, Indian warship had challenged a pirated 'mother ship' in the Horn of Africa region. It had men on board armed with assault rifles and RPG, whose missiles could have seriously damaged the warship. When the pirates resisted, the vessel was fired upon. It sank. Unfortunately, the pirates had locked the fishermen below the deck. They too sank with the ship.

While that interception was in far off waters near the Horn of Africa, three interceptions were in international SLOCs in Indian waters near the Lakshadweep. The first one was when a Japanese vessel *MV Alondra Rainbow* was pirated from waters in South-East Asia. It was intercepted along the Arabian Sea coast. Pirates were arrested and the ship was returned to the owners. Two other interceptions took place in 2011. One vessel was intercepted on January 28. While men on board were apprehended, the vessel sank. The other vessel was intercepted in response to a distress call from a Greek vessel *MV Chios* that it was being chased by pirates. The pirate vessel was tracked by MR aircraft, chased by vessels of Indian Navy and the Coast Guard and intercepted. Pirates surrendered. 28 Pirates were arrested. 24 fishermen from the Thai fishing vessel, *Prantalay,* that was hijacked in April 2010, were rescued.

Interception of *MV Ahat* in January 1993 was also significant from the point of India's state practice. Ships of Indian Coast Guard and Indian Navy had intercepted it on the high seas (some say in territorial waters) and had, thus, denied it freedom of the high seas (or right of innocent passage), and thus violated norms of UNCLOS-III. But, those who criticized Indian action had ignored Article 2, para 16b of India-Sri Lanka Accord of 1987. Under it, India was obliged to offer help, even military help, to Sri Lanka *vis-à-vis* threat posed to it by Tamil militants. That clause, thus, equated the Accord with bilateral military alliance against LTTE. Article 110(1) of UNCLOS-III allows a warship to intercept another vessel even on the high seas under treaty obligations. In the light of issues analysed above, it can be recommended that Indian laws dealing with acts of maritime terrorism need to be streamlined and revamped.

Maritime Enforcement Agencies and the Challenge of Maritime Low Intensity Conflict (MLIC)

MLIC is a new challenge to homeland security posed by NSA and terrorism both indigenous as also foreign sponsored.

Therefore, there is the urgent need to sanitize the adjacent sea space that extends from the shore to at least 100 miles in the sea. It will entail monitoring of movement of vessels including national fishing fleet of various types, as also the capability to intercept suspected vessel in various maritime security zones of India. To achieve these objectives, it is essential that there is effective cooperation in sharing of information and even actionable intelligence, as also in enforcement operations among various maritime enforcement agencies of India.

In this context, two points need to be underlined. The one is that threat posed by terrorists *via* adjacent sea space was not anticipated as a major threat to homeland security. Hence, no maritime enforcement agency had focused its attention on that subject till 2004. Events of 26/11 dramatically highlighted the shortcomings. Now efforts are afoot to provide inputs to these agencies so as to enable them to fulfil their new role more effectively.

The second point worth noting is that till 2004 maritime security was the sole responsibility of the Central Government. After 2004-05, under the new coastal security perspective, coastal states were also provided with a role in that context. This will mean that there is the need to analyse the function of maritime enforcement agencies under two broad heads; those functioning under the Central Government and those that would work under various coastal states. It will also be necessary to find a viable mechanism for synergizing the activities of these agencies at various levels.

Enforcement Agencies under the Central Government

Maritime enforcement agencies that are often quoted in this context are the Navy, the Coast Guard and the Customs (Marine). I have also recommended the establishment of the marine wing of the Central Industrial Security Force (CISF) in the context of basic point security of major ports as also high value offshore oil and gas installations on the continental-shelf.

The Navy primarily focused on defence against state actors. In that context, it had built a fairly adequate blue water capability based upon sophisticated sub-surface, surface and aerial platforms. It had not paid enough attention to the requirements of MLIC or coastal security and, hence, had an inadequate so-called brown water capability.

The Navy was provided with new inputs especially after 26/11 in that context. Navy's new brown water/coastal security concept also led to the formation of the *Sagar Prahari Bal* (SPB). It is supposed to be composed of 1,000 specially trained personnel who would be equipped with 80 or more patrol boats and inshore patrol craft as also with UAVs to enable SPB to monitor adjacent sea space and for enforcement role in sea space of strategic significance like naval bases, ports and similar high value targets. Though the number appears to be large one doubts if it is adequate enough for the Navy to fulfil the role of coastal security on its own. Thus, the Navy will need to synergise its operations with other maritime enforcement agencies.

The Coast Guard was formed to meet specific requirements. Need was felt in mid-seventies to create a specialized force to deal with issues arising due to new developments in maritime international law that were being debated under UNCLOS-III at that time. These issues had also led to the enactment of MZI Act of 1976. Rustamji Committee, that had been entrusted with the task of recommending measures to strengthen steps against smuggling and illegal fishing by foreign vessels in India's maritime zone (EEZ), recommended in January 1977 the creation of a coast guard. An interim Coast Guard was constituted in February 1977 itself. The Indian Coast Guard was formally constituted following the passing of the Coast Guard Act in 1978. It was recognized as an independent armed force under Item 2 of List I of the VII Schedule of the Indian Constitution.

Enforcement responsibilities of the Coast Guard were included in Chapter II and III of the Act. As per Chapter II, its primary role was to ensure the *security* of the maritime zones of India with a view to the protection of maritime and other national interests in such zones. The term security, as noted earlier, was not repeated in Chapter III.

Section 14 (2) in Chapter III lists duties of the Coast Guard. Those relating directly to issues of maritime security concern include:

1. Safety and protection of off-shore oil terminals;
2. Assisting the Customs and other authorities in anti-smuggling operations; and
3. Enforcing provisions of such enactments as are in force in the maritime zones.

Under Section 5(4a) of MZI Act, 1976 contiguous zone is listed as the maritime security zone of India. Interestingly the Coast Guard Act of 1978 had not listed anti-piracy and anti-terrorism operations as duties of the Coast Guard. Like several other duties these too were added subsequently.

The Coast Guard is overburdened with other responsibilities. They included enforcement of various acts of Government of India like the Merchant Shipping Act, the Passport Act, Immigration Act, Foreigners Act, Foreign Exchange Regulation Act etc. The Coast Guard is also empowered to take action against any cognizable offence punishable under any other Act of the Central Government. Thus, it is empowered to act under IPC, CrPC, UAPA, SUA Act of 2002, WMD Act of 2005 etc. Now, the Coast Guard is also entrusted with anti-piracy role, especially after the interception of *MV Alondra Rainbow*. It is the nodal agency in India for the ReCAAP. After 2004, it has been entrusted with the responsibility of combating acts of maritime terrorism. Besides, it is also entrusted with SAR operations and control of marine pollution. The net result is that the Coast Guard is overburdened with diverse responsibilities.

Nature of duties of the Coast Guard necessitated an organizational framework that extends all along the coast of the mainland as also in various island territories of India.

Besides its headquarters in New Delhi, it has four regional headquarters in Mumbai, Chennai, Port Blair and in Ahmadabad that was established recently in the light of greater significance of the water space opposite the coast of Gujarat in the context of coastal security. It has 12 district headquarters and more than 20 Coast Guard stations. For coordinating SAR operations it has three MRCCs and eight MRCAs. It has three pollution control centres. It has one air enclave in Goa and six air squadrons spread all along the country. One more is proposed to be raised in Ratnagiri. Thus, Coast Guard has a multifaceted inter-locked establishment spread along the entire coastline and in Union Territories that strengthens its enforcement role in the context of MLIC.

Its force level comprises of both surface fleet and air wing. Its effective surface fleet includes approximately 13 offshore patrol vessels, 30 inshore patrol craft and SDBs, nine Archer-type fast interceptor craft, eight small patrol boats and six hovercraft. It also operates about 19 Dornier MR aircraft and about 16 helicopters. There were proposals to acquire UAVs as also several medium-lift helicopters and larger MR aircraft. More surface platforms like fast interceptor boats as also aircraft are being acquired to augment its capability so as to strengthen its role in the context of MLIC.

Though Coast Guard's organisational structure and force level are better suited for MLIC operations, even the Coast Guard will need to cooperate/synergise with other enforcement agencies for ensuring a comprehensive coastal security system. The *Customs (Marine)* is entrusted with the task of checking smuggling *via* sea. Over the decades its maritime zone of operation expanded from 3 to 6 n. miles in 1956 and to 12 n. miles in 1967. In 1976, under MZI Act, it extended up to 24 n. miles from the coastline. Thus, its role has expanded greatly over the decades.

The Customs Act, in Chapter IV, Section 11, sub-section 2 defines the role of Customs (Marine) not only as prevention of smuggling, conservation of foreign exchange etc but also *the maintenance of security of India.* This is to be read along with Section 5, sub-section 4 a of MZI Act, 1976 which defines contiguous zone as maritime security zone. Also, all maritime enforcement agencies of the Central Government are expected to enforce provisions of MZI Act 1976. Hence, Customs (Marine) is bound not only under Section 14, sub-section 2 of the Customs Act but also under Section 5(4a) of MZI Act, 1976 to safeguard security in the contiguous zone and, thus, to contain the threat posed by maritime terrorism. It is surprising that these provisions of two important acts of the Central Government have been sidelined even after 2004 and more so after 26/11. Customs (Marine) was to a large extent ignored in the context of coastal security in Phase I (2005-11). One hopes that this lapse will be rectified during Phase II.

Even before MZI Act, 1976 had extended the outer limit of the Customs waters to 24 n. miles, Nag Chaudhury Committee had recommended in 1974 for the establishment of a separate wing of the Customs for enforcement role in the adjacent sea space as also to upgrade the force level. Government of India, in 1974, approved the formation of Customs Marine Organization with HQ in Mumbai. Shore facilities were set up in 1975. The Navy was entrusted with the task of supporting that new organization during the initial phase.

The expanding nature of Customs waters from 3 to 6 n. miles in 1956 had forced the Customs to acquire more suitable vessels capable of operating on the high seas and of intercepting smugglers away from the immediate sea shore. In that context six SDBs (*Sukanya-class*) were acquired from Italy in 1960s. They were found to be inadequate. After 1974, orders were place for *Saab Scania (SS-14)* patrol boats from Sweden. Reportedly, 19 such boats were ordered. Ten of them were acquired in 1975. These patrol boats were armed with light machine gun. They were equipped with echo sounder to search for goods dumped in the sea during the chase, radars and night vision device. These boats were also managed with the help of the Navy. Reportedly, Customs (Marine) had operated about 50 captured *dhows* and they were designated as Customs Auxiliary Craft. *Swallow-class* patrol boats from South Korea arrived in 1980s. They too were managed by the Navy.

Despite a firm start after 1974, Customs (Marine) suffered a series of setbacks due to three reasons. Probably, it was ignored by the parent ministry/department itself. The Navy also overshadowed it. The Coast Guard almost duplicated its role since its establishment in 1977. But, Customs (Marine) has retained its role over the decades. Annual Report, 1987-88, of Ministry of Finance, mentioned a seven-year Customs (Marine) Perspective Plan for modernization. Under that plan 57 new boats were to be acquired. In 1990s, new orders were placed for 60-feet CPL (speed of 20 knots) that were to be built in Kochi. Reportedly there were proposals to acquire 20 fast interceptor boats. About 80 old patrol boats of 80 feet, equipped with radar, were also in operation.

Like the Coast Guard, Customs (Marine) also has a wide organizational set up along the coast of India's mainland and in island territories. It operates not only from major ports but also from minor ports that cater to overseas trade. Thus, it is in a position to strengthen the overall framework of coastal security.

It can, therefore, be recommended that the Customs (Marine) be give a more prominent role in coastal security framework during Phase II of the programme. For that purpose, all efforts should be made to modernize and upgrade its maritime enforcement capability so that it can play its destined role in strengthening maritime security in crucial waters up to the outer limits of the contiguous zone and also effectively cooperate and synergise its role with the Navy, the Coast Guard and the Marine Police.

Two sectors, whose security is the responsibility of Central Government, have no designated agency to manage their maritime security. They are the major ports of India and high value off-shore oil and gas platforms on the continental-shelf operated by public as also private sectors.

The near absence of *port security* mechanism was revealed in 26/11 when foreign terrorists could reach the port area *via* sea without anyone to question them. While several agencies were blamed for security lapse no one pointed even a finger towards the lapse in port security. Has any lesson been learnt from the events of 26/11 in that context or all agencies like the Navy, the Coast Guard and the Marine Police except the port authorities would be blamed for similar lapse in future.

Port security can be divided into two operational zones. The one is the area security which will spill over beyond the immediate environment of the port area. Area security will have to be the responsibility of the Navy and the Coast Guard. The other will be what can be termed as 'basic point' security of the restricted port areas. Most of the steps related to port security are 'land' oriented. It is time that a maritime oriented security setup be installed. It will have its own special characteristics of maritime security framework as well as specialized enforcement agency. Security of major ports is the responsibility of the Central Government and hence it is essential that it looks at the question on a priority basis.

Can any of the enforcement agencies of the Central Government be entrusted with that task? Annual Report of the Ministry of Home Affairs of 2007-08 had a picture of CISF personnel on a boat deployed for port security duty at the Jawaharlal Nehru Port. Can a specialised marine wing of the *CISF (Marine*) be formed and entrusted with the basic point security of major ports of India? Granted that it will also need to coordinate its role with those of other agencies like the Navy, the Coast Guard, Customs (Marine) and Marine Police, a recognized Central Government's agency specifically entrusted with that role can coordinate these efforts more effectively than the *ad hoc* arrangement under which no one is really responsible for coordinating maritime enforcement mechanism in and near the port.

Security of *off-shore high value installations* on the

continental-shelf, like that of major ports, can also be divided into area security and basic point security. Like port security, area security of these offshore installations that are spread over a wide area will need to be entrusted to the Navy and the Coast Guard. But the basic point security of high value installations can be entrusted to CISF (Marine) which will take over security of 500 metre 'safety and protection' zone around each of these structures. Steps can be introduced in that direction during Phase II and if found suitable can be expanded during succeeding years. Services of CISF (Marine) can also be loaned, on payment, to those non-major ports and off-shore installations operated by private sector that wish to avail of their services for maritime security duty.

Maritime Enforcement Agencies: Coastal States

For various reasons, including constitutional and administrative, coastal states had no role in enforcing their criminal jurisdiction even in adjacent territorial waters. Even Tamil Nadu, that was facing the backlash of Tamil insurgency in Sri Lanka, had no effective marine police to enforce law and order in the adjacent territorial waters. For the first time, decision makers in New Delhi realized the contribution that law enforcement agencies of the coastal states can make in strengthening security in waters adjacent to the shore/coast. In that context, the new concept of *Marine Police* was proposed in the first phase of Coastal Security. But, it was seen only as a *supplemental scheme* for strengthening infrastructure of *shore and inland water* (not even territorial waters!)

Details of the creation of Marine Police in all coastal states are available at the level of the Central Government but sufficient data is not available for action taken at the level of various states though they too are expected to contribute to it. As per the Annual Report, 2009-10, of the Ministry of Home Affairs, a sum of ₹ 551 crore was earmarked for a five-year period (First Phase) to be spent on strengthening enforcement capability in all the eight coastal states of India.

Of that, ₹ 400 crore was for non-recurring expenditure while ₹ 151 crore was for recurring expenditure. As per the details provided in the Annual Report of the Ministry of Home Affairs, these coastal states were to be provided support for the establishment of 73 police stations, 97 check posts, 58 outposts and 30 operational barracks. A total of 204 small patrol boats (5 and 12 tons) were to be acquired for operations in inland waters and near the shore line. Besides, 153 jeeps, and 312 motor cycles were to be procured to strengthen surveillance along the shore. Thus, the role of Marine Police, as envisaged in Phase I, was that of a beat constable along the shore and in inland waters.

A question can be raised whether the role prescribed during Phase I will continue to remain the permanent role of the Marine Police or will it be only a first step towards a greater role (at least up to the outer limit of territorial waters) during Phase II. In that case it will be necessary to work out a permanent arrangement for burden sharing between the Central Government and different coastal states. It will also be necessary to give the present *ad hoc* arrangement a constitutional legitimacy for its new role, if necessary, even by amending the Constitution, especially the VII Schedule, List III (Concurrent List) by adding 'maritime security', to the items listed under it, as a common objective to be shared between the Central Government and the coastal states. That will also constitutionally empower the Marine Police of various states not only to cooperate with enforcement agencies of the Central Government but also with those of other/neighbouring coastal states and Union Territories in the larger framework of coastal security.

An analysis of Phase I of coastal security shows that while some of the coastal states like Gujarat and Maharashtra have taken the maximum advantage of the new scheme, other states like Kerala had made a halting progress. It will be important to accelerate the process of involvement of coastal states in the overall framework of maritime security during Phase II. In that context, steps to enhance public awareness and even organized public participation in strengthening maritime security will be useful.

Mechanism of *public participation* at the state level can be at two levels. The one can be at the informal level involving fisher folk operating in the adjacent sea space. They can be encouraged to report anything unusual to the nearest police post. A toll free telephone number will be useful. Marine Police can be the nodal agency and it can either take action on its own or seek cooperation of Central Government agencies like the Coast Guard and the Customs.

The other mechanism will be more formal and will be supportive of enforcement measures of the state governments. There is provision for raising formation of Home Guards at state level. There is also the precedent of Home Guard (Border) that operates in cooperation with BSF along land border. That concept can be extended to create a marine wing of the Home Guard or the *Marine Guard.* Its members can be recruited from among the fishing community.

Those with their own fishing vessels can be given preference. Those selected can be given basic training in the use of GPS for determining exact location on the sea, night vision devices and appropriate communication system for keeping in touch with the coordinating agency like the Marine Police or the Coast Guard. Like the Home Guard, they too can be provided with suitable remuneration with additional incentives for the use of their vessels.

Establishing Marine Guard from among the members of the fishing community from adjacent shore will have several advantages. They are already trained seamen and know the sea space in which they have been operating for years. Since they own their vessels, no extra cost will be incurred in procuring patrol boats except some way of offering financial support for operation of these vessels even while on normal role as local fishing boats. Since these vessels will be fishing boats, they will be operating as such in the designated sea space as a part of their normal routine. Thus, at least one third of the total number can be expected to be 'on duty' at any given time. Even if the first battalion comprises of 300 Marine Guards, approximately 100 trained sea men will be deployed in the adjacent sea space at any given time.

No one can ignore their contribution in the collection and immediate contribution of information to designated agencies so that timely action can be initiated by them. Initially, during Phase II, each coastal state, in consultation with Ministry of Home Affairs, can raise one battalion each of Marine Guard (Home Guard-Marine). If their role is found to be contributive to maritime security, suitable decisions can be taken after the end of Phase-II.

When one analyses the data about the anticipated force level (approximate) of different maritime enforcement agencies capable of taking responsibility of coastal security in the near future one reaches the conclusion that none of them is individually capable of taking on that role effectively. But, collectively, they do possess the minimum capability if they can usefully synergize their operations. That necessitates cooperation and synergy at the level of C3I as also decision making at the higher level and more so in actual operations at the lower level; especially in sub-zones and even at unit level as will be examined subsequently.

New Challenges, New Approaches

Traditional approach to governance in formulation of policy, as also its implementation, is often limited to the level of concerned ministry and the department. That approach is not only inadequate but also counter-productive in the context of sea governance and related issue of maritime security *vis-à-vis* NSA and terrorist. The main reason is that India has no single ministry or department that can take all decisions related to sea governance as also implement them. Given the diversity of issues involved, such a centralized framework for decision making and implementation cannot even be recommended.

There are multiple stakeholders who would like to hold on to their autonomy and who might be far from cooperative if they are forced to follow the dictates of another agency. This will be true both in the field of policy making as well as implementation.

Hence, there is the need for a new approach that would facilitate the creation of a framework that will ensure *willing cooperation and synergy of operation* among multiple agencies that are involved in sea governance as also in maritime security both at the level of Central Government and State Governments.

In 2004-05, when coastal security was being debated, little attention was paid to the question of sea governance. Enforcement activities were to be shared between the Navy, the Coast Guard and the Marine Police in three different zones. In the chain of command the Navy and the Coast Guard worked together and the Coast Guard worked with the Marine Police. The chain of command reflected the traditional leadership role of the senior service over the junior service, not the best way to encourage full cooperation among autonomous enforcement agencies.

One noticed a shift in approach after 26/11 because it focused on the need to involve/coordinate activities of all the stakeholders at the level of the Central Government as also State Governments in the field of shipping, port, fishery, defence, home affairs etc. that was reflected in series of meetings at top level, and involving the Cabinet Secretary, of all concerned stakeholders. There is also the provision for follow up action as detailed in the Annual Reports of the Ministry of Home Affairs of 2008-09 and 2009-10.

Since the broader question of sea governance can no longer be ignored it is necessary to give it a more formal shape. A mechanism needs to be evolved to synchronise action based upon willing cooperation of all stakeholders so as to evolve a new mindset and to dovetail the action of respective stakeholders in the context of better sea governance. The need for the creation of a structure that would lead to cooperation among various stakeholders can be recommended for Phase II of coastal security. It can be termed *National Commission on Sea Governance* (NCSG).

It will not duplicate the functioning of any department but will coordinate functions of various departments in furtherance of more effective sea governance.

To be effective NCSG will:

1. Function under the Cabinet Secretariat.
2. Will have representatives of stakeholders at the level of Central Government, State Governments and private sectors especially those involved in fisheries, port sector (minor ports) and off-shore oil and gas industry.
3. It will hold periodic meetings; bi-annual in the initial period and annual subsequently (beside emergency meet if needed).
4. It will be tasked with:

- Coordination in evolving broad policy of sea governance and role of individual stakeholders in that context, and recommend means of coordination/synergy of operation among immediately concerned stakeholders;
- To constitute, if necessary, committees for facilitating cooperation among concerned stakeholders;
- Revamping/updating of policies and implementation procedures of various departments;
- Formation of a small secretariat under Cabinet Secretariat, with permanent staff to: (a) synchronise the work of committees and the NCSG, and (b) prepare the agenda for the NCSG and for follow-up action;
- Nominating Chairman/Deputy Chairman of NCSG to chair the main session as also various committees, and to supervise the functioning of the Secretariat;
- NCSG to report periodically (quarterly if possible) to Cabinet Secretary on its functioning. The report can also be distributed to stakeholders for information.
- Navy-sponsored programmes of Maritime Domain

Awareness System (MDAS) as also National Command Control, Communication and Intelligence (NC_3IN) can be linked to NCSG since a large percentage of data that goes into MDAS and NC_3IN can be generated only through active cooperation of stakeholders of NCSG.

Second institution that is related to enforcement, National Committee on Maritime Security (NCMS), will concentrate upon broad policy of coordination among various enforcement agencies dealing with maritime security.

The NCMS will comprise of representatives of the Navy, the Coast Guard, the Customs (Marine) and the Marine Police to begin with.

Other agencies like the CISF (Marine) and of the fishery departments can be included if and when formed.

NCMS will be tasked with:

1. Formulating policy on framework of cooperation among various maritime enforcement agencies at national level.
2. Holding periodic meetings, bi-annual to begin with and annual subsequently, to initiate policies as also to review their implementation.
3. NCMS will have a Chairman to preside over the sessions/meetings and to supervise the functioning of the Secretariat.
4. NCMS will help organize seminars/workshops on related topics:

- In cooperation with organizations like the USI, IDSA, NMF etc.;
- Funds can be provided by Ministry of Defence, Ministry of Home Affairs as also by concerned departments like shipping, port authorities, energy etc.; and
- A working committee for the seminar/workshop be constituted comprising of representatives of the stakeholders, funding agency and the organization that is entrusted with that programme.

The working committee will prepare the agenda, list of participants and working papers. It will also prepare the summary of deliberations along with the recommendations. It will assist the organization in preparing the compendium/book of the entire proceeding for wider distribution.

While NCMS will look at the issue at national level, it will be useful to have sub-committees of NCMS at zonal levels (North Arabian Sea, South Arabian Sea and the Bay of Bengal) for discussing problems specific to these zones. Already there is the provision for such cooperation at zonal level. For example, in South Arabian Sea zone, the Navy has been designated as the authority responsible for overall maritime security. Commander-in-Chief Southern Naval Command has been designated as C-in-C Coastal Defence. Navy will be assisted by the Coast Guard, Marine Police and other agencies. For ensuring synergy of action *Joint Operation Centre* has been created in Kochi. It is manned *jointly* by the Navy and the Coast Guard. Information/intelligence is reported to it. It also coordinates enforcement action.

While this is a positive step more needs to be done in that direction at the level of sub-zones and even individual units. Cooperation and synergy of operation will become essential for two main reasons; inadequate force level of individual agencies and compulsions of sharing base infrastructures in isolated areas. This can be best illustrated by giving the example of Beypore in Kerala. That base has the Coast Guard (2PCs), Customs (Marine) (2 PC) and may be Marine Police Station (2 PC). Thus, if these three agencies synergize their operation, at least two patrol boats can be deployed on duty in adjacent waters with two ready for emergency requirements, while two boats can be under repairs. This is often necessary when deployed on sustained operations. Thus, a close rapport among personnel of these agencies and mechanism approved at high level for the synergy of operation will help in overcoming the present limitations of human resources and platforms needed to sanitize the vast sea space of India's coast.

To sum up, one can say that though some halting steps have been initiated to strengthen coastal security, much more remains to be accomplished. In that context, four points need to be underlined. The first is that the target of the threat is the coastal belt of India. The present format of coastal security is Centre-specific with almost all powers and functions vested in Central Government as if Delhi is the potential target. Since the threat is specific to the coastal states and Union Territories, it is imperative that they should be, over the years, given a greater role in combating those threats. In that context it would be desirable to amend Part III of the 7th Schedule of the Indian Constitution and make maritime security a concurrent subject.

The second point that needs urgent attention is the need to bring about some order in the use of adjacent water space, especially by Indian fishermen and sailors. Steps suggested in that context have not succeeded so far. Unless activities of the users of the adjacent sea space is adequately monitored, it will be almost impossible to single out potential criminal elements.

The third point that needs to be addressed deals with the need to evolve a formal mechanism that would involve a section of the local fishing community in keeping an eye on the activities in the adjacent sea space. I have mentioned in this article the need to form a marine wing of the Home Guard (Marine Guard) that will comprise of members of local fishing community who have their own vessels. Their activities can be coordinated by Marine Police who would, in turn, coordinate with the enforcement agencies of the Central Government. It will be the most cost effective way of acquiring human intelligence in a specific zone and at a specific time.

Lastly, there is the need to bring about some form of synergy as regards information sharing and even enforcement operation among multiple agencies operating in a given maritime zone. The total effect of this cooperation will be further enhanced if the scope of that cooperation can be extended to cover the neighbouring maritime zones of adjacent coastal states and Union Territories so as to produce and inter-locked grid.

India has taken some steps in enhancing its coastal

security. More needs to be done. One hopes that over the coming decade, coastal security will become a new source of cooperation not only between the Centre and the State but also among adjacent coastal states and Union Territories. Coastal security is a new concept and one needs to address it with a new and an open mindset rather than searching for solutions in the traditional format which has, at least so far, failed to evolve a truly functional mechanism to ensure security to homeland from threats posed by NSA and terrorists operating *via* the adjacent sea space.

4

India, US and the Indian Ocean: The Strategic Interest and Convergence

S.Y. Surendra Kumar

Indian Ocean is the third largest ocean in the world and is an area of great diversity and contrasts in terms of political, population, culture, economy, environment and complex geopolitical framework. Apparently, for more than centuries, the Indian Ocean was relatively backwater in international geo-strategic affairs. However, since few decades Indian Ocean has gained significance in the international arena for variety of reason such as: The Indian Ocean Region (IOR) presently contains 1/3 of the world population, 25 percent of its landmass, 40 percent of the world oil and gas reserves and continues to be the major source of raw materials. It is also the locus of important international Sea Lines of Communication (SLOCs). The region has emerged as major transport route and export supply area for oil and gas from the Middle East and coal from Australia and South Africa.

Subsequently, more than half of world oil production is transported through Indian Ocean and 36 percent of oil originates from this region. As a result, from the energy and trade perspective the region is now of prime interest for many far-off states in the world like United States, European Union, Japan, China, Russia, Korea, Indonesia, Australia and Iran. At the same time, the region has emerged as most troubled and dangerous region due to many political conflicts and non-traditional security threats, like WMD proliferation, radical terrorism, unstable states, piracy and illicit activities, which poses challenges to international community. Hence, the Indian Ocean is regarded as a very 'active' ocean and perceived by many as the emerging centre of gravity in the strategic world. Against this background, this paper will examine the strategic interest of India and US and the areas of convergence and its limits.

Strategic Interest of India

India's maritime geography consists of 7,516 km. long coastline facing the Arabian Sea on the West, the Bay of Bengal to the East and the vast Indian Ocean in the south. It is close to 200 major and minor ports and a merchant shipping fleet to over 750 ships. [1] Given that Indian Ocean is the backyard of India, its primary maritime interest is to assure national security and secure maritime environment to achieve sustained national development. In this regard from time to time it has enhanced maritime security. At the same time, India's quest to become a regional power is challenged by the interest and presence of many extra-regional powers in the region. Nevertheless, the main strategic interests of India are as follows.

Strategic Ambition

By the virtue of geography, Indian Ocean is India's backyard and is both natural and desirable for India to have predominant influence in this region. It is also the world's only region and ocean named after a single state, thus many argue that Indian Ocean is or should be, India's Ocean. Moreover, India occupies a highly strategic position in the northern Indian Ocean, in way allowing it to control the key SLOCs to and from the Suez Canal, Persian Gulf and Malacca Strait. As a result, many Indian strategic thinkers and Indian establishments have emphasised from time to time that India has legitimate aspiration in emerging as regional hegemony in the region and should have greater role in the Indian Ocean.

For instance, K.M. Panikkar, popularly known as the father of Indian maritime strategy argued that Indian ocean must remain 'truly India' and even advocated the creation of a 'steel ring' around India through the establishment of forward naval bases in Singapore, Mauritius, Yemen and Sri Lanka. [2] Presently, many advocate this strategy to counter China's 'string of pearls'. Furthermore, the Indian Navy's *Maritime Doctrine* (2004), argues for India building maritime power "to control the choke points as bargaining chip in the international power game". [3] Others like Jaswant Singh, the former Indian foreign Minister called the Indian Ocean as India's 'sphere of influence' i.e., India could use the region to achieve its foreign policy objectives.

This was further elaborated by the Prime Minister Manmohan Singh, that Indian Ocean is India's 'strategic footprint', [4] connecting the South East Asia, Far East and beyond, which would strengthen India's successful rise, achieve security ambitions and become the predominant maritime security provider in the region stretching from the Red sea to Singapore. As a result, India has given greater importance to Malacca Strait, since its ability to control the strait is seen as a prerequisite of effective control of effective control of the eastern Indian Ocean. To achieve this, it has developed military facilities in Andaman Island as the base for a new tri-service far eastern strategic command. Subsequently, India is strengthening its strategic relationship with Singapore and Indonesia, and working on the same line with other external powers like US, Australia and Japan. Thus, India's proximity to Indian Ocean has shaped its naval ambition to increase its sphere of influence across the IOR and globe.

In pursuit of its strategic ambition, India has already emerged as reliable player in counter-piracy operations off the Horn of Africa and elsewhere throughout the Indian Ocean, which is well acknowledged by International community and also countries like US, China, Japan so on. Subsequently, it has been actively engaging countries throughout the Indian Ocean region with ship visits, high-level defence meetings, and the provision of military equipment, and it has taken lead in establishing the Indian Ocean Naval Symposium (IONS) in 2008, and organized the MILAN naval exercises held every two years. Thus, India is in progress of achieving its ambition in the region through cooperation, rather than confronting with major powers.

Economic and Energy Security

Economic and energy security is another prime strategic interests for India, as it is the fourth largest economy in the world and the economic resurgence is directly linked to her overseas trade and energy needs, most of which are transported by sea. Moreover, it depends 70 percent on foreign oil and it is estimated to rise to 85 percent by 2020. As a result, many Indian security analysts believe that energy security will be India's prime strategic interest for next 25 years. In its quest for energy and to sustain the economic growth it is highly important for India to protect its offshore oil and gas field; ongoing deep-sea oil drilling projects; building infrastructure of shore and offshore oil and gas wells, pumping stations, telemetry posts, ports, pipeline grids, and refineries. [5] In addition, under the Public-Private partnership, many oil companies have invested billions of dollars in the Exclusive Economic Zones (EEZ) stretching over 2.3 million sq. km., which will meet India energy requirements. Thus, securing these investment, which is crucial for India growth constitute an important strategic interest for India.

Protecting the SLOCs

There are many choke points in the Indian Ocean like Strait of Hormuz, Suez Canal and Red Sea, Strait of Bab-el-Mandeb and Horn of Africa, Malacca Strait, Lombok Strait, Sunda Strait, Six Degree Channel, Nine Degree Channel, Cape of Good Hope, [6] which are vital energy flow points, like US$ 200 billion worth of oil comes out the Strait of Hormuz and US$ 70 billion passes through the Malacca straits, which alone accounts for more than 25 percent of world's maritime trade. As a result, it is the busiest sea lane, [7] and any disruption in traffic flow at these points will prove to be economically disastrous, as it would hit the energy flows.

Presently, the major threats to the SLOCs are piracy, drug trafficking, gun running, human smuggling, pollution, accidents, mines, closure of choke points, inter-state conflicts and territorial disputes. Moreover, there is greater energy demand among India, China and Japan to sustain its economic growth, thus the security of SLOC and choke points of Indian Ocean during the peace, tension or hostilities constitute primary national maritime interest. This was highlighted by Indian ambassador to US, Nirupama Rao in September 2011, that "safety of SLOCs across the Indian Ocean is crucial for the economic growth not just for India and US but for the entire region". [8]

Concerned over Chinese Maritime Power

Generally, Indian analysts have perceived China's policy towards Indian Ocean as directed against India rather than being a legitimate reflection of Chinese interests in its SLOC across the Indian Ocean. China in order to address its energy security needs, has established a substantial naval presence along vital maritime chokepoints, which is popularly known as China's 'String of Pearls", a plan to acquire several strategically placed ports, naval bases and listening posts in friendly countries like Gwadar (Pakistan), Hambantota (Sri Lanka), Sittwe (Myanmar), Chittagong (Bangladesh); electronic intelligence gathering facilities on islands in the Bay of Bengal; funding construction of a canal across the Kra Isthmus in Thailand; a military agreement with Cambodia and building up of forces in the South China Sea. [9] Presently, an attempt is also made to construct a submarine base in the Maldives, to protect the billions of dollars worth trade that pass through strategically sea lanes like the Strait of Hormuz or the Malacca straits to Middle East, Africa and Latin America.

The Chinese government have justified this strategy by emphasising that it imports more than 50 percent of its oil consumption (2010) and Malacca strait is the key choke-point on China's oil supply routes, hence it is in China's interest to develop an alternative ports and pipelines, such as 'sting of pearls', to reduce the criticality of the Malacca Strait and build strategic ties with several countries along the sea lanes from the Middle East to the South China Sea in order to protect China's energy interests and security objectives. Furthermore, Chinese President Hu Jintao in September 2010 stated that "the growth of the Indian navy means that Chinese economic development is potentially at the mercy of India, as well as the US. The forging of Indian security links with Japan and the US is therefore a source of concern". [10] Despite the Chinese justification, India is concerned about Chinese naval presence, which poses a threat to national security and maritime interest of India.

Apart from this, traditionally India's has been a close partner of IOR islands and has always supported numerous endeavours to ensure 'good order at sea', like Indian Navy has assisted the weaker states of the Indian Ocean littoral in building their own capacities by training, advising and providing equipment to safeguard its security such as helping Mauritius to operate coast Guard; strengthening Sri Lanka's ability to control its waters; improving the ability of Mozambique, Madagascar and Maldives to monitor their maritime domain. [11]

However, in the recent time, China is building and strengthening relationship with the Indian Ocean Island like with Mauritius, Seychelles and other African nations which is seen by India as threat to its security and strategic interest. As a result, India has been cautious in allowing China establishing security relationships with Indian Ocean Island and excluded China from regional forums like IONS. [12] Thus, the increasing Chinese naval ambition and presence poses a great challenge to India's dominance in region. Overall, Indian Ocean is important for India from economic, political, legal and military perspective.

Although India is concern over China's maritime power, but in the recent times, India and China's bilateral relations have improved, particularly in the sphere of trade and addressing transnational issues and now even in maritime cooperation. For instance, there are many instances of joint exercises undertaken between both the Navies, however, it was only during the visit of Chinese Premier Wen Jiabao's to India in December 2010, that the new areas such as co-operation in maritime security were raised. Since then both navies have deployed warships in Gulf of Aden for tackling piracy and continue to be committed to freedom of navigation in line with international laws. Most significantly, in March 2012, during the annual meetings of India and China Foreign Ministers, the Chinese Foreign Minister Yang Jiechi presented a proposal on maritime cooperation with India, which was accepted in principle by the India. [13] However, the modalities of cooperation is yet to be worked out, nevertheless mostly it would include joint operations against piracy, sharing of seabed research technology and other common areas concerning both the countries. Thus, these developments has laid a stronger foundation for secure the strategic interest of both countries and also to maintain the good order of the sea.

Strategic Interests of US

Initially, US strategic interest in Indian Ocean was limited, as US was more concerned with Pacific Ocean. However, the Indian Ocean region has only recently become a central focus of US strategic priorities, and even here, only in a piecemeal fashion, with American interests mainly concerned with the threats of non-state actors and fragile or failed states like Somalia, Yemen and Pakistan. Nevertheless, US has emerged as an external actor in the Indian Ocean and has a more significant military presence than before in the Persian Gulf and Arabian Sea, Pakistan, East and northeast Africa, Singapore, and Diego Garcia. In this regard, Robert Kaplan, emphasised the importance of IOR for US-"Indian Ocean is region in which the US will have to keep the peace and help guard the global commons—interdicting terrorists, pirates, and smugglers; providing humanitarian assistance; managing the competition between India and China". [14]

There are many vital strategic interests for US in Indian Ocean such as: (a) to ensure continued access to markets and smooth flow of global energy supply, trade and raw materials through SLOC. Subsequently, it is vital to swing forces from the U.S. Pacific Command through the Indian Ocean to deal with challenges in Southwest Asia, as occurred in Operation Desert Storm (1991) and subsequently Operations Enduring Freedom (2001) and Iraqi Freedom (2003); (b) similar, to India, ensuring the security of maritime chokepoints and SLOCs is vital strategic interest of US; and (c) protecting the critical maritime-related infrastructures like physical and cyber networks, particularly the broadband communication connections between Asia, Europe, and the US that are linked by undersea cables traversing the Indian Ocean. These infrastructure and key resources constitute a significant part of the national economy and security and it also function as critical defence infrastructure, which must be constantly assured for national security operations worldwide. These infrastructures are vulnerable to terrorist attacks in the form of piracy, transnational crimes, drug and arms trafficking, illegal seaborne immigrations, proliferation of WMD. Thus, protecting the infrastructures is vital interest for US; (d) preventing new or established extremist groups from harming the interests of the US or allied Indian Ocean littoral states. [15] Moreover, the region is important for US and its allies as it could become a secondary arena for great power strategic competition in Asia, particularly between India and China, were US can play the role of balancer. Overall, US policy towards Indian Ocean is shaped by maintaining an open Indian Ocean highway, defending chokepoints at either end of the Indian Ocean, and sanitizing the Indian Ocean as a secondary front in broader Asian regional competition. [16]

To achieve these interests, US has developed many strategies which are well reflected in US Navy's "A Cooperative Strategy for 21st Century Sea power" (2007), in which few strategy are relevant to Indian ocean region such as: (a) need for continuous credible combat power in the Western Pacific and the Indian Ocean to protect its vital interest; (b) assure our friends and allies our commitment to regional security, and deter and dissuade potential adversaries and peer competitors; and (c) creation and maintenance of security at sea to mitigate threats short of war, including piracy, terrorism, weapons proliferation, drug trafficking and other illicit activities, [17] since all these are a global common challenges needs maritime cooperation among regional players like India. Even the Pentagon's 2010 Quadrennial Defense Review (QDR) emphasized for more "integrated approach to the region [Indian Ocean] across military and civilian organizations". [18] Overall, US have formulated strategies from time to time to safeguard its interest in the region. One of the vital strategies have been building and strengthening maritime cooperation with regional powers like India, Japan, Australia and Southeast Asian countries.

India-US Maritime Cooperation

India has always opposed the presence of major powers in Indian Ocean region, as it will exacerbate regional insecurity and threaten its regional hegemony. As a result, India did not welcome US presence in the region, even the Sri Lankan proposal (1970s)-the Indian Ocean as a Zone of Peace (IOZP), was rejected by India, as it did not want the entry of US and even Russia into the India Ocean after the British withdrawal. Subsequently, India also feared about the US and its alliances with China and Pakistan, which was threat to India's security. As a result, India initially opposed US presence in India Ocean.

However, with the transformation of Indo-US relation into a strong strategic partnership under the Bush administration,

Indian Ocean emerged as common interest. This was stressed by Secretary of State Colin Powell in 2001 to the US Senate Foreign Relations Committee that "India has the potential to help keep the pace in the vast Indian Ocean area and its periphery...and we should consistently help them in this endeavour". [19] In the process, in 2005, the Bush administration emphasised that it would help India become a major world power in the 21st century, seeking to build India's capabilities as an implicit balance to China. Subsequently, India signed the nuclear deal and 10 year defence agreement with US, which has laid the foundation for stronger partnership in most of key sectors. In September 2011, Robert Blake, the Assistant Secretary of State for South and Central Asia stated "New Delhi as a pillar of stability and prosperity in the Indian Ocean and beyond...said India has long been a maritime power in Asia in its own right and only India itself can charter a path to navigate the geopolitical currents unfolding before us". [20] In addition, US also agreed on strengthening of maritime cooperation through encouraging India's naval ambitions; expansion of its naval capabilities and coordinate its maritime strategy with US in Persian Gulf, South-East Asia and as far as the Taiwan Strait. [21]

Apparently, under the larger strategic partnership, US has encouraged India to increase its naval presence in the north-east Indian Ocean and also assisting in building naval bases. Subsequently, US had conducted frequent joint exercises with Indian navy and sold an American warship for the first time, the 17,000 ton amphibious transport dock USS Trenton. At the same time, the US contactors have been offering India's military advance fighters jets to anti-ship missiles. To expand and strengthen the US-India naval relationship, they undertook many bilateral naval exercises like since the end of cold war, both have carried out 14 series of exercises, of which the last one was a 10-day joint naval exercise Malabar 2011, in the Arabian Sea during April-May 2011. [22]

The main focuses of the operations were on anti-submarine warfare, surface firings and maritime interdiction operations, apart from humanitarian assistance and disaster-relief efforts. [23] The exercise included Indian Navy's advanced guided-missile destroyer, three guided missile frigates, one conventional submarine and several shore-based Sea Harrier fighters. From US Navy side included one guided-missile cruiser, two destroyers, one frigate, one nuclear-powered submarine along with two long-range marine patrol plane P-3s. [24] Interestingly, India now conducts more exercises with the US than with any other country. In addition, both the countries have also undertaken naval exercises at multilateral level like in 2007 and 2009, involving Japan, Australia and Singapore. In August 2010, the 7th MILAN, biennial exercise of the Navies of Asia-Pacific littoral states, was held at Port Blair, in which 12 countries participated, the highest number since 1995, including Australia, Malaysia, Singapore, Indonesia, Thailand, Myanmar, Bangladesh and Sri Lanka and delegations from New Zealand, Vietnam and Brunei. [25]

The Chinese assume that these exercises are design against it, however, the US stated that it was means to rapidly expand the navy-to-navy relationship with India, but underling fact remains, US quest to contain China's growth and influence in ocean, in which India could be strategic partner along with Japan. Thus, all these developments indicate US acknowledging India's rise as a military power in the Asia-Pacific and the dominant role its navy could play in years to come. There are many reasons for increase in India-US naval cooperation like US recognition of India's rise and as a potential strategic partner. Subsequently, US realisation, that multilateralism is the key to deal with regional security challenges and both the countries are concerned about the rising power of China in the Asia-Pacific region and beyond. Thus, India-US strategic partnership has also transformed naval relationship between the countries and provided scope for convergence in the region.

Strategic Convergence

There are many areas of convergence, through which they can achieve their strategic interest in the region such as:

1. From time to time, Indian government has emphasised the need for expanding geographical scope of India's maritime interests, the phrases from "Aden to Malacca" and the 'Suez to the South China Sea' is now part of national security discourse. The former Chief of Naval Staff Admiral Arun Prakash stated, "Indian navy's interest is not restricted to the Indian Ocean and goes beyond". [26] This ambition is well translated through its role during the *Tsunami,* Indian Ocean (2004-05), relief operations in Mediterranean (2006) the continued anti-piracy activity in the Gulf of Aden (since 2008). [27] Thus, India in order to pursue its 'far sea defence' it needs the support and cooperation from major power like US. Moreover, even building 'blue water navy', needs an policy framework to expand capabilities for design, development, and production of naval equipment, and here US also can play a significant role in providing the necessary equipments and weapons to safeguard and strengthen Indian maritime interest and support India's geographical reach.
2. The region represents the most troubled and dangerous area of the world, like in 2009 alone, a total of 170 political conflicts were recorded in the Indian ocean region, representing 46.6 percent of the 36 conflicts worldwide, with 50 percent of all the crises and severe crises in the world, and 19 of the 31 high-intensity conflicts. [28] Of this, terrorism and transnational crime are perhaps the most prominent sources of non-traditional violence and instability in the region. To address these challenges, bilateral, regional and global cooperation is needed.

   Thus, US-India political and military cooperation is vital to counter the very real challenges of international piracy, Al Qaeda and its Linkages, Jemmah Islamiah (JI), an umbrella organisation for a variety of terrorist groups in South East Asia and Islamist terrorism in the Horn of Africa. In this regard, both the countries are working together along with the international community to combat piracy in the Gulf of Aden and off the coast of Somalia. Indian Navy in the recent times has been successful in carrying out anti-piracy patrols like the Gulf of Aden (October 2008), effectively averted numerous piracy attempts and arrested several pirates. Subsequently, continue to provide protection and rendering assistance to merchant vessels irrespective of their nationality like in February 2011, American citizens were lost to an attack by Somali Pirates and in the subsequent month, the Indian Navy neutralized a pirate mother ship and captured 61 Somali pirates, the largest such success in the ongoing anti-piracy operations, getting praise from the International Maritime Bureau (IMB). [29]

Hence, the Indian Navy's success in the recent times and cooperation between both states in overcoming the non-traditional challenges is their interest. This was emphasised by Hillary Clinton, US Secretary of State in July 2011, "strengthening military-to-military ties would assist both to work together in a constructive way on patrolling the seas, combating piracy and providing relief to the victims of natural disasters". [30] Furthermore, both the countries continue to consult on maritime security cooperation in the Indian Ocean Region through forums like Defense Policy Group and its appropriate sub-groups. They are also working towards exchanging views on promoting regional security architecture that enhances maritime security in the Indian Ocean Region.

3. Although, India and the US's relations with China has drastically improved, but they also have shared apprehensions about the People's Liberation Army (PLA) Navy's acquisition trends, capabilities, intentions, and actions in the greater Indian Ocean region, which threatens

their interest at regional and global level. Moreover, US are also concerned about the protection of Taiwan. In addition to China, the US and India are very much concerned with Yemen and Somalia, a fragile states and further deterioration would intensify piracy and allow for greater freedom of action for non-state terrorist actors. Moreover, in the aftermath of American withdrawal from Iraq and Afghanistan, it is unlikely to commit ground forces to stabilize ground realities in Yemen or Somalia, which would give more scope for non-state actors to dominate over sea and given India's geographic proximity to both countries, it will have serious implication on India's security in the region. As a result, the maritime dimension will be vital to any operations and will require strong coordination between the Indian Navy and US navies.

4. The major threat to the collective interests of IOR countries and people is the non-traditional security risks such as the combined impacts of climate change and environmental degradation. In this regard, the Intergovernmental Panel on Climate Change (IPCC) has warned on rising sea temperatures and its impact on monsoon that can create drought, cyclone, intense storm and so on. [31] Moreover, the sea level rise, desertification, and the submergence of islands will lead to migration of million individuals and created environmental refugees, which give rise to additional problems such as health issues, scarce resource competition, and social and ethnic tensions will surface. [32]

The region is prone to frequent natural disaster, locus of 70 percent of the world's natural disasters and overcoming needs a collaborative approach and that is where US can be a great source of help for India in discharging its responsibilities of providing disaster relief. This cooperation has been effective like formation of "Regional Core Group", by US-Japan-Australia-India to address the spearheaded relief work in the wake *Tsunami* in December 2004, in which Sri Lanka, Maldives, Indonesia and southern parts of India were badly affected. Thus, this case demonstrates the effective collaboration between nations for providing disaster relief.

In addition, the ocean resource exploitation in the Indian Ocean also poses a major challenge, as there has been increasing competition for resources due to continued growth and prosperity globally. Apparently, the technological advances are enabling expanded marine activities such as energy development, resources extraction like sea food, minerals etc., and other commercial activity in and under the ocean. Thus, India and the US can assist IOR Island in mitigating these problems.

The Strategic Convergence between India-US maritime cooperation can be further strengthened through an India-US-Australia trilateral strategic dialogue on Indian Ocean. Although, in 2007 attempts were made to institutionalize the US-Japan-India-Australia quadrilateral initiative, however it failed due to change of regime in both Japan and Australia, who had reservation about this alliance; lack of commitment from India, which had agreed only in principle; US was disappointed with response of three countries; and China had raised serious concern about this alliance, as a result this alliance as of now is put on hold, but there are possibilities of this alliance taking shape in near future.

Nevertheless, the India-US-Australia trilateral strategic dialogue on Indian Ocean, could be a significant step for three vital reasons: (a) it will dissuade China or other external powers from seeking parity over India's influence in Indian ocean region, thus securing the highway; (b) the Indian Ocean region has been Beijing's "core interest" and its increasing assertiveness could be countered through this alignment strategies; (c) the alliance will create capacity and norms for security cooperation in response to piracy, terrorism, or other littoral challenges in the Indian Ocean, which needs collective approach and will gradually discourage unilateral power plays by China. [33] Thus, there are potentials of trilateral alliance, but it is yet to take shape.

Although, there are many areas of convergence for India and US in the Indian Ocean region, but there are many limits of this convergence, which would prevent both the nations from achieving their strategic interest. Some of the limits of the convergence are as follows.

Will US Assist India in Countering China?

Many Indian and American analysts argue that both should strengthen its maritime cooperation to contain China's increasing presence in Indian Ocean region. Similarly, it is argued that US is co-opting India to contain China's rise in sea. However, from time to time, US has emphasised that it is neither obsessed with Chinese commercial activities nor concern with string of pearls affecting India's maritime interest, rather US Navy's priority is to improve maritime security against pirates and potential terrorist and proliferation of WMD. Moreover, US naval planning with regard to Chinese naval capabilities is more focussed on a contingency involving Taiwan, and less on containing China in Indian Ocean. As a result, US is more interested in India navy's contribution to combat Somali pirates off the coast of African than assisting India in countering China or assisting littoral states to improve security in the Malacca strait.

India's Concern over US Military Presence

India is also concern about the large U.S. military presence in the Indian Ocean to India's west—in the Arabian Sea and the Persian Gulf. This was stressed by India's *Maritime Doctrine,* that "the unfolding events consequent to the war in Afghanistan has brought the threats emanating on our Western shores into sharper focus. The growing US and western presence and deployment of naval forces, the battle for oil dominance and its control in the littoral and hinterland...are factors that are likely to have a long-term impact on the overall security environment in the Indian Ocean region." [34]

Thus, India is also very much worried about increasing US presence in region, which challenges India's regional hegemony. As a result, many argue that the Indian government is deliberately excluding the US from membership into IONS, when it was started in 2008 on the grounds that the former is not a littoral state.

As of now there are 35 members and 23 have applied for observer status, including US and UK. However, the meeting of INOS in Cape Town, South Africa (April 2012) did not discuss the granting of observe status. Nevertheless, sooner or later India will have no option but to grant US observer status due to the pressure for the INOS members and also due to its own growing strategic partnership with US.

India's Non-committal to PSI

The US is unhappy with Indian's response to the Proliferation Security Initiative (PSI), proposed during the Bush administration. This is a web of partnerships aiming to prevent proliferation at sea, air, land the shipments of WMD, and their delivery systems to terrorists or countries suspected of trying to acquire them. Although, more than 97 countries (Jan 2011) have supported the initiative, and there are 21 Operations expert groups (OEG). However, India participated as an observer in three PSI exercises: Pacific Protector, hosted by Australia in 2006, Pacific Shield, hosted by Japan in 2007, and Maru, hosted by New Zealand in 2008. [35]

Despite this, India is reluctant in joining the US-led PSI. India's reservations are on legitimacy of PSI, that it is not endorsed by United Nations (UN); political sensitivities, technical and diplomatic imperatives. [36] Moreover, PSI is more of an extension of existing US headed military alliances like NATO. In addition, the PSI is aimed directly at Iran and North Korea, apparently, India has a strategic cooperation with Iran and it imports 14 percent of oil. Thus, India not part of PSI continues to be an irritant in India-US relations, which would have impact on maritime cooperation as well.

Concluding Observations

India-US already enjoys significant maritime cooperation and further it can be strengthened by focussing on the Asian and global maritime commons.

Given that, US will continue to be the major power in the region, however the fragile/failed states and the non-state actors have the potential to create serious security problems, as a result, it is in the US interest to strengthen navy-to-navy cooperation with India to maintain regional and global stability, as Indian Navy is one of the key actors in combating terrorism and transnational crimes.

Moreover, US need's to enhance India's naval capabilities in the South China Sea and the Persian Gulf as it also in its interest in countering the China's naval ambition. At the same time, India needs to gain access to U.S. defence technology to facilitate its plans to play a larger role in the Indian Ocean region. Moreover, India also needs US support and cooperation to protect the interest of IOR island, as it involves range of policy instrument like transfer of arms, financial resources and production capacities, failing which will create a vacuum that can be filled by China, which is already happening like India being lukewarm in accepting Sri Lanka's offer to build new port at Hambantota, was taken over by China, which has in way increased its presence in our backyard.

Overall, India's economic prosperity is linked with seas, as more than 90 percent of world trade in commodities and goods continues to flow by the seas, and India is no different. [37] As a result, oceans continue to be the main lifeline for the economic-well being of India. Moreover, as India intents to expand its sphere of influence beyond India Ocean then, it needs to invest heavily in diplomatic initiatives, trade agreements, military exercises, aid funds, energy cooperation and infrastructure building in Indian Ocean as well as in

Pacific Ocean. Subsequently, it should also restructure its maritime ambitions through strengthening its bilateral relations with major powers like China, Russia, Japan, France, Australia and South East Asian nations. At the same time, India along with other major powers should strengthen the existing regional forums like Indian Ocean Rim-Association for Regional Cooperation (IOR-ARC) [India Chairs for 2011 and 2012], IONS and other sub-regional grouping. [38] Finally, if possible, both India and the US should work towards formation of a trilateral cooperation 'US-India-China' for ensuring peace and prosperity in the IOR.

End Notes

1. Devbrat Chakraborty, (2010), "Regional Maritime Security Environment: An Indian Perspective", in Sam Bateman and Joshua Ho, (eds.), *Southeast Asia and the Rise of Chinese and Indian Naval Power*, London: Routledge, p. 155.
2. K. M. Panikkar, (1962), *India and the Indian Ocean: An Essay on the Influence of Sea Power in Indian History*, Bombay: George Allen and Unwin, p. 15.
3. David Brewster, (2010), "Australia and India: the Indian Ocean and the Limits of Strategic Convergence", *Australian Journal of International Affairs*, 64 (5): 554.
4. Ibid, p. 555.
5. Vidhan Pathak, (2009), "China and Francophone Western Indian Ocean Region: Implications for Indian Interests", *Journal of Defence Studies*, 3 (4): 90.
6. Ministry of Defence, (2007), *Freedom to Use the Seas: Indian Maritime Military Strategy*,", New Delhi: Integrated Headquarters Ministry of Defence (Navy).
7. Vidhan Pathak, op. cit. 5, p. 91. Sheldon W Simon, (2011), "Safety and Security in the Malacca Straits: The Limits of Collaboration", *Asian Security*, 7 (1): 27-43.
8. "India, U.S. Agree to Enhance Maritime Security Cooperation: Nirupama Rao", 28 September 2011, Available at http://www.thehindu.com/news/international/article2492815.
9. Amardeep Athwal, (2008), *China-India Relations: Contemporary Dynamics*, London: Routledge, pp. 30-76.
10. "India, US need to partner to balance China in Indian Ocean",

The Indian Express, 2 September 2010. Available at www.indianexpress.com/news/india-us-need-to-partner-to-balance-china-in-indian-ocean/676275/2

11. C. Raja Mohan, (2010), "India and the Changing Geopolitics of the Indian Ocean", *Maritime Affairs*, 6 (2): 9.
12. The Indian Ocean Naval Symposium is a voluntary initiative consist of 35 members, seeks to increase maritime cooperation amongst navies of the littoral states of the Indian Ocean Region by providing an open and inclusive forum for discussion of regionally relevant maritime issues and, in the process, endeavours to generate a flow of information between naval professionals that would lead to a common understanding and possible agreements on the way ahead.
13. Praveen Swami, "No more at Sea" *The Hindu,* 6th March, 2012, p. 12.
14. Robert D. Kaplan, (2009), "Centre Stage for the Twenty-first Century", *Foreign Affairs,* March/April Vol. 88, Issue 2, p. 18.
15. James R. Holmes, Andrew C. Winner and Toshi Yoshihara, (2010), *Indian Naval Strategy in the Twenty-first Century,* London: Routledge, pp. 106-125.
16. Michael J. Green and Andrew Shearer, (2012) "Defining Indian U.S. Indian Ocean Strategy", *The Washington Quarterly*, Vol. 35, No. 2, p. 178.
17. Bronson Percival, "Growing Chinese and Indian Naval Power: US Recalibration and Coalition Building", in Sam Bateman and Joshua Ho, op. cit. 1, p. 37. Also see Andrew S. Erickson, (2008), Assessing New US maritime Strategy: A Window into Chinese thinking", *Naval War college Review*, 61 (4): 35-53.
18. Michael J. Green and Andrew Shearer, op. cit. 16, p. 175.
19. Washington File, (2001), 'Powell statement before Senate Foreign Relations Committee', 17 January. Available at http://usinfo.org/wf-archive/2001/010117/epf301.html.
20. "India Pillar of Stability in Indian Ocean Region: Robert Blake", 28 September 2011, http://articles.economictimes.indiatimes.com/2011-09-28/news/30212790_1_maritime-power-pillar-robert-blake.
21. Ashley Tellis, (2002), "South Asia", in Richard Ellings and Aaron Friedberg (eds.), *Strategic Asia 2001-2002: Power and Purpose*, Seattle: National Bureau of Asian Research, p. 224.
22. The Malabar exercise was conducted in 1992, 1995, 1996, 2002,

2003, 2004, 2005, 2006, 2007 (twice), 2008, 2009, 2010 and 2011). Twelve exercises were conducted off Indian Coast and two in the Pacific Ocean. Although, this exercise is primarily a bilateral exercise, but Japanese Navy, Australian and Singapore Navies also participated on few occasions.

23. Balaji Chandramohan, "US courts India in the Indian Ocean", Available at http://www.atimes.com/atimes/South_Asia/LE06Df02.html.
24. "Indian Navy starts Annual Joint Exercise with U.S. Navy", 24 April 2010. Available at http://english.peopledaily.com.cn/90001/90777/90851/6962009.html.
25. "Indian Navy: 2010 Year-End-Review", 5th January 2011. Available at http://www.defencetalk.com/indian-navy-2010-year-end-review-31032/#ixzz1r3CITuuf.
26. Walter C. Ladwig (2009), "Delhi's Pacific Ambition; Naval Power, Look East and India Emerging Influence in the Asia Pacific", *Asian Security,* 5 (2): 91.
27. C. Raja Mohan, op. cit. 11, p. 7.
28. Christian Bouchard and William Crumplin, (2010), "Neglected no Longer: The Indian Ocean at the Forefront of World Geopolitics and Global Geostrategy", *Journal of the Indian Ocean Region,* 6 (1): 27.
29. Sameer Sexane, "One Ocean, Two Shades: Perception about the Indian Ocean". Available at www.usnwc.edu/Lucent/OpenPdf.aspx, James R Holmes, (2010), "Tackling Somali Piracy Ashore: Maritime Security and Geopolitics in the Indian Ocean", *Strategic Analysis,* 35 (5):717-727.
30. "India, US talk Maritime Security" (2011), *The Times of India,* 20th July. Available at http://articles.timesofindia.indiatimes.com/2011-07-20/india/29794460_1_maritime-security-indian-ocean-region-military-to-military-ties.
31. Lee Cordner, (2010), "Rethinking Maritime Security in the Indian Ocean Region", *Journal of the Indian Ocean Region,* 6 (1): 70.
32. Conference Report, (2010), *Maritime Challenges and Priorities in Asia,* Singapore: S. Rajaratnam School of International Studies.

33. Michael J. Green and Andrew Shearer, op. cit. 16, p. 185.
34. Government of India, Ministry of Defence, *Annual Report 2004–05,* New Delhi: Ministry of Defence, p. 46. Available at www.meaindia.nic.in.
35. Charles Wolf, Brian G. Chow and Gregory S. Jones, (2008), *Enhancement by Enlargement: The Proliferation Security Initiative,* Santa Monica, RAND Corporation, p. 36.
36. Sameer Sexane, op. cit. 29, p. 19.
37. C. Raja Mohan, op. cit. 11, p. 4.
38. C. Raja Mohan, (2010), *India, US and the Global Commons,* Washington: Centre for a New American Security, p. 8.

5

India's Maritime Interests and the Growing Influence of China in the Indian Ocean

Chandrakant Yatanoor

Introduction

Immediately after Independence in 1947, India was preoccupied with stabilising the economy and feeding the country's teeming millions. Though, a handful of the intelligentsia had realised the importance of the seas for India, the economic and strategic philosophy adopted by the government prevented making any adequate investments required to set up the maritime infrastructure. Maritime interests of India had indeed taken a backseat with administrative issues worrying the thinkers. The three wars, which India fought with its neighbours also contributed towards a continental outlook. During the Cold War era, India remained non-aligned, the then existing altercation between the two super-powers (referring to United States of America and the former Soviet Union) provided a semblance of balance and security in the maritime sphere, although an uneasy one.

With the collapse of the Soviet Union in the late eighties, there was a fundamental overhaul in the international order. The USA being the only super power was working towards strengthening its security alliances with a view to retaining its superiority. This provided US the prospect to create pressure points, enforce, engage or infringe militarily, where other options would fail. It became thus important for India, more than ever, to formulate a strategy to safeguard its maritime interests. Territorial Integrity is the primary criterion which is taken up as a governing factor in maritime Indian interests. With piracy, militancy and terrorism raking the country's borders, Indian military forces are always up in arms to safeguard the country's emergency interests. This has become more important because of the growing influence of China in the Indian Ocean region.

Most analysts of Indian foreign and security policy, whether at home or abroad, would argue that the organizing principle of India's international relations is the notion of 'strategic autonomy'. But how credible is the notion of 'strategic autonomy' at a time when the Indian economy is globalizing and is becoming one of the worlds largest? Just as the mantra of 'self-reliance' is no longer a hallowed concept in our economic strategy, 'autonomy' can no longer be the organizing principle of our foreign and security policy.

Today, India's economic growth and prosperity are tied very deeply to resources and markets outside its borders. As a result, India's own security perimeter has widened rapidly and its interests are more widely dispersed around the world. Autonomy is for weak powers who are trying to insulate themselves from the regimen defined for them by the great powers. For many decades, India has seen itself as a weak developing state that must protect its territory, interests and freedom of choice from being trampled upon by the great powers. If India itself were to emerge as a great power, it is not impossible to see that Delhi's task will be to contribute to the management of the international order and not seeking autonomy from it.

The mental leap from being a 'rule-taker' to a 'rule-maker' will not come easily to Delhi's decision makers. But, the international pressure on India to take a larger role in the region and the world will be relentless. As in the case of China, so in the case of India, the compulsion will be to act as a 'stakeholder' rather than a 'free rider'. [1] This will be especially true of the maritime domain where the weight of growing naval power is now consequential for the ordering of the security complexes in the Indian and Pacific Oceans.

Since Independence, India's traditional impulse was to protect its own territory and the waters around it. The Partition of the subcontinent and the creation of new borders made internal conflict in the subcontinent a perennial one; the emergence of China as a new land neighbour after its control of Tibet added to India's security burdens. If India's land forces were weighed down by the defence of its borders, India's naval strategy too was guided by the imperative of protecting the territorial waters and its large exclusive economic zone. As the logic of economic globalization unfolded over the last two decades, the Indian naval leadership began to invent a new maritime strategy that is in tune with its new circumstances.

Not surprisingly since the late 1990s, the two Prime Ministers we have had—Atal Behari Vajpayee and Dr. Manmohan Singh—repeatedly underlined the expanded geographic scope of India's maritime interests. The phrases from 'Aden to Malacca' or 'the Suez to the South China Sea' were re-injected into the national security discourse. That this is not an empty talk is reflected in the operations of the Indian Navy that has frequently shown the Tricolour in waters as far apart as the North Atlantic and the South Pacific and from the Mediterranean to the Sea of Japan. More importantly, anti-piracy activity in the Gulf of Aden (since 2008) and relief operations in the Mediterranean (2006) and the Indian Ocean (2004-05) have underlined the growing capacity of the Indian Navy and the new political will in Delhi to act far from its shores. Like India, China too is following the logic of what it calls 'far sea defence'. [2] The difference, however, is in the level of political and policy commitment to the construction of a maritime grand strategy. In China, President Hu Jintao underscored the relationship between Beijing's expanding global interests and the 'historic missions' of the PLA Navy amidst China's rise on the world stage. [3]

What is missing in Delhi is that passion for maritime

strategy among its political leadership and the business-as-usual approach by the bureaucratic leadership of the government. For example, building a blue water navy needs a policy framework to expand capabilities for design, development and production of naval equipment. Unlike China which has dramatically expanded the indigenous naval production base, India is yet to promote a sustainable one. Successful power projection also depends on reorienting the armed forces to develop expeditionary capabilities.

Despite two centuries of expeditionary operations under the Raj and half a century of international peacekeeping operations, the word 'expeditionary' remains a taboo in Delhi's discourse. The notion of 'power projection' continues to sit uneasily with our political classes who feel more comfortable with the old verities of third worldism. Power projection also needs a more vigorous military diplomacy that can reinforce the navy's capability to operate far from our shores. This would mean creation of arrangements for friendly ports and turnaround facilities in other nations that will increase the range, flexibility and sustainability of Indian naval operations.

No great power has built a blue water navy capable of projecting force without physical access and political arrangements for 'forward presence'. Having long rejected 'foreign bases' in the Indian Ocean, it is somewhat discomforting for our political and strategic communities to even contemplate the new imperatives. The proposition that China is building a 'string of pearls' along vital sea lines of communication in the Indian Ocean has had the merit of forcing open a whole new debate. Some analysts outside India are beginning to talk, somewhat prematurely, of a 'necklace of diamonds' emerging in India's own plans for power projection. The idea of such a necklace is not new. Sardar K.M. Panikkar, who remains an inspiration for Indian naval thinking, emphasized the need for a ring of bases in the Indian Ocean to secure the nation. [4] It is not clear if there is the political will and bureaucratic capacity in Delhi today to think clearly about the logic of power projection and the imperatives of forward presence.

India's Maritime Interests

Once, Pandit Jawaharlal Nehru had famously stated that: "...We cannot afford to be weak at sea. History has shown that whatever power controls the Indian Ocean, has in the first instance, India's seaborne trade at her mercy, and in the second, India's very independence itself". [5] In this context, national security encompasses certain economic factors, which bear mention here. India's fortunate geographic location, astride the major sea-lanes of the world, point to the crucial relevance of its role in ensuring the free flow of oil and commerce from the Gulf to the Asia-Pacific region. The criticality of the sea-lanes from the Persian Gulf to the Straits of Malacca is evident from the fact that of the US$ 200 billion worth of oil coming out of the Strait of Hormuz annually, US$ 70 billion passes through the Straits of Malacca, mainly bound for China, Japan and South Korea.

India is currently at a very energy-intensive stage of its development. Between 1990 and 2003, oil consumption in India (and China) grew at an average rate of 7 percent, against just 0.8 percent for the rest of the world. Today, India imports over 70 percent of its oil requirements and it is estimated that by 2050 India will be the largest importer of oil in the world. Imagine then, the effect of higher oil prices combined with a possible threat to their security. A quick calculation of loss to the national GDP in such a circumstance is in itself justification enough for investment in a strong navy. A new development is our acquisition of oil and gas fields across the globe. Today, Indian companies operate tank farms in Trincomalee and oil and gas fields in the Sakhalin Islands, Egypt, Sudan and Myanmar. While the Indian Navy is at this moment, not mandated to provide security for these assets, the billions of dollars of investment does warrant some thought about its protection and security. A strong maritime force with adequate reach and endurance is a logical choice.

A quick look at our Overseas Trade. India is now projected to become the fourth largest economy in the world by 2020, after China, Japan and the US. India's exports for 2008-09 were over US$ 95 billion. This figure is almost double our exports just five years ago, and it is estimated that it would double again in the next five years. The tremendous scope for further growth can be imagined when we consider that our present share of the world trade is only 0.9 percent. Another facet of the ocean, which presents the prospect of wealth and prosperity, and yet contains the seeds of future conflict, is undersea resources. India has a mineral rich EEZ extending over 2 million sq. km. and the successful exploitation of these could lift us from economic backwardness.

Lastly, India's merchant navy, though small for our needs and size, remains a major factor in our maritime security planning. Relatively speaking, it constitutes a little over one percent of the world shipping tonnage, and our ships are able to carry only about a third of our own foreign trade. In absolute terms however, India's growing fleet of over 600 ships is quite large, and operates out of 12 major and 184 minor ports. The security of these ports, our merchant ships and the sea-lanes that they ply on represent vital maritime interests for us.

Having seen our maritime interests, now we can come to know the political, economic and security objectives that India can seek to achieve through the exercise of a maritime strategy.

Political, Economic and Security Objectives of Maritime Power

Maritime strategy has a direct relationship, not just with the overall military strategy, but also with a nation's economic and diplomatic initiatives. So, let me analyse first to the security objectives of our maritime strategy. During the long years of peace, we need to project power and show presence;

catalyse partnerships through our maritime capability; build trust and create interoperability through joint operations and international maritime assistance. Occasions may arise when a state is required to use coercion to achieve national interests, and maritime power is best suited for a graduated escalation.

The political (or diplomatic) objectives of our maritime strategy are to build strong relations with our immediate neighbours and countries of strategic interest in the Indian Ocean Region. Government of India set up a new organisation at NHQ under a Rear Admiral, to give concrete shape to such initiatives in close coordination with the diplomatic establishment. An example of this in the post-Cold War years is the Indian Navy's role in improving our relations with the US through the Malabar Exercises with the US Navy and with ASEAN through the biennial gatherings named "MILAN" with Bay of Bengal Rim navies in Port Blair. [6]

Apart from this, navies are ideally suited for "winning friends and influencing people". During the time of Sunami it has provided a classic demonstration of the positive role that navies can play. Witnesses to this are thousands of people whose lives were touched by the assistance provided by individual sailors. From medical assistance, to cleaning of wells, to restoration of infrastructure and supply of food and water, they did it all. Ever since, the navy has been receiving accolades for the fine job done by our men, not only in India but also in Sri Lanka, Indonesia and the Maldives. Consequently, an integral part of our maritime strategy will be the capability to provide humanitarian assistance, particularly in our island territories, and if required, to our friends abroad. Catering for our needs alone is, however, not enough. Smaller nations in our neighbourhood as well as nations that depend on the waters of the Indian Ocean for their trade and energy supplies expect that the Indian Navy will ensure a measure of stability and tranquillity in these waters.

Hence, our strategy also needs to ensure that we cater for adequate capability, in concert with our Coast Guard, to the constabulary role. Apart from combating piracy and terrorism at sea, this also includes responsibilities of surveying the waters around us, providing SAR facilities to those in distress, coordinating navigational warnings over a vast oceanic area and a myriad of minor, but vital tasks that keeps the global maritime industry and economy. With this let us something about what should be the composition of our maritime force?

Composition of India's Maritime Force

It is an accepted tenet that in international relations, there are no permanent friends or enemies, only permanent interests. The order of battle of the Indian Navy is not configured on the basis of perceived threats to our security, but on the basis of our long term interests, the capabilities existing in our neighbourhood and the likelihood of emergent challenges. This holds good, not just for adversaries, but for all countries whose actions may impact on us. The underlying premise is that if a capability is available or being developed by a country with which we share boundaries or interests, it could have a bearing on our security, should circumstances or intentions change over time. To cater for all the contingencies outlined above, the Indian Navy needs to field a three-dimensional blue water force with the capability to operate across the entire spectrum of conflict. The capabilities required to meet the challenges will include:

1. Prolonged surface operations at extended ranges and periods.
2. Submarine operations in coastal waters and on the high seas.
3. Anti-submarine warfare capability to counter enemy submarine threat.
4. Capability for combined operations with multinational forces and ability to execute out of area contingencies—either alone or under a UN mandate.
5. Joint operations at theatre level with the other two Services, which will require an amphibious and a stand-off

land attack capability.

6. Last, but not the least, a sea-based strategic deterrent capability. [7]

To meet the requirements of the force levels (including two carrier groups) which we hope to field by 2015, there are currently on order, 21 ships and 6 submarines. We already have approvals for another 15-20 ships, but a lot depends on the production rate of our shipyards, and how much our private industry can contribute. The former Russian 44,000 ton VTOL carrier Admiral Gorshkov was acquired in 2003 and is currently undergoing modernization and conversion to a new configuration in the northern Russian port of Severdovinsk. This configuration involves installation of a ski-jump forward and a set of arrester wires aft, and is known as STOBAR for "short take off but arrested landing". [8]

The keel for a second such ship, the Indigenous Aircraft Carrier (IAC) was laid in Kochi in April 2006, with a completion date of December 2012. For obvious reasons, this ship will have the same STOBAR configuration and operate the MiG-29K too. At 37,500 tons the IAC is smaller than the Gorshkov, but as the biggest warship ever built in India, will certainly pose a challenge to our ship designers and builders. In a parallel technology initiative, Indian aircraft industry has embarked on a project to design a STOBAR version of the indigenous Light Combat Aircraft designated LCA (Navy) which we plan to induct on both our carriers by 2015.

There are some priority areas for the Indian Navy for the immediate future. Foremost among them is the ability to operate in a secure, networked environment. Today, the Indian Navy has weapons of formidable range and our naval forces are deployed across vast distances from the Arabian Sea to the Bay of Bengal and the farthest reaches of the Indian Ocean. The intention here is to network all our forces, in all three dimensions, with our command centres, so that whatever data is available to one unit is available to the entire fleet. Networking will help us extend our vision beyond a single unit's capability and in synergizing the strengths of our naval assets. Aerial surveillance of our area of maritime interest is another priority area. We must have sufficient knowledge at all times, of what is happening in the maritime domain of our interest. Currently there are some voids in our maritime surveillance capability, but it seems that this is being addressed on priority.

Geo-Economic Interests

UNCLOS III (United Nations Convention on the Law of the Sea) grants coastal states with sweeping powers within the Exclusive Economic Zone (EEZ), including rights for the purpose of exploring and exploiting, conserving and managing the ocean resources, living or non living. UNCLOS III bestows upon India almost 3.1 million sq. km. of EEZ after taking into account the continental shelf. Protection of the living and non-living resources in this vast EEZ is in India's vital maritime interest.

Oil and Natural Gas

It has been estimated that the continental shelf around India up to a depth of 200 metres can have an approximate potential oil reserve of 1 billion tonnes and natural gas reserve of around 271 billion cubic meters. Under India's maritime interests, the stupendous discovery of Bombay High has been the biggest oil find in the country and it rates as one of the six biggest fields in the world. After Bombay High, surveys have led to the discovery of many satellite fields, like Panna, Bassein, Heera, Tapti, Mukta, and Leela. The discovery of major oil fields off the Andhra Coast, Cauvery Delta and in other areas of Bay of Bengal, further protection and security have been accounted for as a key governing factor in maritime strategy.

Deep Sea Mining

India's contribution in deep sea mining has been recognised with the status of a `pioneer investor`. The country has been given the right of deep-sea bed mining in the equatorial Indian Ocean, an area of 1.5 lakh sq. km. about 2500 km south of India. In order to evenly exploit Indian maritime interests, the country have started to tap resourceful areas underwater in search for more options. Ocean bed mining activity at present is limited to exploration, research and development, but not exploitation. The National Institute of Oceanography, India's only oceanographic institute, is, however, conducting extensive research in this field.

Fishing

Indian maritime interests very much is rested in fishing, both deep sea and shallow. The seas are an excellent source of nutrition. India is auspicious to have an abundance of fish in its waters. India is looking towards a yet unrealised achievement of 3.92 million tonnes, including 2.28 million tonnes (58 percent) from the coastal waters and 1.64 million tonnes (42 percent) from offshore. Protection of this vast resource is considered cardinal.

Port Infrastructure

Another factor, which affects the trade potential of India, is its port infrastructure. There are 12 major ports and 185 minor ports in India. The World Bank has approximated that India's present port handling capabilities could be boosted by around thirty to thirty-five, by a thorough overhauling of existing port management practices. Indian ports handle seven to eight containers in an hour, making port infrastructure a vital governing factor counted under Indian maritime strategies. Advancement has been made with the development of ports such as Paradip, Mangalore and Ennore. Headways have also been made in the mushrooming of private ports, especially in Gujarat.

The Oceans as a Resource

The oceans of the world bring together nations as they provide the path for people and trade to move from one country to another. The Indian Ocean extends India's neighbourhood to beyond the normally accepted concepts of land borders, to far away nations like South Africa and Australia. Maritime interests of India thus are often focused on various outlandish subjects.

China's Growing Influence in the Indian Ocean

China's growing naval presence in and around the Indian Ocean region, beginning in areas such as China's Hainan Island in the South China Sea, should be troubling for India. Of particular note is what has been termed as China's 'string of pearls' strategy, some elements of which are no doubt hyped, that has significantly expanded its strategic depth in India's backyard. It is possible to explain the construction of these ports and facilities by China along India's periphery on purely economic and commercial grounds, but regional and global powers like the US, Japan and India inevitably view the sum total of China's diplomatic and military efforts in the Indian Ocean as projecting power vis-à-vis competing rivals.

Moreover, most of Chinese naval facilities in the Indian Ocean are dual use in nature and no serious strategy can discount their future military use. China is merely following in the footsteps of other major global powers who have established military bases abroad to secure their interests. There is only one kind of great power, and one kind of great power tradition. China is not going to be any different. The sooner India acknowledges this, the better it will be able to manage China's rise and protect its own vital interests.

In a move that may cause unease in India, China recently on 12 December 2011, announced that it will set up its first military base abroad in the Indian Ocean island of Seychelles to "seek supplies and recuperate" facilities for its Navy. [9] The naval fleet may seek supplies or recuperate at appropriate harbours in Seychelles or other countries as needed during escort missions. China has already cemented its foothold in the Indian Ocean by signing contract with the UN backed

International Seabed Authority to gain rights to explore polymetallic sulphide ore deposit in Indian Ocean over the next 15 years.

The contract awarded to a Chinese association exclusive rights to explore a 10,000 sq. km. of international seabed in the southwest Indian Ocean. The base in Seychelles is regarded significant by analysts as China is about to launch its first aircraft carrier. It is currently undergoing final trials. Playing down its significance, Chinese Defence Ministry statement said that, it is international practice for naval fleets to re-supply at the closest port of a nearby state during long-distance missions. Apparently, commenting on a recent report that China will establish a military base in Seychelles, the statement said that, Chinese naval fleets have re-supply facilities at harbours in Djibouti, Oman and Yemen since China sent its first convoy to the Gulf of Aden in 2008. [10]

The decision to establish its first naval base abroad was taken during Chinese Defence Minister, Gen Liang Guanglie's goodwill visit to Seychelles during the first week of December 2011. During the visit, Seychelles Foreign Affairs Minister, Jean-Paul Adam said that, his country has invited China to set up a military base on the archipelago to beef up the fight against piracy. "We have invited the Chinese government to set up a military presence on Mahe to fight the pirate attacks that the Seychelles face on a regular basis," [11] Adam was quoted as saying in the media reports. "For the time being China is studying this possibility because it has economic interests in the region and Beijing is also involved in the fight against piracy," he said. [12]

During Liang's visit, the two sides exchanged views on their countries' and armies' cooperation, as well as on the global and regional situation, state-run Xinhua news agency reported. Seychelles appreciates China's efforts to maintain safe navigation on the Indian Ocean, as well as the support it has granted to Seychelles. Seychelles also invited China's navy to re-supply and recuperate in the country during escort missions.

Conclusion

India remain concerned about the rising power and influence of China, now the world's second largest economy, projected to surpass the U.S. in size as soon as 2020. India has for some time been alarmed by China's military links with Pakistan and its growing presence in the Indian Ocean. We are fortunate that a far sighted naval leadership launched the navy on the path of self-reliance nearly 40 years ago. Our shipyards have delivered to us till today, over 80 warships, of which the latest warship has an indigenous content of 85 percent.

As we know, our shipyards have reached a level of competence where the Indian Navy has today on order with them, 21 vessels which cover the full spectrum of warship building: from patrol boats, landing ships and corvettes, to frigates, destroyers and an aircraft carrier; and of course, submarines in a few years time. We have also aggressively sought out centres of excellence, whether in the public or private sectors, and Indian industry now supports our warship building endeavours by producing ship-building steel, propulsion systems (steam and diesel), gear boxes, gun mounts, torpedo tubes, power generation, air conditioning, hydraulic, pneumatic and hundreds of other ship-board systems. Having said that, we must also admit that total self-reliance is a goal that is still very distant: that is if we want to aim for it at all. We have, and we will continue to have platforms, weapons, sensors and systems of foreign origin in our inventory for a long time to come.

After the break up of the USSR, we learnt many bitter lessons about the pitfalls of dependence on foreign sources: uncertain availability, arbitrary pricing, and doubtful quality. With all this at the back of our mind, we have embarked on a deliberate programme of indigenisation and NHQ has recently put in place a dedicated Directorate of Indigenisation to synergise our endeavours in this direction. The Government having permitted private participation in defence production, we need to work out methods of creating public-private synergy in the form of partnerships, joint ventures or in any other form. This will provide impetus to innovation and bring economy and efficiency in defence production.

In the coming decades, India will be among the foremost centres of power—economic, technological and cultural. This needs to be matched by a concomitant accretion of military power, of which the maritime power will be a critical dimension. Indian Navy can be the catalyst for peace, tranquillity and stability in the Indian Ocean Region, across a wide range of conditions and circumstances that one can envisage in peacetime. It can be used to engage other maritime nations and extend a hand of friendship and co-operation. Its robust presence in a particular area or region could contribute to stability and ensure peace. Lastly, it can act as a strong deterrent with the ability to prevent conflict, or to respond, should it become necessary. We are confident that the maritime strategy that India will craft will protect our interest and that will be equal to the challenges of our times.

End Notes

1. Vice Admiral Suresh Bangara (Retd.), "Shaping India's Maritime Strategy-Opportunities and Challenges, in *Indian Maritime Doctrine,* April 2004, Ncw Dclhi, pp. 25-26.
2. Ibid.
3. The Indian Express, April 28, 1989.
4. The Hindu, June 13, 1991.
5. Dutt V.P., "India and China: A Leap into the Future", *World Focus*, No.12, June 1998, pp. 69-70.
6. Gopalji Malviya, "Sino-Indian Relations: Security Environment in the Nineties", Publication Division, University of Madras, 1992, p. 91.
7. Ibid., p. 93.
8. Vice Admiral Suresh Bangara (Retd.), "Shaping India's Maritime Strategy-Opportunities and Challenges, in *Indian Maritime Doctrine,* April 2004, New Delhi, pp. 25-26.
9. http://www.dailystar.com.lb/Opinion/Commentary/2011/Nov-03/152973-wary-of-chinas-growing-influence-its-southern-neighbors-court-india.ashx#ixzz1ikZMnK2F.

(The Daily Star:: Lebanon News :: http://www.dailystar.com.lb)

10. Ibid.
11. The Indian Express, December 4, 2011.
12. Ibid.

6

Maritime Dimensions of Energy Security: China and South China Sea

C. Vinodan

The rise of China and India as major global economic powers, the continued growth in Western energy demand, challenges of global climate change and instability in key oil-exporting regions are dramatically transforming global energy landscape. Prospects for stable production are increasingly linked to internal political issues and the regional ambitions of major suppliers. These dynamics will affect the global balance of power, as energy security is becoming a more important factor in countries' national security and economic development calculations. Without adequate and affordable energy to underpin the economic growth of a country, its sustenance and indeed its very survival is at risk. Given the fact that energy is simultaneously (either implicitly or explicitly) linked to maintaining social cohesion, the economic well-being of a country and the military might of a state, it is considered to be the *sine qua non* of national security.

To that extent therefore, all states, whether developed or developing, rising or declining, energy producing/exporting or energy importing, need energy to survive. Energy therefore is an incredibly important component of national security, understood here both in the traditional and non-traditional sense, where the state and the individual are referents, respectively. This paper examines China's behaviour in the South China Sea disputes through the lens of its new energy security strategy. The South China Sea, potentially rich in energy resources and straddled by international waterways, is beset with territorial and maritime disputes. The strategic and economic significance of the South China Sea has led to a contest over features dotting the semi-enclosed sea.

With shipping routes potentially endangered by maritime border disputes, freedom of navigation is therefore a main concern of countries that use vital shipping lanes in the South China Sea. The risk of conflict in the South China Sea is significant not only for regional security but also invite global ramifications. The paper argues that China is exhibiting a more assertive posture to bolster its strategic position in the South China Sea. China, Taiwan, Vietnam, Malaysia, Brunei, and the Philippines have competing territorial and jurisdictional claims, particularly over rights to exploit the region's possibly extensive reserves of oil and gas. Freedom of navigation in the region is also a contentious issue, especially between the United States and China over the right of U.S. military vessels to operate in China's two-hundred-mile exclusive economic zone (EEZ). These tensions are shaping—and being shaped by—rising apprehensions about the growth of China's military power and its regional intentions. This paper also examines the dimensions of maritime security interests of various actors in the South China Sea. It finds that multiple stakeholders pursuing diverse interests have yet to close the gap between goals and means of achieving maritime security.

Energy Security and Conflict

Energy security can be defined as a condition in which a nation and all (or most) of its citizens and industries have access to adequate energy resources at reasonable prices for the foreseeable future, free from serious risks of major disruption of service (Hancher and Janssen, 2004). Insecurity can arise from various causes, such as geopolitical instability, natural disasters, terrorism, poor regularity designs, or a lack of investments (Redgwell, 2004). The literature on energy security suggests that different countries have developed different strategies for securing their energy supply. The UN-mandated and US-led coalition's campaign to secure Kuwaiti sovereignty in 1990 and 1991 can be understood within this context. The US and others prevented Iraq from becoming the second-largest oil producer in the world, controlling the Persian Gulf transit and threatening Saudi Arabia, the largest oil producer, militarily. It is also argued that the US and UK's military intervention in Iraq in 2003 can be evaluated in this context. As the argument goes, especially after the 9/11 attacks, the nature of US-Saudi relations has become ambiguous in ways that might have led the US and UK to unlock the Iraqi oil potential for world markets by removing the Baath regime.

Many aspects of modern life, economies, and the relations between states are shaped by the development of energy resources and technologies. The reliance on energy in every field of life has made energy security tremendously important for states and societies. Especially for modern militaries, securing energy resources has become of utmost importance since the beginning of the twentieth century. Therefore, "second only to national defence," energy security has become a primary concern for the survival and wellbeing of both developed and developing nations. (Hamilton, 2005: xxi)

History proved that First and Second World Wars in the twentieth century were also linked with energy use. Winston Churchill's decision to use petroleum by replacing coal for the British Navy to maintain its hegemony before World War I shaped the course of the war; it also led the Allies to invade the oil-rich territories in the Middle East. Energy resources were even more important in World War II. One of the major reasons that Japan attacked the US was the latter's oil embargo against the former's empire. The Axis powers, lacking substantial energy resources, based their strategies on first gaining access to energy-rich areas, such as Romania and the Caspian Sea. The Allies, on the other hand, "floated to victory on a sea of oil" and used nuclear power for the first time to conclude the war. (Barton et al. 2004: 3)

The modern concern with energy security began with the

Arab-Israeli war of 1973-74 and the Organization of Arab Petroleum Exporting Countries (OAPEC) and Organization of Petroleum Exporting Countries (OPEC)'s use of the "oil weapon." OPEC's boycott of major energy-importing countries in Europe and the US has shown how important it is for modern societies to secure their supply of energy; it became clear that an energy crisis can hurt everyone in society, including government, business, and individuals. Consequently, securing energy resources has become a key aspect of foreign policy making of major powers since the 1970s. With the collapse of the Soviet Union in 1991, the concerns for energy security acquired a new dimension.

The newly independent energy-rich ex-Soviet republics in the Caspian basin have become a playground for great-power rivalry. The US and EU, both having suffered from dependency on Middle Eastern energy in the 1970s, have begun increasing their political and economic influence on the region to gain access to energy resources. "The New Great Game" was coined as a term to describe the rivalry between the Western powers and a weakened Russia for the control of the Eurasia region and its energy resources (Kleveman, 2003). Since energy-hungry China has begun pursuing aggressive foreign policies to secure the supply of energy to its growing market, this rivalry has taken a "tripolar" shape.

China's search for energy security has come under close international scrutiny in recent years. This is partly because of the economic impact on other countries–most notably changes in the price and availability of some energy resources. But there are also important political dimensions to these debates. For example, supporters of a liberal global order are concerned that China is undermining attempts to pressure authoritarian states to reform. If such states don't like the conditions that accompany aid and economic relations with the West (or more correctly, some in the West), then if they have things that the Chinese want they can deal with them instead. They might insist that you don't have political relations with Taiwan, and want guarantees that their investments are safe, but they won't pressure you to liberalise your political or economic systems. And as an added bonus, the repayment terms of Chinese development loans are often cheaper than those offered by places like the World Bank.

China's Growing Energy Needs and Maritime Policy

The geopolitics of energy insecurity has emerged as a key theme of national priority in the contemporary world. The world has entered a new era of more of dramatic transition, heralding a century of serious energy uncertainty. Major powers are moving from a position of relative energy independence to one of significant dependence on imports. Security for Asia's major energy sea-lanes—running from the Hormuz Strait, into the Indian Ocean, through the Malacca Strait to Singapore, and into the South China Sea—currently lags behind the growing criticality of these waterways. Key economic powers in the region depend on sea-lane transport for the vast majority of their oil supplies, which in turn help to fuel their economic growth.

The growing mismatch between the importance of the sea-lanes and the stress on and vulnerability of the system has contributed to rising energy insecurity in the region. The majority of the world's rising consumption of energy, and oil in particular, is occurring in Asia. Limited regional oil production means that Asia increasingly relies on imported oil, primarily from the Middle East. Close to 90 percent of the energy that China, Japan, and South Korea import must pass through the Southeast Asian sea-lanes. (Storey, 2009a, p. 36) Continual access to these energy supplies is critical for sustained economic growth in Asia, which has been a source of stability in the region.

In the last two decades, Asia's economic growth has diverged from that of other developing regions. Since the mid-1980s, economic growth in emerging Asia (including China and India) has been much stronger than elsewhere. Such growth has benefited from economic integration with the global economy. From the mid-1990s, China and India started to make their mark in the world economy. In 2009, according to World Bank, the Asia and Pacific region accounted for almost one-third of global GDP, while 54 percent of the region's GDP comes from just China and India. [1]

China has experienced rapid economic growth over past decades. In total economic size, China has quickly caught up with other large economies. In 2008, it overtook Germany to be the second largest economy in the world, and in 2010 it surpassed Japan to be the second largest economy. China has enjoyed rapid economic growth ever since it embarked on reform and opening up to the world in 1979, although the speed has varied from time to time. The surge forward was particularly impressive from the start of twenty-first century until the financial crisis, with the economy zipping along at a double-digit growth rate.

In recent years, its economy has turned into a driving locomotive for the entire Asian continent. Undoubtedly, the country has become an important factor in global politics and economics with a tremendous impact on the political, social and economic development of all other states on our planet. Today's emerging new world order is unimaginable without China playing a crucial role in it (Hauser and Kernic, 2009). China has achieved remarkable economic growth during the past three decades, with Real Gross Domestic Product increasing at an average annual rate of over 10 percent between 1978 and 2008. (World Bank, 2009) China's rapid growth since 1978 has been highly dependent on energy. As its economy has expanded, energy use has increased by over 200 percent and by nearly 150 percent per capita, with over half of this growth occurring in the years since 2001.

This tight connection between growing energy use and economic development means that energy policy is a central concern of the government. Following its economic development, China's demand for energy, particularly oil, has skyrocketed. According to IEA research, almost half of global oil demand growth in the next five years will come from China. Looking farther ahead, the scenarios in the IEA's *World Energy Outlook, 2010* (IEA, 2010a) shows China importing 79 percent of the oil it consumes by 2030, and accounting for a larger increment in oil demand than any other country.

Maritime Dimensions of South China Sea Dispute

Maritime security concerns in the South China Sea are increasing for several reasons: higher volumes of shipping traffic, protection of exclusive economic zone resources, piracy, terrorist threats, greater international scrutiny of ports and shipping, and the modernization of regional naval and coast guard forces. Coastal states and international user states have many overlapping interests in the South China Sea, for example, in promoting safe navigation through its busy sea-lanes. (Rosenberg and Chung, 2008) On other issues, in particular, anti-piracy or anti-maritime terrorism measures, they have different views about the seriousness of the threats and the responses necessary to address them. Maritime security in the South China Sea faces a number of challenges, ranging from lower-level non-traditional threats to traditional politico-strategic considerations, including the potential for conflict between regional states over territory or marine resources and the possibility of conflict between major powers.

At the highest level of the threat spectrum, the possibility of conflict between major powers is also rarely absent from such an important sea area, which involves some of the world's busiest and most important sea lines of communication (SLOC). There are many reasons, why efforts to address and ameliorate challenges to order, security, and well-being in a semi-enclosed sea area, within which many of those challenges are transnational, ought to be shared cooperatively between littoral states. However, the political sensitivities involved in Southeast Asia, where national interests often clash, or at least diverge, as much as they are shared, make the achievement of a "stable maritime regime," extremely unlikely. [2]

The South China Sea is a large space linking southern China and Taiwan to peninsular and archipelagic Southeast Asia and peninsular and continental Southeast Asia to archipelagic Southeast Asia. The South China Sea is categorized as semi-enclosed sea under the United Nations Convention on the Law of the Sea (the LOS Convention). [3] It is surrounded by six countries—China, Vietnam, the Philippines, Brunei, Malaysia, and Indonesia—and has an area of 648,000 square nautical miles, twice the area of the Sea of Japan. [4] The South China Sea also constitutes a vital section of the seaborne trade route linking: both Europe and the Middle East to Northeast Asia; Southeast Asia to Northeast Asia; and much of Southeast Asia to the Pacific Ocean and North America. [5] The geography of the South China Sea area is an important factor in a strategic analysis. Its central location in East Asia ensures its importance for trade and strategic communications.

Its complexity ensures both physical dangers for the safety of navigation and political dangers as a source of international dispute. The South China Sea is semi-enclosed by eight littoral polities: Brunei, China, Indonesia, Malaysia, the Philippines, Singapore, Taiwan, and Vietnam as well as Cambodia and Thailand within the Gulf of Thailand. The geographic limits of the South China Sea are poorly defined and to some extent contested. [6] Such contested claims and counter claims led to the regional actors to engage in militarization especially in naval modernization. A leading factor in the South China Sea has been the disputes over the territorial features and, as a consequence, the potential maritime jurisdiction to which such features may be entitled, including the related living and nonliving marine resources.

Questions exist over the extent of possible hydrocarbon resources in the central South China Sea. Another factor often overlooked is the South China Sea's importance as a fishing ground, accounting for 10 percent of the global catch, [7] with the annual harvest of around 5 million tonnes representing the fourth largest of the world's 19 major fishing areas. [8] The centrality of China's role as a claimant state, and the linkages between its interests in the South China Sea and the development of Chinese maritime power and its overall ambitions for regional hegemony, make the disputes important beyond the limited face value of a few small, scattered islands, rocks, and reefs—or even potential energy resources.

China has long been wary of the strategic presence of opposing hegemonic powers in Southeast Asia, who might exploit Chinese weaknesses at sea to apply pressure on China from its southern maritime periphery. China's strategic ambitions in the South China Sea therefore involve the extension of its defensive perimeter, countering the presence of other major powers, countering threats to its territorial and maritime interests by other claimants, and, ultimately, seeking some measure of maritime command over the area to enforce its hegemonic pretensions.

Furthermore, China also has an interest in being able to exert control over East Asian sea-lanes, both to safeguard its own oil supplies and to threaten the economic lifelines of Taiwan and Japan if necessary. A permanent strategic presence in the South China Sea, particularly if it can successfully enforce its territorial claims, might conceivably provide China with such ability in the future. The establishment of bases, staging, and surveillance posts along the vital sea-lanes has been described as China's "string of pearls" strategy. [9] China has over a period of more than three decades slowly built up its military facilities throughout the South China Sea, including in the Spratlys.

In recent years, it has significantly enhanced bases, in particular, on Hainan Island and in the Paracel archipelago. There have also been reports that the People's Liberation Army (PLA) Navy intends to bolster its forces in the area, with a senior PLA officer suggesting that the security situation was "very grim," requiring China to deploy more ships to the disputed region, and to enhance the militarization of occupied features in the Spratlys, including constructing a port for naval vessels and an airport on Mischief Reef, a Chinese occupied reef that lies inside the EEZ claimed by the Philippines. [10] Chinese strategists also noted the geopolitical importance of controlling Taiwan and the Taiwanese-occupied islands in the Spratlys if China is to establish a dominating position into the "southernmost reaches of the South China Sea."

Another driver of naval modernization is the likelihood that these factors have led to a degree of hedging by the Southeast Asian littoral states against strategic uncertainty or the possibility of a significant conflict. Although rarely stated by the regional states, it is fair to suggest that the most likely contingencies that might directly affect the South China Sea area involve China. The possibilities include a conflict over Taiwan, with Japan *or* the United States, Chinese moves in the Spratlys or against Vietnam, or the external consequences of internal instability within China itself.

Although less likely to lead to armed conflict, the region is also rife with longstanding local rivalries. [11] Naval modernization in the South China Sea states thus cannot be attributed to any single factor. While each individual state may have its own priorities, all of the issues discussed above influence most of the littoral states of the South China Sea to a greater or lesser extent. However, the fluid state of great power relations and the rise of China should not be discounted as a leading driver of at least some of the higher end war fighting capabilities being procured, such as submarines.

China's Strategy in the South China Sea

China is both a coastal state with an extensive coastline and EEZ resource claims as well as a user state with a large shipping fleet and a growing dependence on energy imports. An energy importer since 1993, China's high energy demand has prompted it to intensify offshore exploration, including a tripartite seismic survey in the South China Sea with the

Philippines and Vietnam; to acquire or invest in exploration and production projects overseas; to enter into supply contracts with countries as diverse as Angola, Australia, Iran, Sudan, and Venezuela; and to establish a strategic oil reserve. China considers any interruption of tanker traffic through the South China Sea would have immediate negative effects on China's industrial, urban, and transport sectors.

The economic dimension of China's maritime security interests, including in the South China Sea, is underscored by the fact that 90 percent of its foreign trade is seaborne. (Sakhuja, 2001) The South China Sea also presents a potential opportunity for China to use its territorial claims to gain control of oil/natural gas reserves to deny access to or disrupt supplies. The region contains the heavily disputed Paracel and Spratly Islands with overlapping claims to various areas and energy exploration blocks by China, Taiwan, the Philippines, Vietnam, Indonesia, Malaysia, Brunei, and Thailand. [12] Over the last 20 years, there have been at least 10 documented disputes over energy exploration rights and 17 military confrontations in the South China Sea and its territories. [13]

Some confrontations have resulted in deaths while most have merely jeopardized attempts to exploit energy resources, most significantly between China, Vietnam, and the Philippines. Ultimately, China's extensive claims raise US suspicions over its intent to potentially control the South China Sea and its resources. Such suspicions have evoked strong criticism from the US which espouses "to intercede to ensure safe passage through international waters" as prescribed by the 1982 United Nations Convention for the Law of the Sea (UNCLOS). [14]

Under the UNCLOS, states have sovereign rights to explore, exploit, conserve, and manage the natural resources within an EEZ which can range to 200 nautical miles (nms) beyond a state's territorial sea. [15] China's loose interpretation of the UNCLOS has permitted it to claim territory and establish an EEZ that stretches to nearly 1,000 nms beyond mainland China and encroaches upon the sovereignty of its neighbours. Notably, most of the Spratly Islands are submerged at high tide and don't meet the legal criteria necessary for EEZs. [16]

Furthermore, although a signatory to the UNCLOS, China unilaterally established its own measure through its 1992 Law on Territorial Waters and their Contiguous Areas. This solidified the Chinese claim to the Spratly and Parcel islands as well as empowered the People's Liberation Army (PLA) to employ force to defend the islands. [17] Citing this, UNCLOS, and historical records, China claims ownership of roughly 80 percent of the South China Sea including areas that encompass existing oil fields operated by Brunei and Indonesia. China bases such claims on historical references to exploration, naming, utilization, government jurisdiction, and acceptance of the Japanese surrender following World War II to validate its sovereign control of the area, yet this isn't codified anywhere in international law. [18]

The rise of China in to global prominence and its ambition to assume superpower status prompted to enhance its economic, military and diplomatic activities in the larger East Asian region. For China, the South China Sea dispute represents the kind of challenge that could determine whether or how China will indeed ascend to superpower status. Regrettably, China does not yet recognize the extent to which its aggressive course in the South China Sea is damaging its diplomacy with neighbouring countries.

First, sovereignty disputes with some ASEAN neighbours have severely weakened China's standing in the region and beyond. The deterioration of China's relationship with the West after the 1989 Tiananmen Square incident should be a strong reminder to Beijing of its recent strategic errors in judgment. During that period, ASEAN played an important role as a conduit for China to the outside world. Indeed, it is in large part due to China's relationship with ASEAN that China was able to gradually resume normal diplomatic relations with the West. China's current assertiveness in the South China Sea is now slowly but surely eroding its positive image with its ASEAN neighbours as a peacefully rising power.

Without exception, countries within Southeast Asia and beyond are very cautious of China's rise. Even as China's national economic and global stature increase, its influence, image and "soft power" abroad is declining dramatically. China's aggressiveness has resulted in the United States reprioritizing its global strategy with its "pivot" or "rebalance" toward the Asia-Pacific region. This policy adjustment by the United States has given Chinese policymakers serious reason for concern and activated the fear that China might again end up being contained in much the same way as the former Soviet Union during the Cold War. China now sees "US hands" in both its internal and external affairs.

Throughout the region, US allies including Japan, South Korea and the Philippines have all upgraded their already strong military cooperation with the United States. If China continues to ignore the interests or concerns of its neighbours who have a stake in the South China Sea, its aggressiveness is likely to galvanize increased regional cooperation with the United States. Troubles with close neighbours also affect the image and position of China in the world. The most important condition for any country aspiring to ascend to global power status is to maintain good relations with its neighbours. However, if China is unable or unwilling to maintain a cordial relationship with its closest neighbours, how can countries further field trust and respect this aspiring superpower?

As long as China is unable to maintain a significant level of trust and friendship with its neighbours, benevolent global power status for China is likely to remain a pipe dream. China's dramatic assertion of unilateral sovereignty over the South China Sea has adversely affected the peaceful environment China desperately needs to become a global power. If conflict does break out, it is likely to have a sustained, widespread and long-term detrimental impact on the regional economic and security situation in the region.

China itself would severely be impacted as nearly 80 percent of its oil imports and the majority of its goods, imports and exports, flow through the Strait of Malacca and other South China Sea routes. Central to the dispute is China's claim of sovereignty over the U-shaped line that it claims to have inherited from the Kuomintang government, and which was only officially submitted to the UN Commission on the Limits of the Continental Shelf in 2009. As the lines are not based on any legal foundation and have no specific geographical coordinates, they leave room for inconsistent explanations from China.

It should be noted that the Chinese U-shaped line covers 80 percent of the South China Sea, while China only administers 15 percent of that area. China's unilateral claims of sovereignty over the years to the South China Sea has made the majority of Chinese citizenry mistakenly believe that China does indeed own the entire area within the U-shaped line and that the line makes up China's southern border. However, newly discovered maps in 1904 dating from the Qing Dynasty do not show the Paracel and Spratlys Islands. Instead, it is Hainan Island that is depicted as China's southern most borders. Unfortunately, this U-shaped line is now very much like a bone contention in the emerging security environment. How China overcomes its miscalculations in its South China Sea policy will significantly influence Chinas rising profile in the emerging world order. Its handling of sovereignty disputes with some of its neighbours, however, has already weakened its standing in the Far East and beyond.

India's Stakes in the South China Sea Dispute

The South China Sea is a strategic waterway providing the key maritime link between the Indian Ocean and East Asia. Sea lines of communication (SLOCs) of the South China Sea are a matter of life and death for the Asia Pacific countries, and SLOC security has been a fundamental factor contributing to regional economic development. As the eastern gateway to the Indian Ocean (IO), South China Sea (SCS) is India's strategic left flank. And, more than half of India's interests pass through or are located in the South China Sea. India has had civilizational contacts and relations, predating the middle ages, with most of the South China Sea littoral nations. The geo-strategic significance of the South China Sea lies in the fact that it is the eastern access to the Indian Ocean.

India established a presence in the South China Sea in the early days of the "Look East" policy, conducting its first-ever joint naval exercises with Indonesia (1991), Malaysia (1991), and Singapore (1993). In 2001, India held separate bilateral exercises in the South China Sea with the Vietnamese and South Korean navies. Singapore, which during the Cold War had considered the Indian navy to be a threat, reversed course in 1996 and signed an agreement on military cooperation with India. The Indian navy now conducts exercises regularly with Singapore.

Thailand has developed a complementary "Look West" policy and has become an increasingly close ally of New Delhi. Coordinated naval patrols are an element of this closer relationship. India's ties to Vietnam were greatly strengthened in 2000 following the visit of the Indian defence minister to Vietnam. [19] India has entered into bilateral defence cooperation agreements with Malaysia, Singapore, Laos, and Indonesia. It has also provided military aid to the armed forces of Myanmar and Thailand. India's current maritime doctrine states that "the Indian maritime vision for the first quarter of the 21st century must look at the arc from the Persian Gulf to the Straits of Malacca as a legitimate area of interest." [20] While India's naval chief, Admiral Arun Prakash, indicated in 2005 that India had no intention of patrolling the Malacca Strait, this view changed in 2006 when New Delhi signalled its willingness to help patrol the strait subject to an invitation from the littoral states. [21]

India's rapid rise to strategic prominence in the region has been aided by its absence of any history of disputes in the region. It has no territorial claims in the region. Unlike Japan, China, or the United States, India is perceived as having no strategic ambitions in the region. It is seen as a power that could balance China's rise without posing a direct threat. However, as its trade with ASEAN and China grows, India has an increasing economic incentive to keep regional SLOCs open for international shipping. India is now embarking on Phase II of its "Look East" policy, expanding its scope to include Australia, China, Japan, and South Korea.

More emphasis will be placed on security cooperation, including joint operations to protect sea-lanes and the pooling of resources against common threats. The military contacts and joint exercises that India launched with ASEAN states on a low-key basis in the early 1990s are now expanding into full-fledged defence cooperation. [22] Bilaterally, India regularly engages in naval exercises with the US, French, British, Russian and Singapore navies and on an opportunity basis with the Indonesian, Japanese, Philippines, Vietnamese, Saudi Arabian, German, Omani, Iranian and PLA navies. It is noteworthy that India's policy of bilateral naval engagement with a power such as the US is no different at all from that with the regional or other powers. India is also distancing from the emerging rivalry of the US and China over South China Sea. The challenge is for India to become a responsible balancer within the international order by effectively partnering with the key players to manage an increasingly insecure world.

As a resident power in the Indian Ocean region which is still growing, India has new responsibilities in the 21st century. These relate not only to defending her own national interests but also to ensuring security and order in her maritime neighbourhood. The Indian Maritime Military Strategy identifies the South China Sea and the Pacific Ocean as 'secondary areas' of operational interest for the Indian Navy. It elaborates, "Areas of secondary interest will come in where there is a direct connection with areas of primary interest, or where they impinge on the deployment of future maritime forces". Around 55 percent of India's trade in the Asia Pacific transits through the South China Sea region.

For India, the South China Sea region serves as a strategic link between the Pacific and the Indian Oceans whose security is vital for the smooth flow of her sea borne trade. India's new energy foreign policy also gives priority for active engagement with the South China Sea littorals to commercially participate in exploration of the vital energy resources. Any attempt by China or any other external actors to unilaterally seek to change the status quo will have the potential to impinge upon India's commercial interests relating to energy security and the navigational prerogative to freely use the South China Sea as provided for by the international law.

India should also play a proactive role both strategically and diplomatically to ensure peace and order in this vital region. India's policy towards the nations involved in the South China Sea imbroglio would be to respect their viewpoints and persuade them to resolve their issues bilaterally. While not interfering in the ongoing bilateral or regional dialogues is the right policy for India, she should also hedge her bets and be ready to safeguard her own national interests. India should, therefore, extend full support to reducing friction in the region. This would be best done through principled negotiation and peaceful resolution of all potential conflicts under a defined set of rules.

Conclusion

The South China Sea is a strategic waterway providing the key maritime link between the Indian Ocean and East Asia. Sea lines of communication (SLOCs) of the South China Sea are a matter of life and death for the Asia Pacific countries, and SLOC security has been a fundamental factor contributing to regional economic development. The rise of China, as a reckonable power in the global order, is one of the defining features of the 21stcentury world order. China's unprecedented economic growth and modernization have accelerated China's demand for energy resources, especially oil. Recently, China emerged as the world's largest consumer of oil surpassing the United States and now imports over 50 percent of its oil requirement. Concern about energy insecurity has resulted in the establishment of new priorities and objectives for China's international economic interactions, focusing on the search for secure and reliable sources for the long-term.

As the global demand for energy rises, China's geo-strategy includes more assertive policies in the vital strategic regions of the world. China's "Go Out" economic policy and its mercantilist approach to controlling energy resources combined with aggressive trade agreements that include weapons, advanced technology, and/or loan deals for oil reflect China's growing energy security dilemma. The South China Sea's vast energy resources in the heavily disputed Spratly and Paracel Island regions stand to raise the stakes of interested parties including the US and India. Given China's rise and its territorial claims to not only the islands, but the vast majority of the South China Sea and its resources, it remains unclear whether such claims will become a platform for cooperation or conflict. China had showed its assertiveness in the South China Sea through a tough posture instead a conciliatory approach of diplomacy and economic integration with its Southeast Asian neighbours.

Other South China Sea states are also asserting their own claims and developing their own naval capacity, albeit to a lesser degree than China. As the eastern gateway to the Indian Ocean, South China Sea is India's strategic left flank. And, more than half of India's interests pass through or are located in the South China Sea. Like all other law abiding nations, India is particular about the freedom of navigation in the maritime commons. In her view, it is of paramount importance that status quo be maintained in respect of freedom of access and passage within the South China Sea. How China overcomes its miscalculations in its South China Sea policy will significantly influence Chinas rising profile in the emerging world order. Its handling of sovereignty disputes with some of its neighbours, and differences with the US have already weakened its standing in the Far East and beyond.

End Notes

1. Gross domestic product (GDP) is the sum of gross value added by all resident producers in the economy plus any product taxes and minus any subsidies not included in the value of the products (World Bank, *World Development Indicators Online, 2010*).
2. Michael Leifer, "The Maritime Regime and Regional Security in East Asia," *Pacific Review* 4 (1991): 126-136. See also, more recently, Sam Bateman, "Building Good Order at Sea in Southeast Asia: The Promise of International Regimes" in *Maritime Security in Southeast Asia*, eds. Kwa Chong Guan and John K. Skogan (London: Routledge, 2007), pp. 97-116.
3. United Nations Convention on the Law of the Sea, 1833 *U.N.T.S.* 397, Article 122.
4. J.R.V. Prescott, *The Maritime Political Boundaries of the World* (London: Methuen, 1985), p. 209.
5. John H. Noer, with David Gregory, *Chokepoints: Maritime Economic Concerns in Southeast Asia* (Washington, DC: NDU Press, 1996), figures 17-20, 63-66.
6. For example, the International Hydrographic Organization (IHO) has been trying to revise its published 1953 South China Sea limits for over 20 years. The revised 2002 edition of its *Limits of Oceans and Seas* publication remains in draft form only. The 2002 draft edition excludes significant areas incorporated within the 1953 edition: the Natuna Sea in the south (this revision seems to approximate Indonesia's archipelagic baselines); the Gulf of Tonkin in the west (in addition to the already excluded Gulf of Thailand); and the Taiwan Strait in the north. This article takes no position on the limits of the South China Sea, simply noting the problematic nature of definition. Nevertheless, no matter where exactly the limits are drawn, it is a large body of water encompassing a surface area of approximately 2.7 million to 3 million square kilometres. For a discussion on the geographical scope of the

South China Sea, See Nien-Tsu Alfred Hu, "Semi-enclosed Troubled Water: A New Thinking on the Application of the 1982 UNCLOS Article 123 to the South China Sea," Ocean Development & International Law 41(3), 2010, pp. 281-314, and 299-301.

7. Clive Schofield, "Dangerous Ground: A Geopolitical Overview of the South China Sea" in *Security and International Politics in the South China Sea: Towards a Cooperative Management Regime*, eds. Sam Bateman and Ralf Emmers (London: Routledge, 2009), pp. 14-18.
8. United Nations Environment Programme (UNEP), *Global International Waters Assessment. South China Sea: Regional Assessment 54* (Kalmar, Sweden: University of Kalmar, 2005), pp. 40-41.
9. This term was coined by a U.S. report, *Energy Futures in Asia*, produced by consultants Booz Allen Hamilton for the Office of the Secretary of Defence. A string of ports, bases, and listening posts stretching from the entrance to the Persian Gulf through to the South China Sea constitute the so-called "pearls." The report was first publicised by Bill Gertz, "China Builds Up Strategic Sea Lanes," *Washington Times*, 18 January 2005.
10. L.C. Russell Hsiao, "In a Fortnight: PLA General Advises Building Bases in the South China Sea," Jamestown Foundation, *China Brief*, 24 June 2009, pp. 1-2.
11. Some of these are historically based, such as between Singapore and Malaysia; related to territorial or maritime disputes, such as that between Indonesia and Malaysia over the Ambalat offshore development area on the east coast of Borneo; or both, such as the nascent Philippine claim to Sabah or the long-standing enmity and distrust between Vietnam and China. Religious and ethnic factors may also play a role in some rivalries. Even though many of the rival states would never admit to it, such relationships are factors in military modernization.
12. China's historical claims to the South China Sea date back to the Han and Ming Dynasties. For a detailed discussion on the Spratly Island dispute and territorial claims, see Michael W. King, *United States and the Spratly Islands: Six Actors, Which Stage?* Strategy Research Project (Carlisle Barracks, PA: U.S. Army War College, November 24, 2001) 1-21; Also, see Country Analysis Briefs, South China Sea available at

http://search.usa.gov/search?affiliate=eia.doe.gov&v percent3Aproject=firstgov&query=spratly+islands (accessed January 17, 2011).
13. For a detailed listing see Country Analysis Briefs for the South China Sea available at http://search.usa.gov/search?affiliate=eia.doe.gov&v percent3Aproject=firstgov&query=spratly+islands (accessed January 17, 2011).
14. Daniel T. Kate, and Nicole Gaouette, "Clinton Signals U.S. Role in China Territorial Disputes After ASEAN," July 23, 2010, available at http://www.bloomberg.com/news/2010-07-23/u-s-says-settling-south-china-sea-disputes-leading-diplomatic-priority-.html (accessed March 24, 2011).
15. Article 57 of UNCLOS prescribes a 200nm limit to any Exclusive Economic Zone (EEZ). See http://www.un.org/Depts/los/convention_agreements/convention_overview_convention.htm (accessed March 21, 2011).
16. "Why ASEAN Should Align themselves Against China," January 31, 2008 available at http://www.paracelspratly.com (accessed February 21, 2011).
17. Michael T. Klare, *Resource Wars: The New Landscape of Global Conflict* (New York, NY: Henry Hold and Company, LLC, 2001), p. 121.
18. Xavier Furtado, "International Law and the Dispute over the Spratly Islands: Whither UNCLOS?" *Contemporary Southeast Asia*, December 1999, pp. 386-404.
19. Faizal Yahya, "India and Southeast Asia Revisited," *Contemporary Southeast Asia* 25 (2003): 7.
20. Integrated Headquarters, Ministry of Defence (Navy), *Indian Maritime Doctrine. INBR 8* (New Delhi: Integrated Headquarters, Ministry of Defence, 2004), 56.
21. "India Has No Intention of Patrolling Malacca Straits," *Daily Times,* 23 July, 2005.
22. India-ASEAN Summit, *India-ASEAN Summit Declaration, 30 November 2004*, New Delhi.

References

Barton, B., Redgwell, C., Ronne, A., and Zillman, D.N. (eds.) (2004), *Energy Security: Managing Risk in a Dynamic Legal and Regulatory Environment*. Oxford: Oxford University Press.

David Rosenberg and Christopher Chung, Maritime Security in the South China Sea: Coordinating Coastal and User State Priorities, Ocean Development & International Law, 39:51-68, 2008.

Hamilton, L.H. (2005), Foreword. In J.H. Kalicki and D.L. Goldwyn (eds.) *Energy and Security: Toward a New Foreign Policy Strategy.* Washington: Woodrow Wilson Centre Press, p. xxi.

Hancher, L., and Janssen, S. (2004) Shared Competences and Multi-Faceted Concepts–European Legal Framework for Security of Supply. In B. Barton, C. Redgwell, A. Ronne, and D.N. Zillman (eds.) *Energy Security: Managing Risk in a Dynamic Legal and Regulatory Environment*. Oxford: Oxford University Press, pp. 85-119.

Hauser, Gunther/Kernic, Franz (eds.), China: The Rising Power Frankfurt am Main, Berlin, Bern, Bruxelles, New York, Oxford, Wien, 2009, 215 p. 1).

International Energy Agency (2007), *Toward a Clean, Clever and Competitive Energy Future–IEA Report to G8 Summit in Heiligendamm, Germany 2007.*

Klare, M.T. (2008), *Rising Powers, Shrinking Planet: The New Geopolitics of Energy.* New York: Metropolitan Books.

Kleveman, L. (2003), *The New Great Game: Blood and Oil in Central Asia.* New York: Grove Press.

Nye, J. (2005), *Understanding International Conflicts: an Introduction to Theory and History.* New York: Pearson/Longman.

Redgwell, C. (2004), International Energy Security. In B. Barton, C. Redgwell, A. Ronne, and D.N. Zillman (eds.) *Energy Security: Managing Risk in a Dynamic Legal and Regulatory Environment.* Oxford: Oxford University Press, pp. 17-46.

Vijay Sakhuja, "Maritime Power of People's Republic of China: The Economic Dimension," *Strategic Analysis* 24 (2001): 2024.

Yunchang Jeffrey Bor and Zhong Xiang Zhang (2010), Energy Economics: Asian Energy in the Context of growing Security and Environmental Concerns, Amsterdam.

Zweig, David, and Jianhai Bi (2005), China's Global Hunt for Energy. Foreign Affairs 84 (5): pp. 25-38.

7

Growing Convergence between India, Australia and the United States in the Asia-Pacific

Josukutty C.A.

The Asia-Pacific region is fast becoming the next great theatre in world politics. It is the region that is readying itself to stage transformations in global power political equations between an emerging China and a declining United States (hereafter US). A remarkable feature of the emerging scenario in Asia-Pacific is the growing convergence between and among India, Australia and the US. This growing collaboration is based on the logic that these countries face a number of common challenges and have opportunities that are defined by shared values and threat perceptions. The proximity between Australia and US in political and strategic arena is well founded and will continue to be so given the demographic and geographic context. India and the US, after the cold war estrangement, have moved closer politically and strategically in a short span of time. Relationship between India and Australia, though marred by historical and cold war equations, is steady and progressing with intense desire for comprehensive collaboration in manifold ways.

The bilateral upswing in the relationship between these countries have been readying the ground for greater trilateral understanding which would enable them to collaborate and act together to address current and future challenges more effectively and exploit the opportunities to the benefit of all. What is all the more important is the fact this burgeoning relationship is getting shaped by the growing integration of the

Pacific, especially Western Pacific and Indian Ocean regions into one maritime strategic system. Indian Ocean and India-Pacific are pivotal to the maritime strategy of Asia-Pacific.

The decision of the US to devise a new security architecture in Asia and the support the initiative has received among the countries of the region to the embarrassment of China is ripening the region for a new cold war. The key argument made here is that the kind of relationship envisaged is not in India's long term interest in the context of a rising Asia. The paper attempts to study and analyze the factors that bring these countries together, the interests of Australia and US in forging and cultivating this relationship, the implications of this relationship as far as India is concerned and, its impact on India-China relations and on Asia at large.

Significance of the Asia-Pacific Region

The Asia-Pacific region, stretching from the Indian subcontinent to the western shores of the Americas, spans two oceans the Pacific and the Indian that are increasingly linked by politics, trade and strategy, is fast becoming the new great theatre in world politics. It is home to almost half of world population and some of the world's busiest ports and critical lines of commerce and communication. It includes many of the key engines of the global economy, as well as the largest emitters of greenhouse gases. It is home to emerging powers like China, India, and Indonesia. The region generates 30 percent of global exports and holds two-thirds of global foreign exchange reserves. [1] It is estimated that over the next decade all of Asia may contribute between one-half to two-thirds of world economic growth. [2] For exporters, the dynamic India-Pacific and East Asia economies represent growing markets for consumer goods and services, capital goods, and infrastructure construction expertise.

The Asia-Pacific Economic Co-operation (APEC) has become one of the most influential economic organizations in the world as well as the premier forum for facilitating trade, investment and economic growth in the Asia-Pacific region. [3] Growing number of multilateral and regional institutions such as The Association of Southeast Asian Nations (ASEAN) add to the vibrancy of the region. Moreover, the Indo-Pacific region is becoming significant for the fact that trade volumes between East Asia and South and West Asia have been growing much faster than, and now far outweigh, those across the Pacific. [4]

It is a region of unprecedented transitions and unsettled questions where many of the greatest opportunities as well as challenges of the 21st century lie. The region has been witnessing transformations in global power political equations between an emerging China and a declining US. Politically, Asia is the most contested and disputed continent in the world. World's most critical 'hotspots' and 'flashpoints' such as Afghanistan and Pakistan as the epicentre of international terrorism, uneasy bilateral relations between India and China, China and Japan, India and Pakistan, Australia and Malaysia, China and its South East Asia neighbours, nuclear flashpoints in Korea, India-Pakistan-China, Iran and Israel are prone to unpredictable events with deleterious consequences.

Adding to this is the growing rivalry between China and the United States. China's assertion as the pre-eminent power of Asia and the US reiteration as the guarantor of peace and stability in the Asia-Pacific have all the ingredients of a cold war graduating into a hot war. The US considers Asia-Pacific as an area of vital national interests and it is revamping its efforts towards an Asian architecture. Ben Rhodes, US Deputy National Security Advisor for Strategic Communications, said Asia-Pacific is fundamental to US' ability to achieve some of its top priorities, whether it is doubling exports and achieving balanced and sustainable growth or fighting terrorism and combating climate change. [5] Hillary Rodham Clinton, the US Secretary of State, referring to the Asia-Pacific region wrote in the November, 2011 Issue of Foreign Policy Magazine, "from opening new markets for American businesses to curbing nuclear proliferation to keeping the sea lanes free for commerce and navigation, our work abroad holds the key to our prosperity and security at home". [6]

Shared Values, Common Threats and Strategic Build-up

India, Australia and the US are three important countries of the Asia-Pacific region by virtue of their shared values, opportunities and the threats that confront them. They represent the best and the largest democracies in the world. If the US and Australia constitute two of the best run democracies, India is the largest democracy—a model and inspiration for the emerging democracies across the world. All the three have been among the core group of participants in the US initiated Asia-Pacific Democracy Partnership, the Bali Democracy Forum and promoters of 'maritime democracy'.

They are strong, vibrant, secular and multi-cultural economic and political systems with a free press and an independent judicial system. The values and principles of rule of law, human rights and liberalism constitute the bases of governmental and societal organization in these countries. A strong and influential Indian diaspora and large numbers of Indian students going to Australia and the US for education, are significant factors in the growing co-operation. The growing trade and economic relationship adds to the burgeoning relationship in a big way. Australia is a time-tested traditional ally of the US whereas India is a post-cold war recruit.

After the end of European domination of Asia by the Second World War, US forward-deployed military forces, alliances, and extended nuclear deterrence was the bedrock of geo-political stability in the Western Pacific and the Indian Ocean. But this region, though has US presence since the 19th century, was not the primary focus of its foreign policy endeavours till recently. The gradual build up of a number of common security threats such as conflicting maritime claims, piracy, trans-national and home grown terrorism, nuclear proliferation, missile defence system and maritime trade security demanded greater collaboration among the countries of the region.

Above all, what worries all the three simultaneously is the rise of China and its maritime claims in the Asia-Pacific and especially in South-China Sea and in India-Pacific. China has been raising objections to the presence of US and Indian maritime movements in the region. China's increasing assertiveness in the sea waters is seen as a challenge to free trade and larger security in the region. The economic resurgence of Asia and the rise China as pre-eminent economic and political power with the potential to challenge US predominance in the region prompted it to shift the pivot of its global activism to the Asia-Pacific. This larger threat scenario and the shared values and interests between India, Australia and the US constitute the context and rationale of the trilateral strategic and security partnership in the Asia-Pacific. [7]

Maritime Security and Trade

Growing trade and economic relationship between the three and the benefits accrue from it constitute one of the strongest and most prospective bases of the trilatcral relationship. Bilateral trade between India and Australia has been growing rapidly, and have crossed the US$ 20 billion mark. At present India is Australia's fourth-largest trading partner. Similarly, the US is India's second largest trading partner. In these circumstances, undefined and contested maritime boundaries in the Asia-Pacific have the potential to turn volatile at any time.

Bilateral and trilateral coordination and cooperation in defence and security matters between the US, Australia, and India are on the increase and it would help maritime security and freedom of navigation in the entire Asia-Pacific. Since 2009, there have been a series of maritime incidents in which Chinese naval or paramilitary vessels and aircraft have challenged or harassed American, Indian, Japanese,

Vietnamese, and Philippine vessels in the South China Sea, East China Sea, and Yellow Sea far seaward of China's 12-nautical-mile territorial limits. China also is reported to have elevated the South China Sea to one of its geographically determined "core interests" in 2010. [8]

China insist that it would handle differences on its maritime boundaries with countries like Vietnam, Philippines, Brunei and Malaysia bilaterally. The US, India and others made the point at the East Asia Summit in Bali in May 2011 that issues involving maritime boundaries and freedom of navigation have to be settled in conformity with the provisions of the UN Convention on the Laws of the Seas. Roughly 40 percent of India's trade with the United States traverses through the South China Sea. Moreover, its entire trade with Japan and South Korea traverses through waters claimed by China to be areas of its "core interest". [9]

Indo-Australian trade depends heavily on sea traffic through the Indo-Pacific region. Two-thirds of Indian oil and gas imports transit the Indian Ocean, and most of Australia's resource exports transit East-Asian waterways to China, Japan, South Korea, and Taiwan. [10] The burgeoning Australia-India energy and resource trade is also primarily seaborne. India is understandably wary of China's growing role in the Indian Ocean, particularly China's interest in developing major port facilities in South and South-East Asia.

The Indian Navy is expanding its activities eastward to cope with expected increasing Chinese naval activity in the Bay of Bengal and Indian Ocean and to enable India to project power into the Asia-Pacific. India has also carefully cultivated ties with the countries of the Indian Ocean rim, including Mauritius, Maldives, Seychelles, and Madagascar. It has provided these countries with naval support, such as offshore naval patrol vessels, staff, and training. In February 2008, India convened the Indian Ocean Naval Symposium (IONS), inviting participants from the littoral states, including Australia, to discuss maritime security. [11]

India also is pursuing better ties with several Southeast Asian navies, notably Vietnam, to balance Chinese naval power and protect access to the Indian Ocean. New Delhi initiated a security partnership with Hanoi in 2000 that emphasized defence training, supply of advanced weaponry, and the potential for India to gain access to the South China Sea through the Cam Ranh Bay naval and air base. [12] It is essential to balance the Chinese naval presence in the Western Pacific and to counter China's 'String of Pearls Strategy' encircling India.

Piracy

Countering piracy is an urgent necessity to ensure unimpeded trade and commerce in the Asia-Pacific. Somali piracy is a growing threat in the Arabian Sea off India's west coast. India has engaged in anti-piracy operations since 2008, disrupting around 30 piracy attempts and arresting more than 120 pirates. [13] India is also responsible for securing the exclusive economic zones of Maldives, Seychelles, and Mauritius. India, Australia and the US have immense scope in joint efforts in meeting the challenge of piracy as the Somali pirates have expanded their activities to the Asia-Pacific.

Counter Terrorism

Transnational terrorism and home-grown terrorism is major concern for India, Australia and the US. Home-grown terrorist groups, often inspired by global terrorist groups, threaten most of South Asia. Such groups and "lone wolf" terrorists are also a matter of great concern in the US and several other Western nations. Islamic terrorists groups in Indonesia and Malaysia pose challenge to Australia. Transnational terror groups such as Lashkar-e-Taiba, Jemaathe Islamiyah, and other groups and individuals that are loosely or closely affiliated with Al-Qaeda.

Nuclear Scenario

Asia is the nuclear flashpoint of the world. The China-

Pakistan collaboration in nuclear and missile development and active programs in Iran and North Korea are major concerns for the US, Australia, and India. These developments have far-reaching potential to alter the military balance and peace in Asia. It is equally important for India, the US, and Australia to coordinate their positions on Iran. India is keen to work with Iran, given its growing demand for energy resources, but is uncomfortable with Iran's clandestine nuclear activities, especially when they have been linked to Pakistan. These three countries can collaborate in devising global responsibilities towards nuclear disarmament.

Nature and Goals of US-Australia-India Convergence

The growing convergence between Australia, India and the United States has identified a number of interests and goals as bases of its collaborative enterprise. Its stated goals include a regional order based on freedom of navigation, maritime security, free and open commerce, rule of law and, above all, security in Asia. This includes ensuring that regional security forums engage with pressing problems, such as putting in place a multilateral mechanism to reduce the risk of conflict in the Asia-Pacific.

The United States wants to maintain a forward deployed military presence in the region that both reassures friends and reminds others that America will remain the ultimate guarantor of regional peace and stability. As per the "United States and the Asia-Pacific Region: Security Strategy for the Obama Administration", the following strategic imperatives guide US policy in the region: reaffirm US leadership and to restore its moral authority; reaffirm and reinvigorate the network of US alliances that continue to serve as the foundation upon which a broader strategy must be built; maintain strategic equilibrium while integrating rising powers in ways compatible with US interests; retard the proliferation of Weapons of Mass Destruction; and actively participate in the region's multilateral economic, political, and security structures to address both traditional and non-traditional security challenges. [14]

To address these imperatives, the US envisages six key lines of action in the Asia-Pacific: strengthening bilateral security alliances; deepening working relationships with emerging powers, engaging with regional multilateral institutions; expanding trade and investment; forging a broad-based military presence; and advancing democracy and human rights. [15] Accordingly the focus is to build a web of partnerships and institutions across the Asia-Pacific that is as durable and as consistent with American interests and values as the web built across the Atlantic. The aim of US forward diplomacy is regional security, heighten prosperity, and support stronger democratic institutions and the spread of universal human rights in the Asia-Pacific region. [16]

Strengthening bilateral relations with traditional friends like Japan, South Korea and, Australia is an important aspect of the US strategy. With this aim in mind the US has been entering into security pacts, joint military exercise and strengthening military bases in the region for a broadly distributed military presence in the region. It has security pacts with Japan, Australia, South Korea, Taiwan and Philippines and conduct regular joint military exercises between and among these countries. United States territory of Guam, a far-reaching strategic enclave in the Pacific much like the island of Diego Garcia in the Indian Ocean, is a major military station for overseas military commitments. Air Sea Battle,' the US Defence Departments special strategy for Asia is an instrument with which American military power plan to address 'asymmetrical threats in the Western Pacific-an implicit reference to China. [17] The announcement in November 2011 to station US marine in Darwin, Australia is a continuation of this militaristic as well as a strategic logic.

The US has enhanced its engagement in Asia-Pacific multilateral organizations towards the development of the regional institutions and architecture. The US is very committed to the APEC and has strong relations with the ASEAN, the ASEAN Regional Forum (ARF), the ASEAN Defence Ministers Meeting (Plus), the East Asia Summit (EAS), Lower Mekong Initiative (LMI) and, the Pacific Island Forum (PIF).

The fear of China's dominance is at the centre of US foreign policy of the Asia-Pacific region. [18] America's participation in the first ASEAN "Defence Ministers Plus" meeting (ADMM+) in 2010, the East Asia Summit (EAS) for the first time in 2011, reaffirming of the 60-year-old security pact between the United States and the Philippines, the creation of an American-led regional trade pact that pointedly excludes China for the present, the decision to station US marine at Darwin in Australia and, US motivated democratic reforms in Myanmar are considered by Beijing as a tactic to weave American noose around China. [19] The 2011 East Asia Summit held at Bali is a significant development in this respect. Despite Chinese reservations, five ASEAN member-states—Singapore, Philippines, Brunei, Vietnam and Thailand—together with India, Australia and the US raised the issue of maritime boundaries and freedom of navigation. [20] Washington justifies its build-up in the region by citing China's increasingly menacing claims on the region's contested waterways. China's growing military capabilities, particularly in the field of ballistic missiles and stealth strike aircraft, have placed current US bases in Japan and South Korea in the radius of attack. Potentially, it challenges America's military pre-eminence in Asia in half a century. The fear of China's dominance is at the centre of U.S. foreign policy of the Asia-Pacific region. [21]

The US shift of focus to Asia-Pacific region has an underlying economic and political dimension. According to the US, its economic prosperity, pre-eminence in global politics, the security of the United States in the 21st century will depend on the course of events in East Asia, and most importantly on how the region will accommodate itself to the rising power and economic strength of China. [22] In the words of Hillary Clinton, "Harnessing Asia's growth and dynamism is central to American economic and strategic interests and a key priority for President Obama". Open markets in Asia provide the United States with unprecedented opportunities for investment, trade, and access to cutting-edge technology.

Our economic recovery at home will depend on exports and the ability of American firms to tap into the vast and growing consumer base of Asia. [23] Strategically, maintaining peace and security across the Asia-Pacific is increasingly crucial to global progress, whether through defending freedom of navigation in the South China Sea, countering the proliferation efforts of North Korea, or ensuring transparency in the military activities of the region's key players. Pentagon strategists say the aim is to "dissuade, deter and defeat" regional aggressors.

Indian engagement in security institutions focused on the Asia- Pacific region has long been fitful but has gathered pace in recent years, consistent with India's Look East policy and the post-cold war improvement in the Indo-US relationship. At present many consider India as a strategic partner of the US in the emerging world. The Defence Framework Agreement signed in 2005, the Civilian Nuclear Agreement of 2008, joint military exercises, collaboration through multilateral institutions in Asia and a host of agreements ranging from agriculture to democracy have improved Indo-US relations tremendously. In many instances India has followed a pro-US policy to the embarrassment of China and traditional friends like Iran. [24]

In the words of India's Foreign Secretary, "Indo-US partnership is important for building a stable, prosperous and secure Asia-Pacific region or the Indo-Pacific region...as we now have growing strategic and security engagement in the region". [25] This is further cemented by the reference to India in the US Department of Defence Comprehensive Strategic

Review-2012': "The United States is also investing in a long-term strategic partnership with India to support its ability to serve as a regional economic anchor and provider of security in the broader Indian Ocean region." [26] It is argued that the US move to create a naval base in northern Australia close to the South China Sea could bring more strategic and business opportunities to India. The first piece of evidence has come by way of Australia's decision to sell uranium to India. [27]

According to China expert Subramanian Swamy, "Japan, Vietnam and Indonesia will feel more secure. India and Indonesia can get together to control the Malacca Straits, which is the route though which 90 percent of Chinese goods to East Asia passes". [28] Washington's move has put the US navy within easy sailing reach of Vietnam, which is involved in a serious territorial dispute over oil-rich islands in the South China Sea. The old US led alliance order is proposing more and more trilateral dialogues such as the first-ever India-Japan-US trilateral meeting in December 2011 which professed to protect core Indian interests. [29] The US sees India as a party to the containment of China through bilateral and multilateral mechanisms.

Australia is a key partner of the US led alliance in Asia and it has a central role in Australian security and defence strategy. In a Testimony before the House Committee on Foreign Affairs Subcommittee on Asia and the Pacific in March 2011, Kurt M. Campbell, US's Assistant Secretary, Bureau of East Asian and Pacific Affairs, stated that Australia remains a strategic anchor for regional stability and plays an incredibly important role in maintaining global security, US and Australian forces fight side-by-side, extending a legacy of cooperation that goes back a century, and Australia is the largest non-NATO contributor to the coalition effort in Afghanistan. [30]

The 25th Australia-US Ministerial Consultations (AUSMIN) in November, 2010, announced the launch of the Australia-US Force Posture Review Working Group, which envisages expanded US-Australia military cooperation to optimize US force posture in the Asia-Pacific region. [31] Australia has long been an active participant in and builder, along with the US, of Asia-Pacific regional organizations, including APEC, the ASEAN Regional Forum (ARF), and the East Asia Summit. Of late the US is expanding its alliance with Australia from a Pacific partnership to an Indo-Pacific one, and indeed a global partnership and it considers Australia's counsel and commitment indispensable from cyber security to the strengthening of regional architecture in the Asia-Pacific. [32]

In fact, China's rising power is fundamental to US-Australia alliance. [33] In strategic and security realms, during the Cold war days, Australia followed a policy of "Forward Defence," where Australia sought to protect itself from hostile regional forces by closely aligning itself with the US. [34] In the 2000 defence white paper, there is a visible shift away from this old policy of Defence of Australia to more offensive-minded Australia Defence Force. The goal is to be adaptable and versatile in meeting and sustaining the demands of diverse operations and the potential threat of great power confrontation in the Asia Pacific between China and the US. [35] White paper released in May 2009 titled, "Defending Australia in the Asia Pacific Century: Force 2030", emphasizes its security apprehensions further.

Essentially, the paper is based on the assumption that China will increasingly dominate the region, alongside India and a re-emerging Russia. While championing the importance of the United States' nuclear umbrella to regional stability, the paper assumes that the US conventional role and capability will diminish. As a result, Australia will be forced to become more self-reliant. [36] It suggested that "over the period to 2030, the Indian Ocean will join the Pacific Ocean in terms of its centrality to our maritime strategy and defence planning." [37]

Australia needs the US presence in the Asia-Pacific mainly

for two reasons: first, to secure its trade routes as well as offshore areas potentially rich in gas; second, to ensure military, technological and intelligence support and protection from the US. That support is necessary to enhance its capabilities in an area where the potential for conflicts exists, including a possible maritime confrontation with China. [38]

In the early years of the post-cold war period Australia was reluctant to the idea of India as a partner. Nonetheless, it began to support US agenda of cultivating New Delhi as a partner for the new century. Today, India and Australia co-operate in various multilateral forums and are members of the G-20, Commonwealth, IOR-ARC, ASEAN dialogue partners, ASEAN Regional Forum, Asia Pacific Partnership on Climate and Clean Development, core group of first responders to the 2004 Tsunami in South-Asia and have participated in the East Asia Summits and as members of the Five Interested Parties (FIP) in the WTO. Australia is an important player in APEC and supports India's membership of the organization. In 2008, Australia became an observer in the SAARC and supports India's candidature in an expanded UN Security Council.

This desire for greater collaboration with India is reflected in the Australian decision to lift ban on uranium sale to India which in Prime Minister Julia Gillard words, "a decision that is in our nation's interest, a decision about strengthening our strategic partnership with India in this, Asian century." [39] To the leftist opposition to lift the ban on uranium Gillard said "India is in a class of its own." [40] What Ms. Gillard left unsaid has been detailed in an Australian government's approach paper on the defence architecture, which suggested the beginning of a US-Australia-India trilateral dialogue. In future this could expand into joint naval operations and theatre missile defence between India, Australia and the US.

An Indian defence Ministry release laid out the contours of the expanded relationship: "Both sides agreed that challenges in the area of maritime security, like piracy and freedom of navigation, are important issues which required concerted efforts of the global community." [41] As such Canberra is eager to complement the rise of India in Asia's power dynamics with a serious strategic partnership. Both the countries see each other overwhelmingly as factors for stability in the shared Indo-Pacific region.

The defence and security relationship between India and Australia have the most intriguing potential of any area, with the capacity to significantly enhance both Indian and Australian geopolitical, strategic and security interests, working to build a rule-based maritime order in the Indian Ocean, and supporting one in the South China Sea. [42] The Joint Declaration on Security Cooperation between Australia and India, made in November 2009, is part of a number of security agreements being entered into across the Asia Pacific. This trend has included the establishment of the Trilateral Security Dialogue among Australia, the United States and Japan (which was upgraded to foreign and defence ministerial level in 2006), the 2007 Australia-Japan Security Declaration and the 2009 Australia-South Korea Security Declaration, as well as a mooted security declaration between Japan and South Korea. [43]

China with its growing military power, combined with differences over values, poses fundamental security anxieties to Australia. Australia is developing a hedging strategy based on its assessments of present and future capability of China and other major players in the region. [44] This hedging strategy involves increasing Australia's own military weight, intensifying the US alliance, and building security links with large democratic Asian partners, including India. [45] The growing strategic and security relationship between India and Australia has to be seen in this background.

These bilateral and multilateral security mechanisms are to be seen as an expansion of the US "hub and spoke" alliance system that has existed in the Asia-Pacific since the 1950s, in which the United States formed the centre of a series of bilateral alliances with key allies in the Asia-Pacific (most notably Japan, Australia and South Korea). [46] This system has been evolving in recent years through the development of additional security frameworks that facilitate direct dialogue and cooperation between US allies.

Both the US and Australia want India to be a party to this emerging strategic partnership to counter the rising Chinese threat—politically, economically and strategically. Essentially, it is a strategy of `containment' aimed at China. China considers these steps as reminiscent of the 19th and early 20th century efforts by the Western powers to corner it and is inimical to peaceful development in the Asia-Pacific. [47]

The US and Australian policies towards Asia-Pacific have two main goals. The primary goal is to contain China. Second is to exploit the economic opportunities offered by rising Asia. The strategy adopted is to enter into bilateral and multilateral security and strategic alliances with countries of the region and multilateral organizations. Both the US and Australia want India to be an active partner in this endeavour. The rationale offered is the security, peace and prosperity of the region. To a great extent India has complied with the US-Australian plans for greater co-operation and friendship in the region. The question that the new found relationship raises is what are its implications for India and the region.

Implications of Australia-India-US-Convergence

Adverse Impact on India-China Relations: India's most important relationship in the contemporary times is with that of China. There is already a feeling that India is teaming with the US and its allies in Asia for the containment of China. The Australian Defence White Paper 2009 portrayed China as the primary threat. [48] The US views China as the major economic and military challenge to its hegemonic ambitions in the 21st century. Therefore it is reinventing the 'hub and spoke' alliance system that it practiced in Asia during cold war days with the aim of containing China. The US treaty alliances with Japan, South Korea, Australia, the Philippines, and

Thailand are the fulcrum for its strategic turn in the Asia-Pacific and these leverage US regional presence and enhances its regional leadership at a time of evolving security challenges. [49]

China increasingly suffers from geopolitical claustrophobia. It sees its environment turning increasingly sceptical, if not hostile, to its rise and that wrangling over territorial interests or regional influence leads its neighbours to call on the US to keep China in check. Australia, in spite of its strong economic and cultural (strong Chinese community in Australia) relations with China, is an active partner of US machination and it is likely to gain from such a tie up. Whereas India's case is different, India's relationship with China is important economically, politically and culturally. India's economic prosperity and regional and global ambitions depends to a great extent on the kind of India-China relationship. China is a great economic and political opportunity for India. A hostile relationship with such an important neighbour will certainly go against India's larger interest at home and abroad.

Doom and Gloom for Asia

The Western countries headed by the US could dominate world politics after the Second World War because they worked as a united front. Europe registered tremendous economic progress as they stopped fighting among themselves learning lessons from devastations of the first and second world wars. Also it must be remembered that European powers lost their domination of world politics as they fought among themselves on flimsy grounds which could have been avoided through sensible diplomatic means.

After the Second World War, the US replaced Europe in Asia as the dominant power, and thereafter regarded itself as having the right to force Asian countries into following policies that benefit US and NATO interests rather than their own. [50] The US alliance knows that if the Asian powers, especially Beijing and Delhi act in concert, they would lose its hold on Asia and its markets and resources. So a divided Asia and not a united Asia serves Western interest in a better way. [51] The most important thing that emerging Asia should try to do is to avoid the fate of the early 20th century Europe. In India, many regard China as a threat, just as many in China regard India as a threat. Asia should learn from Europe's lessons in co-operation, rather than their lessons in conflict. Friendship between India and China is a pre-condition for a rising and united Asia.

The Asian century will never become a reality if the two giants of Asia move in opposite directions. Rather, it will provide another opportunity for the West to divide and rule Asia that they so successfully implemented during the days of colonialism. Asia is the most contested and divided continent in the world. India entering into any sort of security or military alliance with the US will sharpen existing animosities and rivalries in Asia into unmanageable levels, particularly India's relationship with China, Pakistan and Arab countries. Many countries in Asia which include, the Chinese and some ASEAN members, such as Indonesia, fear that a more significant presence of the US Navy could destabilize the region. [52] India joining the US and Australia led Western machinations would be all dooms and glooms for Asia.

Incompatible Alliance

The Indo-US and Australian convergence is an incompatible alliance. The level and degree of co-operation and understanding between and among these countries are of a different genre. The relationship between Australia and the US is time tested and historically inherited and has been consolidated by ethnic and racial considerations. Australia and the US belong to the same race and colour. Race has always been a factor in international relations and special relations among countries of the Western white ethnicity is a reality.

The relationship between Australia and the US is bonded

by their common European origin and racial identity. It is similar to the special relationship and 'racialised peace' between the US and Britain in which the American and British foreign policy elites framed themselves as members of a single supreme and messianic Anglo Saxon race. [53] Even now race continues be a factor as could be derived from Obama's May 2011 address to the British parliament in which he referred to the domination of the world by the Anglo-Saxons. [54]

One of the reasons for the lacklustre relationship between India and Australia during the cold war was its Western white identity and the poor state of relationship between India and the US led Western countries. Australia was a country that followed a proud 'White Australia Policy' for a long time and its immigration policy searched initially for fair-skinned Europeans. [55] As such it was isolated from its neighbours for most of the time as a 'White Western country' in 'Brown Asia'. Most of the security alliance and pacts that Australia signed have been with Western countries to ensure security with Asia.

Some analysts say that Australia was West's early warning system in Asia. [56] The prospects of relationship between India and Australia always depended on the nature of relationship between India and the West. The new found warmth in the relationship between these countries is a marriage of convenience and not a natural alliance of democracies or like minded states. It is the pressures of the circumstances that prompted these countries to form security alliances and initiate strategic negotiations. Australia was historically "protected" by the British Empire and after the Second World War this historic responsibility has been carried out by the hegemonic Anglo-Saxon Americans. In short, the relationship between Australia and US is a 'special relationship' spanning over centuries and consolidated by their common Anglo-Saxon origins. India is a misfit in this configuration. In other words, there is a big cultural and political gap between Australia and the US on the one hand

and India on the other hand.

Incongruent with India's Basic Foreign Policy Precepts

Even after the end of Cold War and the post-Cold War shift in India's foreign policy priorities, the basic principles and impulses of India's foreign policy remain almost the same. An intense desire for an independent foreign policy, which many analyst call 'strategic autonomy' and an aversion to military and security alliances are still very strong. India is not used to it and has not been a party to any military and strategic alliances. Therefore, becoming a part to an Asian security architecture is odd to Indian foreign policy practices and precepts.

Conclusion

Entering into any sort of security alliances with USA and Australia beyond economic is detrimental to India's interest. The relations between Australia and USA in the Asia-Pacific is special. India is new entrant into this category of alliances and security architecture. The efforts to enter into defence agreements under the guise of bilateral agreements is also not in India's long term interest. The best thing is to engage in bilateral diplomatic relations with a strong economic content and build its own security infrastructure. India becoming a party to Asian security architecture being envisaged by the US would not contribute to peace and prosperity neither in India nor in Asia.

End Notes

1. Cossa, Ralph A., Glosserman, Brad, et al. (2009), *The United States and the Asia-Pacific Region: Security Strategy for the Obama Administration,* http://csis.org/files/media/csis/pubs/issuesinsights_v09n01.pdf accessed on 12-11-2011.
2. http:www.parl.org.ca/content/SENCommitte/352/fore/rep/repjim97notes.htm accessed on 24-03-2012.
3. *China attaches great importance to Asia-Pacific regional*

cooperation, Peoples daily online, Nov.12.2010 http://english. peoplesdaily.com.in, accessed on 17-02-2011.

4. *India and Australia in the Asian Century*, Keynote Lecture by Professor the Hon. Gareth Evans AO QC, Chancellor of The Australian National University, Professorial Fellow at The University of Melbourne and former Australian Foreign Minister, to the Australia India Institute and University of Calcutta Conference The Asian Century–Security, Sustainability and Society: An India Australia Dialogue, Kolkata, 5 December 2011, http://report.heritage.org/sr0099 accessed on 11-1-2012.
5. *Asia-Pacific region holds vital importance to US: Obama Administration,* March 16 2010, http://www.indianexpress.com/news/asiapacific-region-holds-vital-importance-to-us-obama-admin/591423/0 accessed on 21-04-2011.
6. Rodham Clinton, *Hillary, America's Pacific Century*, http://www.state.gov/secretary/rm/2011/10/175216.htm accessed on 12-10-2012.
7. The decision of the U S in 2012 to open a naval training centre at Darvin in Australia close to South-China Sea is seen as an effort to contain China in its neighbourhood.
8. Curtis, Lisa, Lohman, Walter et al. (2011), *Shared Goals, Converging Interests: A Plan for U.S.-Australia-India Cooperation in the Indo-Pacific*, The Heritage Foundation, Washington D.C. http://report.heritage.org/sr0099, accessed on 11-1-2012.
9. Parthasarathy, G, *Arrogance of China*, http://www.dailypioneer.com/columnists/item/50633-arrogance-of-china.html, accessed 12-12-2011.
10. Ibid.
11. Ibid.
12. Ibid.
13. Ibid.
14. Cossa, Ralph A., Glosserman, Brad, et al., *op. cit.*
15. Rodham Clinton, Hillary, *op. cit.*
16. http://www.state.gov/p/eap/rls/rm/2011/03/159450.htm accessed on 27-02-2012. Asia Overview: Protecting American Interests in China and Asia, Testimony, Kurt M. Campbell, Assistant Secretary, Bureau of East Asian and Pacific Affairs, Testimony Before the House Committee on Foreign Affairs Subcommittee

on Asia and the Pacific Washington, DC, March 31, 2011.

17. Glain, Bstephen,(2011), *Choosing Arms Over Diplomacy: America Errs in Asia* http://www.nytimes.com/2011/12/16/opinion/sunday/costly-military-expansion-in-asia.html?nl=todaysheadlines&emc=tha212 accessed 16-12-2011.
18. Baroud, Ramzy, '*U.S. flirts with risky cold war in warm waters* http://www.japantimes.co.jp/text/eo20120227rb.html, accessed on 28-02-2012.
19. Glain, Bstephen, *op.cit.*
20. http://www.dailypioneer.com/columnists/item/50633-arrogance-of-china.html accessed 12-12-2011.
21. Baroud, Ramzy, *op. cit.*
22. Rodham Clinton, Hillary, *op. cit.*
23. Rodham Clinton, Hillary, *op. cit.*
24. India's Vote with the US in the UN resolution on Syria in March 2012 and its vote against Iran in ıAEA in November 2009.
25. http://www.indianembassy.org/prdetail1860/speech-by-foreign-secretary-of-india,-mr.-ranjan-mathai-at-the-center-for-strategic-and-international-studies-(csis),-washington-dc-on-february-6,-2012-on-andquot-percent3Bbuilding-on-convergences percent3A-deepening-india-u.s.-strategic-partnershipandquot percent3B accessed on 13-02-2012.
26. Department of Defence, (2012), USA, *Sustaining U S Global Leadership: Priorities for Twenty First Century Defence*, http://www.defense.gov/news/Defense_Strategic_Guidance.pdf accessed on 25-04-2012.
27. It is to be noted is that the Australian decision to review and change its policies regarding the sale of uranium to India was announced during US President Barack Obama's visit to Australia.
28. Dasgupta, Saiba, *US naval move in Australia may help India take on China,* http://articles.timesofindia.indiatimes.com/2011-11-17/china/30409385_1_india-china-south-china-sea-china-expert accessed on 15-1-2012.
29. Jha, Saurav, *India-Australia Relations and the Obama Pivot to Asia,* World Politics Review, 10th January, 2012, *www.worldpoliticsreview.com* accessed on 15-2-2012.
30. *Asia Overview: Protecting American Interests in China and*

Asia, Testimony, Kurt M. Campbell, Assistant Secretary, Bureau of East Asian and Pacific Affairs, USA, Testimony before the House Committee on Foreign Affairs Subcommittee on Asia and the Pacific Washington, DC, March 31, 2011 http://www.state.gov/p/eap/rls/rm/2011/03/159450.htm accessed on 27-02-2012.

31. Ibid.
32. Rodham Clinton, Hillary, *op. cit.*
33. Medcalf, Rory, *Australia's Uranium Puzzle: Why China and Russia not India?* Australia India Institute, Spring 2011, Vol. 1, p. 10.
34. Snyder, Craig A. '*Strategic Posture Review: Australia*', World Politics Review, 01 May 2009, *www.worldpoliticsreview.com* accessed on 15-3-2012.
35. Ibid.
36. Hunt, Luke, *Against the Ropes: Australian Defence Policy* , World Politics Review, 03 August 2009, *www.worldpoliticsreview.com* accessed on 17-3-2012.
37. Australian Department of Defence, (2009), *Defending Australia in the Asia Pacific Century: Force 2030*, http://www.defence.gov.au/whitepaper/docs/defence_white_paper_2009.pdf. accessed on 14-1-2012.
38. Tofani, Roberto, *East Asia Summit: U.S. and China, With ASEAN in the Middle* 23 Nov 2011, World Politics Review, *www.worldpoliticsreview.com* accessed on 2-12-2011
39. Vinod Kumar, A, *Uranium from Down Under: Can Madam Gillard Pull it off?* November 21, 2011.IDSA Comment. http://www.idsa.in/idsacomment/UraniumfromDownUnderCanMadamGillardPullitoff_avkumar_211111 accessed 19-01-2012.
40. Ibid.
41. Ibid.
42. India and Australia in the Asian Century http://report.heritage.org/sr0099 accessed on 11-1-2012 op.cit.
43. *Japan, South Korea Eye Security Declaration,* The Yomiuri, Shimbun, 9th January 2010 http://newsonjapan.com/html/newsdesk/article/78985.php accessed on 19-12-2011.
44. Ibid.
45. Ibid.
46. Brewster, David (2010), *The Australia-India Security*

Declaration: The Quadrilateral Redux? Security Challenges, Vol. 6, No. 1, pp. 1-9.

47. Fraser, Malcolm, *The new Asia needs better than obsolete Cold War-era concepts*, The Daily Star, December 12, 2011, http://www.dailystar.com.lb/Opinion/Commentary/2011/Dec-12/156598-the-new-asia-needs-better-than-obsolete-cold-war-era-concepts.ashx#axzz1ulE7JLQi accessed on 12-01-2012.
48. Medcalf, Rory (2009), *Problems to Partnership: A Plan for Australia-India Strategic Ties*, Lowy Institute, Policy brief, November www.lowyinstitute.org, accessed on 18-02-2012.
49. Rodham Clinton, Hillary, *op. cit.*
50. Nalapat, M.D., *Asia should ignore 'divide and conquer' tactics*, Global Times, December 28, 2011.
51. The western countries have always been against the rise of Asia and Asian countries. The reports regarding the protests movements against the kundakulam nuclear power plant being aided by the US and Scandinavian countries is testimony to the fact. Western powers have made umpteen efforts not to let Asian countries reap the benefits of higher technology, followed a policy of balancing one against the other, India against Pakistan and recently India against China, they engage with the emerging powers with the policy of hub and the spoke and off-shore balancing at different levels. One can also study BVD spy Frits Hoekstra's book, a senior BVD officer who quit the service in 1987; to understand the level of complicity of Dutch with American agencies to create disruption in third world. For more details see
http://ariseasia.blogspot.in/#!http://ariseasia.blogspot.com/2012/02/koodankulam-protests-church-and-western.html
Koodankulam Protests, Church and Western NGOs-Citizen's Probe.
52. Tofani, Roberto, *East Asia Summit: U.S. and China, With ASEAN in the Middle*, 23rd November 2011, World Politics Review, *www.worldpoliticsreview.com* accessed on 17-2-2012.
53. Srdjan Vucetic, (2011), *A Racialised Peace? How Britain and the US made Their Relationship Special*, Foreign Policy Analysis, (2011), Vol. 7. No. 4, Columbia, p. 416.
54. http://www.newstatesman.com/2011/05/nations-rights-world-united accessed on 10-03-2012.
55. Robin Jeffrey, *Australia-India: reimagining the relationship,*

Current affairs and culture from Australia and beyond, 15 February 2010 . http://inside.org.au/australia-india/ accessed on 14-04-2012.

56. Barber, Lionel, *Asia's Rise, the West's Fall*? Financial Times, Sydney, 17 November 2011, http://aboutus.ft.com/2011/11/17/the-2011-lowy-lecture-lionel-barber-asia percentE2 percent80 percent99s-rise-the-west percentE2 percent80 percent99s-fall/#axzz1ulGA9exS accessed on 12-01=2012.

8

India's Two Decades of Naval Engagement with ASEAN

S. Utham Kumar Jamadhagni

Relation Review

With the unveiling of the *Look East Policy* a drastic change in the orientation of India's foreign and economic policy took place with sights set on strengthening the relations with these countries that have had strong cultural ties. Trading relationships between India and some ASEAN member countries can be traced back more than a thousand years and have profoundly affected one another's linguistics, religion, culture and business. South-East Asia has been a destination of Indian migrants for centuries. India's cultural, trade and religious ties with South East Asia in general dates back to 1 A.D. The contact began with migrants from Gujarat settling in these areas. Later from South India, trade relations began and flourished till 7th century. Indian ports like Mahabalipuram sent spices like cinnamon and pepper to the islands of Java, Sumatra, and Bali. [1] The successful integration of the local Southeast Asian trade network into the Indian Ocean economic world was done by South Asian mariners and merchants. This facilitated the "selective adoption of South Asian religions, cultural forms and technology by the people of Southeast Asia." [2]

Cultural and religious influence from Hinduism and Buddhism followed the traders. In fact, the most successful empires in Southeast Asia were those of Hindu kings like Sri Vijaya. The cultural influence in literature, music, dance, rituals and religious practices are evident to this day. Some of the greatest literary works of Southeast Asia are based or are heavily drawn from Hindu epics like Ramayana and Mahabharata. Ancient art forms that define Indonesian ethos like *Wayang Kulit* or shadow puppetry, the *Barong* mask dance and the *Sendratari* art forms base their narrative in the Ramayana and Mahabharata. Several translated versions of these epics are replete throughout this region's history.

ASEAN is close to India geographically—India shares land borders with Burma and Thailand, and sea borders with them as well as Malaysia and Singapore. The "Look East" policy took this into account and the potential role the diaspora could play in bridging the gaps between India and their host countries. [3] This policy sought to foster closer links with ASEAN in strategic, political and economic fields. Not only was it an attempt to exhibit India's trade and investment potential, it also attempted "to carve a place for India in the larger Asia-Pacific". [4] India's attitude towards ASEAN during its early years of independence was ambivalent but not hostile.

The Indian leadership viewed ASEAN as an American "imperialist surrogate" while ASEAN dubbed India as the "surrogate of the Soviet Union". The signing of the Friendship Treaty with the Soviets, India's stand on Afghanistan and India's recognition of the Hang Samarin Government in 1981—all led to estrangement between India and ASEAN. India's decision not to participate as a dialogue partner in 1980 was a further setback. The expansion of the Indian Navy in the early 1990s and the military assistance provided to Maldives had led to adverse propaganda in Australia and ASEAN. It is only after some Joint Naval exercises with the South East Asian nations and the collapse of the Soviet Republic, India's efforts to improve relations with ASEAN gained momentum.

India-ASEAN relations have deepened and intensified significantly in recent years. India became a sectoral dialogue partner of ASEAN in1992. In 1995 this was upgraded to full dialogue partnership. It participated in the ASEAN Ministerial

Meeting (AMM), the Post Ministerial Conference (PMC) and the ASEAN Regional Forum (ARF) in July 1996. Since 2002, India has annual summits with ASEAN along with China, Japan and Republic of Korea. These political level interactions are further strengthened through the Senior Officials' meetings, as also specialized working groups in functional areas. [5] In the words of Prime Minister Dr. Manmohan Singh, "India's Look East policy is not merely an external economic policy, it is also a strategic shift in India's vision of the world and India's place in the evolving global economy. Most of all it is about reaching out to our civilisational neighbours in South East Asia and East Asia". [6]

Political Relations

Independent India supported the self-determination efforts of countries like Indonesia. In fact, Indonesia was also a founding member of the Non-aligned Movement (NAM). [7] But the relations soured in the late 50s. Southeast Asia was caught in the Cold War tangle and attempted to shore up its security. Interestingly India was to be part of this arrangement. Jawaharlal Nehru on the other hand, was vehemently opposed to the Philippines proposal of forming a regional defence pact. SEATO or the Southeast Asian Treaty Organisation in the eyes of Nehru was an anti thesis of Panch Shila (the five principles of state policy including non interference in the internal affairs of other states) and an intrusion upon the sovereignty of India". [8] During the 1962 Sino-Indian conflict when India expected support, she suffered blight from the indifference of Southeast Asian countries especially in the context of creation of the Jakarta-Peking-Hanoi axis.

In the mid and late 1960s, the Southeast Asian countries wished to invite India to become a member of ASEAN for which India was neither prepared nor in a mood. Thus, an opportunity to forge strong ties was missed. [9] However, the relations reached a new low during Sukarno's reign. The 1965 Indo-Pakistan war took place at a time when New Delhi and

Jakarta possessed different world views. This period saw increasing alignment between Indonesia and China and rapport with Pakistan. There were reports of vague threats from President Sukarno to aid the Pakistanis. It was later learnt that Indonesia promised MIG 19 and MIG 15 jet fighters during the conflict. [10]

According to Air Marshal Asghar Khan of Pakistan, Sukarno offered even to seize Andaman and Nicobar islands as a diversionary tactic. [11] There were reports of Indonesia lending a flotilla with a pair each of submarines, missile carrying boats and vessels. [12] The effect was the sensitization of the Indian defence establishment to the potential threat from Southeast Asia and highlighted the need for an increased naval presence in Bay of Bengal. [13]

The renewed focus through Look east policy has attempted to engage ASEAN countries in economic, strategic and political fields. It is interesting to note that for the past three years, the chief guests at India's Republic Day parade have been Southeast Asian leaders. Some of the countries have enhanced relationship to strategic level.

Trade Ties

On the economic front, ASEAN figures in the list of India's biggest trading partners. The trade relation with this region has grown by leaps and bounds. Trade volumes with the ASEAN countries have more than doubled in a decade. From a mere US$ 1484 million in 1993 Indian market has emerged as one of the largest importers of South East Asian goods with imports touching US$ 18,928 million in 2006. [14] The trade figures for 2011 were US$ 58 billion. The recently concluded Free Trade agreements with countries like Thailand and Singapore are set to contribute to this trend. Expanding markets and larger import flows imply not only economic prosperity but also vulnerability at sea.

Realising the potential India has stepped up its interaction in trade and other areas. Indian companies have begun investing in banking, mining, oil and gas, iron and steel, aluminium, automotive, textiles, IT and telecommunications. [15] With a fast growing economy, India's energy needs are bound to grow and countries in ASEAN might turn out to be a vital alternative source. Apart from importing raw materials like rubber and metals, India plans to procure natural gas through an undersea pipeline from Southeast Asia to the Nicobar Islands. [16] India has also signed preferential trade agreements which have slashed import duties on several products like seafoods, chemicals and apparel on both sides. [17]

Malacca Milieu

Strategically and economically too there is a commonality. The world's three important choke points namely Malacca straits, Sunda and Lombok straits are situated in this region. Of these Malacca, the second busiest shipping lane in the world sees 50,000 ships pass through it every year. It is the shortest route between the Indian and Pacific Ocean. More than half of the world's oil travels through these waters. Nearly 40 percent of India's sea trade volume passes through these straits. The 800 km. stretch seaway is very narrow at some points. Thus any disruption in traffic through these straits would spell disaster to world economy. This makes the safety of sea lanes of paramount interest and concern.

Conquering Piracy

One of the most important concerns in the maritime realm is piracy. Between 2002 and 2006 two-thirds of all reported piracy and sea robbery attacks in Southeast Asia, earning them the unenviable reputation of being the world's most pirate-infested waters. [18] In the first quarter of 2009, the International Maritime Bureau (IMB) reported that the number of pirate attacks around the world nearly doubled, to 102 incidents, compared with the same period last year; only one of them occurred in the Strait of Malacca. [19] The Malacca straits were the worst piracy prone region for long. However the joint patrolling by Malaysia, Indonesia and Singapore known as MALSINDO has effectively countered this menace. The coordinated patrol of the Malacca straits under the MALSINDO or Malaysia, Singapore and Indonesia joint agreement of 2006 and the Eyes in the Sky Program (EiS) initiated in 2005 involved joint aerial surveillance aimed at containing piracy and terrorist attacks in the Straits and provide safety for ships plying here. But this was also restricted by the stipulation that air patrols cannot go beyond 3 miles of each other's borders. [20] This effort is often cited as the principal reason for a fall in piracy incidents in this region.

South East Asian states like Indonesia, Malaysia and Philippines are home to a considerable number of groups, which have similar ideologies like Al-Qaeda. These countries also have contact points between offshoots of Al-Qaeda and terrorist groups in South East Asia in various places. As terrorism displayed a tendency to globalize, South East Asia has turned into a stage for global war against terrorism. The Bali bombing, which is blamed on Jemaah Islamiah (JI), a terrorist group based in Indonesia, marks the onset of a spiral of violence.

Groups like Indonesia based Gerakan Aceh Merdeka (GAM), Malaysian-based Kumpulan Mujahideen Malaysian (KMM), Philippine-based Moro Islamic Liberation Front (MILF) and Abu Sayyaf Group (ASG) have the ability to manoeuvre at sea. The tanker *Penrider*, which was attacked in the straits of Malacca in August 2003, is suspected of being intercepted by GAM. [21] The MILF is connected with JI and Al-Qaeda and even before the war on terrorism in Afghanistan, more than 1000 Muslim rebels were thought to be already Al-Qaeda trained. [22] Presence of all these groups in straits of Malacca, which has been considered as a 'Lifeline of Indian Ocean" is under threat.

There are several separatist outfits like Jemaah Islamiaya (JI) the Garekan Aceh Merdaka (GAM) the Abu Sayyaf group and other organisations active in Southeast Asia. Many of these groups are said to possess substantial maritime capabilities. Since 2000, Al-Qaeda, the Moro Islamic Liberation Front, the Abu Sayyaff Group, Jemaah Islamiyah, the Kumpulan Militant Malaysia, the Gerakan Aceh Merdeka, and Laskar Jihad have all been suspected of planning or executing maritime attacks. Others have used or could possibly use piracy to fund their activities. [23] In March 2003, the Indonesian tanker *Dewi Madrim* was hijacked and steered the ship for an hour allegedly as a dry run for future terror attacks. [24] However, scholars like Sam Bateman dismiss these as mere media hype [25] The tentacles of terror could also spread far with networking with other Islamic terrorist organisations like the Al-Qaeda. The relief over reduction in number of piracy attacks in these waters in the recent years is offset by the pattern of attack. Now, the organized pirate gangs attack medium-sized vessels, including cargo ships, bulk carriers and tankers. In these cases, a vessel and its crew is held hostage for a limited time, or the entire vessel is hijacked by pirates and is then turned into a 'phantom ship'. [26]

The transnational maritime crimes are no longer local acts but highly sophisticated and precise using latest technology, weapons and other equipment. Pirate gangs are feared to be associated with arms smugglers, drug traffickers funding and arming them. Groups like Indonesia based Gerakhan Aceh Merdeka (GAM) and such others have the ability to manoeuvre at sea. GAM was also frequently linked with acts of maritime piracy against international shipping in the Strait of Malacca. [27] In August 2003 for example, the tanker Penrider was suspected to be intercepted by GAM in the Malacca Straits. [28]

Not only is the sea lane security important to ASEAN nations, it is imperative for India too. India's island territory of Andaman and Nicobar Islands are closer to ASEAN countries than to the Indian mainland. The Nicobar Islands are just 98 nautical miles from the Banda Aceh province of Indonesia. Both countries share around 300 nautical miles of maritime border. There is no maritime boundary dispute between the two countries. Notably, India settled its maritime boundary with Indonesia as early as 1974 following an agreement over the area between Great Nicobar and Sumatra islands. [29]

A 1977 treaty extended this line into the Andaman Sea and the Indian Ocean. [30] In 1979, the agreement over the trijunction point between India, Indonesia and Thailand came into force. [31] For long, India has neglected the strategic importance of the far flung island territory. The Chinese foray into gaining access to the Indian Ocean through leverage from military and economic aid to littorals all around India have woken her up to the looming threat. Thus, India established a separate tri-service command here.

The Andaman and Nicobar joint service command, at first called the Far Eastern Naval Command, was established only in 2001. This set off concerns within Southeast Asian region especially Malaysia, Thailand and Indonesia on her present growth and "future intentions". [32] An Indonesian naval delegation later visited the A&N naval installations convincing them that a strong Indian Navy could be a positive factor in the safety and security of the region. Some of the 562 islands in the Andaman and Nicobar group are uninhabited making them safe havens for poachers and other Violent Non-state Actors (VSNAs). The proximity of these islands to the international trading route is also of concern as there are reports of dangers of collision, oil spills and marine pollution.

Sea Lane Security

As neighbouring maritime regions, India and Southeast Asia view the security of sea lanes, prevention of the use of the sea for nefarious activities and increasing vigilance against maritime terrorism as common maritime objectives. Since they are island nations, maritime security is at the forefront of Southeast Asian political concerns. The geo-strategic location of Malacca straits as the gateway to the east and the passage of a quarter of world trade through it also indicate its vulnerability. Also container ships are slow moving and hence very vulnerable and could even turn into a weapon of mass destruction. [33] In the same way, a 9/11 like incident of using a ship to destroy ports or refineries could be catastrophic. [34]

With emerging global economic powers like China, India in Asia the intensity of cross maritime communication between the Pacific and the Indian Oceans is certain to increase. Given their location and capabilities, India and Southeast Asian countries have a critical role to play as sentinels guarding these vital lifelines. [35] The region's economy is maritime-based. India too possesses a rich maritime tradition and is even today a predominantly sea faring nation. The dependence on the sea becomes more acute due to the large quantities of oil that India imports. The volatility of the oil market and growing world dependence of the energy resources of the Persian Gulf makes preservation of the sea lanes of communication a vital necessity. India straddles these sea lanes. [36]

While countries like Indonesia are energy niche economies, India is a net importer. With uninterrupted vigil of the far flung island coastlines being almost impossible, the vulnerability to terrorist attack is high. Thus the safety of the sea lanes is essential for national security too. These waterways also have a military value as they are the fastest way to deploy navy units from Indian Ocean to Pacific Ocean and vice versa. [37] The navies thus come to play a very important role in maintaining peace in the region. There has been extensive interaction between the Indian navy and navies of Southeast Asian countries individually.

Joint Naval Exercises

The nature of prevailing transnational and cross border threats warrants that countries in a region cooperate to control and finally weed out the menace. Earlier military threats emanated from other states and were clearly demarcated. With the rise of maritime security problems like piracy, arms and drug smuggling and trafficking, illegal immigration and maritime terrorism that respect no boundaries, states are left with no choice but to seek the help of others within and out of the region. The widening of security paradigm to encompass challenges of pollution, energy demand and supply, economic security and several other human related issues has meant the consideration of issues that are foreign in source and or solution. The pan regional threats like over-fishing that could affect the marine resources of a region are also noted with concern. The joint naval exercises reflect this reality in that it has manifested into search and rescue operations, patrolling of dangerous waterways, associating with hitherto remote nations and the focus on specific issues facing the cooperator.

The plethora of regional and extra regional military exercises by the Indian navy, army and air force in the recent are rudimentary steps towards cooperation in the military arena in the south Asian region. Owing to the transnational character of sources or solutions to threats and the inadequacy in numbers, sophistication or range of individual national armed forces in combating these threats are the twin movers of this rationale. Such exercises are aimed at achieving coordination at the operational levels and learning or sharing the separate experiences in facing or dealing with the threat. The threat of maritime terrorism is further aggravated by the threat of the WMDs falling in the hands of terrorists obtained from the theft of vessels ferrying such material. With containerization of sea borne trade and the Flags of convenience concept now allowing concealment of ownership, piracy together with maritime terrorism concoct a dangerous mix.

Singapore

The Indian navy has one of the oldest formal maritime cooperative mechanisms with Singapore. The Singapore, India Maritime Bilateral Exercises (SIMBEX) began as early as 1993 in the Andaman Islands has over the years, grown in scope and complexity, evolving to advanced naval warfare exercises covering the air, surface and sub-surface dimensions.

[38] The focus of late has shifted to surface firings, anti-air engagements to anti-submarine warfare and maritime patrol aircraft operations. [39]

This year's exercise included missile firing manoeuvres too. Singapore has emerged as India's staunchest supporter for the latter's geo-strategic initiatives and the military presence in the Asian region, and provided a strong platform for India's integration with the East Asian economies. [40] Singapore can be seen to be one of the closest. In what began as anti submarine warfare training, the naval engagement has grown to unique access to Indian naval bases. Singapore has also been a consistent supporter of a greater role for India in ASEAN's fora. In fact, India joined the ARF upon Singapore's nomination and backing.

Indonesia

India's first-ever naval exercise outside the Commonwealth was with Indonesia. [41] India has been supplying naval equipment and proposes to enhance cooperation in this field by joint production and transfer of technologies. Apart from this the two countries have established frameworks to deal with non-traditional security issues like terrorism and maritime piracy. Since 2002, India has been conducting coordinated patrols (INDINDOCORPAT) with the Indonesian navy to tackle maritime concerns like piracy, arms and people smuggling and also to enhance security in the Andaman Sea. [42] India has also been conducting bilateral Search and Rescue Operations with Indonesia named Indopura SAREX (Search and rescue exercise). Since 1997, the bilateral SAREX has been converted into a multilateral maritime operation comprising of India, Indonesia, Malaysia and Singapore. [43]

Indian naval ships have been paying goodwill visits to Indonesian ports. Coordinated patrol with Indonesia called 'INDINDO Corpat' along the International Maritime Boundary Line (IMBL) between India and Indonesia is done twice annually since its inception in 2002. [44] The Joint Working Group on terrorism since 1995 and the SAREX operations are illustrations of the deep relationship between the two countries. In times of crises like the tsunami, India assisted Indonesia by sending medicines and food supplies under Operation Gambhir.

Thailand, Vietnam and Cambodia

With an aim to prevent piracy and arms smuggling, India signed a MoU with Thailand in 2005. [45] The Royal Thai Navy also conducted coordinated patrols from 2005. [46] With the aim of preventing the use of Thai waters to transport weapons, Thailand and India held a joint naval exercise to boost cooperation in curbing arms smuggling. Under the exercise, the Thai Navy had also been ordered to patrol isolated islands and search for hidden arms caches as part of the drive against arms smuggling. Weapons have on occasion been seized in large numbers in the South, believed to be either destined for rebels fighting in Indonesia's Aceh province, or for Tamil rebels in Sri Lanka. [47] India and Thailand also jointly patrol the international maritime borders in the Andaman Sea. Vietnam has also offered permission for Indian naval ships to drop anchor at the Na Thrang port in the South China Sea. [48] Vietnam has also expressed interest in procuring the Brahmos supersonic missile. With the aim of preventing the use of Thai waters to transport weapons, Thailand and India held a joint naval exercise to boost cooperation in curbing arms smuggling.

The Indian Navy has not only initiated several maritime security and capacity building measures such as countering piracy by joint exercises, but also participated in *Tsunami* relief measures in 2004-2005 in Sri Lanka, Indonesia and Maldives. In addition, India is closely monitoring the activities of the other countries that are organizing joint surveillance; and entering into comprehensive security agreements that ensure safety of the area and increase regional cohesion. India has also initiated actions with other maritime partners similar to the comprehensive cooperation efforts between India and the US for a secure maritime domain. [49]

Joint exercises with Malaysia included live fire drills. [50] Malaysia showed the newly procured Scorpene submarine to India en route its maiden journey to Malaysia. [51]

Indian Ocean Naval Symposium

Regional cooperative security frameworks are the most suitable forms or mechanisms since the 'local' element in problems and their solutions can be incorporated. Use of imported models that do not consider the cultural and geo-strategic uniqueness of the Indian Ocean region can only serve to be counter productive. Some recent efforts like the IONS initiative incorporate these features. Conceived as a "non-hegemonic, consultative, cooperative and inclusive regional forum" [52], IONS was inaugurated on 14 February 2008 in New Delhi. As a regional forum that brings together Chiefs of various Indian Ocean Navies, IONS aims to facilitate "flow of information and opinion" [53] that would lead to appropriate response to present and future challenges. A naval symposium is a working model that would form "the lowest possible level for a security regime" [54] As it is not a political forum and does not require intense institutionalisation or complicated legal obligations it might prove useful. The Indian Chief of Naval Staff, Suresh Mehta has emphasized that the symposium aimed at "interoperability among the region's navies to tackle terrorism, piracy and natural disasters". [55]

MILAN

A biennial gathering of navies of the Indian Ocean Region initiated by the Indian Navy, MILAN began in 1995 with Indonesia, Singapore and Thailand as participants other than Sri Lanka. This has now grown to include 16 nations. The most recent MILAN exercises were held in February this year at Port Blair.

As a regional power, India and such other countries must seize the moment to forge new partnerships and revive existing ones to provide shape to a working regional cooperative mechanism.

India is also a signatory of a regional cooperation agreement on combating piracy and armed robbery against ships in Asia (ReCAAP). [56] India's security assistance in the Malacca Straits could be in the form of a 'convoy protection scheme'. The establishment of a Regional Marine Training Centre has been discussed at the ARF Workshop and the ARF Senior Officers Meeting. The centre is expected to establish common understanding and common procedures. [57]

Multilateral naval engagement has also been an item of discussion. In an effort to protect the sea lanes, India has even proposed joint patrol in and around the Malacca Straits, but some Southeast countries have shown reluctance in allowing extra-regional navies in the Straits. India has time and again offered to share its expertise but with a measure of caution. In the words of the then Defence Minister Pranab Mukherjee such offer for help was subject to the "desire of the littoral states". [58]

The willingness to assist was expressed much earlier during the ASEAN plus 3 meetings in Jakarta in July 2004. In April 2002, Indian naval ship *INS Sharda* escorted American commercial vessels carrying high value goods transiting through the Malacca Straits. While India is conscious of the sensitivities of the regional countries that are apprehensive of extra regional navies staking a claim in Southeast Asian regional security, there is acknowledgement that continuous air surveillance of Malacca straits would require a large fleet of maritime patrol aircraft and UAVs that are non existent in Southeast Asian armoury. [59]

Red Tide

Yet another area of common concern is the perception of the threat posed by a rising China. The growing Chinese influence through economic and military relations with Myanmar and all other countries of the Southeast Asian region is another area to be watched. Not only is China one of the largest trading partners of each of these countries but it has also extended cooperation in the military field to modernize aging equipment and overcome budgetary restrictions. [60] All over the Indian Ocean, China has opted to develop existing ports or establish new ones. The Gwadar port in Pakistan, Hambantotta in Sri Lanka [61], Sittwe, Coco islands in Myanmar, Thailand, Indonesia, and her extensive commercial relations with African countries is seen to be to gain access to the all weather ocean—the Indian Ocean not just for economic but strategic reasons too.

The development of ports and other facilities by China is however, seen to be a containing strategy that would check India's expanding influence in the region. [62] China is witnessing unprecedented demand for energy to sustain its economy and thus has huge stakes in protecting the energy routes passing through Southeast Asia. Ironically, the Southeast Asian countries themselves are cautious about China's recent forays. Some of the ASEAN leaders have expressed discomfort at China's growing clout, fearing that China may, as in the past become a source of destabilization and bullying in the region. [63] It is here that India is seen to be an essential component.

India is often viewed as a counter weight to future Chinese expansionism in Southeast Asia. India was invited to join regional security mechanisms which India has earlier turned down. But now India is a member of the ASEAN Regional Form (ARF) and other arrangements. Countries like Indonesia have lent strong support to make India a member of the East Asian Summit community. The two neighbours could thus shape the emerging security architecture in the region thereby not allowing China to dominate or such architecture assuming any character detrimental to either's interests.

Defence Sector

While the trade sector has seen robust relations, the defence related ties are yet to move to the next level of greater cooperation that of the operationalised type where states not only modify policies to meet preferences of other states but also cooperate in exchange of information. Defence ties are being strengthened and the possibility of joint production of weapons and military equipment is being explored. India had proposed a draft Memorandum of Understanding on Defence Cooperation in 1995 with the focus on supplies, technologies, joint production and joint projects. Although the MoU has been signed by both the countries, it is yet to be ratified by the Indonesian Parliament. India and Indonesia signed a Bilateral Agreement on Cooperative Activities in the Defence field in 2001. [64]

Indonesia has expressed interest in importing batteries for torpedoes, engines for Parchim-class corvettes, repair facilities for Type 209 submarines etc. The supersonic anti-ship missile, Brahmos jointly developed by India and Russia has also attracted the attention of Indonesia. The co-production of radars, electronic equipment and artillery weapons is also being looked into. [65] In November 2005 it was agreed with the then visiting Indonesian President, Mr. Susilo Bambang Yudhoyono, that the two countries would hold an annual "strategic dialogue" at the level of senior officials. The first such dialogue was held in the first half of 2006.

Ongoing Joint Efforts

The 16 member (the ASEAN members plus China, South Korea, Japan, Bangladesh, India, and Sri Lanka) ReCAAP or Regional Cooperation Agreement on Combating Piracy and Armed robbery against ships in Asia agreed in 2004 to deal specifically with piracy emphasising the importance of sharing information on imminent piracy attacks is an example of such effective mechanisms.

Prompt humanitarian assistance by India especially with the help of the naval establishment is also yet another cooperative arena. In the aftermath of Tsunami of December 2004, India launched Operation Ghambir in January 2005 and sent food and medical supplies amounting to US$ 1 million to Indonesia through its hospital ship *INS Nirupak* and a corvette *INS Khukri*. President Yudhoyono during his visit to India the same year and the Indonesian Vice President Dr. Jusuf Kalla, during his January 2007 visit, expressed their country's gratitude for India's assistance in Tsunami relief operations. India also donated US$ 2 million in relief assistance following the major earthquake in Northern Sumatra in March 2005. India delivered US$ 2 million worth of relief assistance to Indonesia after the earthquake in Java in May 2006. A medical team from the Indian Navy also engaged in relief work in the affected areas after these disasters. [66] Thus in reply to the prevailing strategic environment, India has initiated several maritime security and capacity building measures including joint exercises and assistance in the form of tsunami relief.

India-ASEAN Summit

In an effort to further cement ties with ASEAN countries India has been convening India-ASEAN Summit annually since 2002. At the Second summit in Bali, Indonesia in 2003 India acceded to the Treaty of Amity and Cooperation in Southeast Asia (TAC) and also signed a Joint Declaration for Cooperation in Combating International Terrorism, with the aim of strengthening cooperation in the fight against terrorism. India has now appointed an Ambassador to ASEAN. However we are yet to open a mission for the multilateral organization. China has already done so. India held a commemorative Summit on December 20-21, 2012 in New Delhi to mark the 20th anniversary of India-ASEAN dialogue relations.

An Eminent Persons Group has also been established to review the 20 year relations, think of ways to deepen the relations by taking into account the various steps that have already been taken through formal agreement and documents. In the third summit in Vietnam in 2004, the ASEAN-India

Partnership for Peace, Progress and Shared Prosperity was signed. [67] The objective of the joint statement in the field of anti-terrorism is to also deal with among others, drug and human trafficking, arms smuggling, and sea piracy all of which possess a maritime element. A plan of action to implement this was also drawn for 2004-2009 and one for 2010-2015 too.

ADMM +

The first ASEAN Defence Ministers' meeting with ASEAN countries plus the US, China, Russia, Japan, India, South Korea, Australia and New Zealand, was held in Hanoi on October 12, 2011. It would meet once in three years and discuss non traditional security agenda. There are now separate working groups to deal with for maritime security, humanitarian assistance and relief, counter terrorism, military medicine and peace keeping operations. [68] The focus on 'non traditional security' issues is to attract consensus and agreement. [69] Though it is unlikely that ADMM Plus would address bilateral conflicts among member states it could emerge as an institution "promoting practical cooperation" [70] among armed forces of different states.

While India is a member of this group India's role has to be more active. A recent extension to the plan of action for years 2010-2015 for the ASEAN-India Partnership for Peace, Progress and Shared Prosperity looks at promoting the ADMM+ as "as a useful platform for dialogue and security cooperation, in particular for forging practical cooperation to address the security challenges facing the region". [71] This document also specifically mentions maritime safety and search and rescue by mutual sharing of experience, cooperating in the technological areas and exchange visits of concerned authorities.

This forum gains added impetus with the ASEAN Community becoming a reality by 2015. India could also look to utilize other mechanisms that have been recently created like the ASEAN Peacekeeping centres network and the Network of ASEAN Defence and Security institutions. With the wide experience in peacekeeping that India has, she could offer.

Conclusion

India has had extensive contact with many regions of the world, especially Southeast Asia. This is reflected in the area of naval interaction too. Ever since becoming a full-dialogue partner of ASEAN in 1995, India has gradually increased the manner of naval engagement. While it might be strong at the individual bilateral level, that with ASEAN is yet to reach full fruition. India has continued to engage the Southeast Asian region in the maritime realm. The tailor-made naval exercises like the coordinated patrol exercises with Indonesia, or the deep ties nurtured with the constant friend in Singapore signify the range of activities India has been engaging in. The periodic conduct of exercises in the South China Sea considered an area of possible future conflict can be seen as a test of India's power projection capabilities. The just concluded SIMBEX was held in the Andaman Sea and Bay of Bengal from 21st March to 1st April 2012. [72] There are also new initiatives with countries like Burma. India's humanitarian assistance through its naval assets especially during the tsunami and such other natural calamities has also cemented ties.

However, this also highlights the lacunae or deficits in such exchanges. While agreements on cooperation in defence technology have been signed by many of the Southeast Asian neighbours, no concrete progress has been made. Joint development or production is still a drawing board idea and much needs to be done in the field of anti-piracy activities. The India-ASEAN Summit and the ADMM+ are steps in the right direction in creating greater scope for widening nature of engagement in areas including the naval sector. It is hoped that this year's bi-decennial celebration would spur additional impetus to the maritime security realm. Being a neighbouring region with no apparent conflict over maritime boundaries and a convergence of interest in maintaining safety of sea lanes including the prevention or at least control of maritime terrorism as well as keenly watching China's efforts at engaging ASEAN both as opportunity and threat, India should enhance cooperation in all sectors of mutual benefit especially using its naval infrastructure.

End Notes

1. http://www.hinduwisdom.info/Seafaring_in_Ancient_India.htm.
2. Kenneth McPherson, "The Indian Ocean: A History of People and the Sea", New York, 1993, p. 77.
3. Dong Zhang, "India's Look East Policy: Strategies and Impacts", *AUSAID Working Paper*, September 2006, p. 15 http://www.ausaid.gov.au/publications/pdf/india_east.pdf.
4. Whither, "The Look East Policy: India and Southeast Asia", *Strategic Analysis,* Vol. 28, No. 2, April-June 2004, p. 337 http://www.idsa.in/system/files/strategicanalysis_naidu_0604.pd
5. C.S. Kuppuswamy, India's Look East Policy-A Review, February 12, 2010 http://www.southasiaanalysis.org/papers37/paper3662.html.
6. C.S. Kuppuswamy, India's Look East Policy-A Review, February 12, 2010 http://www.southasiaanalysis.org/percent5Cpapers37percent5Cpaper3662.html.
7. Laxman Bahroo, "India Looks East", *Bharat Rakshak Monitor*, Vol. 3(3), November-December 2000.
8. Yagama Reddy, A Semblance of Unison in the Security Perceptions of India, Southeast Asia and Australia, Paper in the seminar "Maritime Security: Emerging Trends", University of Madras, December 2004.
9. A.N. Ram, Historical Perspectives: Looking East, A Symposium on the need to refocus our foreign policy, March 2000 www.india-seminar.com/2000/487/487 percent20ram.htm.
10. http://www.bharatrakshak.com/IAF/Books/Reviews/804-IPAW65.html.
11. Mohammed Ayoob, India and Southeast Asia: Indian Perceptions and Policies, Institute of Southeast Asian Studies, Singapore, 1990, p. 41.
12. http://www.pakistanideology.com/pakistan-news/usa-who-

helped-us/

13. For a detailed account of the threat from Indonesia refer, Hiranandani, Transition to Triumph History of the Indian Navy 1965-75, http://indiannavy.nic.in/t2t2e/Trans2Trimph/chapters/3_1965 percent20war1.htm.
14. *ASEAN Statistical Yearbook 2006*, http://www.aseansec.org/Stat/Table21.pdf.
15. "Relations between RI and India Reach Historic High" in 2009, *The Jakarta Post*, April 1, 2004.
16. Indonesia-India Relationship Moving into Splendid Phase: Envoy, *The Jakarta Post*, 15 August 2008 http://www.asianinfo.org/asianinfo/indonesia/pro-history.htm.
17. India, Indonesia get into free trade mode, October 4, 2010 http://www.domain-b.com/economy/trade/20101004_india_indonesia.html
18. Ian Storey, "Maritime Security in Southeast Asia: Two Cheers for Regional Cooperation", *Southeast Asian Affairs*, Vol. 2009, p. 38.
19. Michael Schuman, How to Defeat Pirates: Success in the Strait, *Time*, April 22, 2009, http://www.time.com/time/world/article/0,8599,1893032,00.htm l?xid=rss-topstories-cnnpartner.
20. "Balancing Powers in the Malacca Strait", *Global News Journal*, March 7, 2010 http://blogs.reuters.com/global/2010/03/07/balancing-powers-in-the-malacca-strait/
21. "More Regional Cooperation Needed to Combat Piracy", Radio Singapore International, 13 August 2003.
22. Barry Desker and Kumar Ramakrishna. "Formulating an Indirect Strategy in Southeast Asia", *The Washington Quarterly*, Spring 2002.
23. John Bradford, "The Growing Prospects for Maritime Security Cooperation in Southeast Asia", *Naval War College Review,* Summer 2005, Vol. 58, No. 5, p. 70.
24. Simon Elegant, Dire Straits, *Time*, November 29, 2004 http://www.time.com/time/magazine/article/0,9171,832306,00.ht ml.
25. Sam Bateman, Sea Piracy: Some Inconvenient Truths, *Disarmament Forum*, 2, 2010, United Nations Institute for

Disarmament Research (UNIDIR), p. 13.
26. Carolin Liss, The Privatisation of Maritime Security-Maritime Security in Southeast Asia: Between a Rock and a Hard Place? Working Paper No. 141, February 2007, Asia Studies Centre, Murdoch University p. 3, http://wwwarc.murdoch.edu.au/wp/wp141.pdf.
27. Dana R. Dillon, "Democratic Indonesia as a Security Partner", Backgrounder No. 1800, *The Heritage Foundation*, September 24, 2004 pp. 7-8, http://www.heritage.org/Research/Reports/2004/09/Democratic-Indonesia-as-a-Security-Partner.
28. S. Utham Kumar Jamadhagni, Alternative Maritime Security Perspectives for the Indian Ocean, Paper for seminar, Kolkata.
29. P.S. Jagota, Maritime Boundary, Martinus Nijhoff Publishers, The Netherlands, 1985 p. 79.
30. www.dtic.mil/whs/directives/corres/20051m_062305/india.doc.
31. Limits in the Sea, No. 93, Continental Shelf boundaries: India-Indonesia-Thailand, Office of Geographer, US Department of State, August 17, 1981 http://www.state.gov/documents/organization/58818.pdf.
32. T.R. Ford as quoted in V. Suryanarayan, Andaman and Nicobar Islands: Gateway to Southeast Asia, *Dialogue*, Volume 4, No. 4, April-June 2003.
33. Michael Richardson, A Time Bomb for Global Trade, Institute of South Asian Studies, Singapore, 2004.
34. Rommel Banlaoi, "Maritime Terrorism in Southeast Asia: The Abu Sayyaf Threat", *Naval War College Review*, Autumn 2005.
35. Shyam Saran, Rising Indonesia, http://www.business-standard.com/india/news/shyam-saran-rising-indonesia/395353/, Business Standard, May 19, 2010.
36. Mihir Roy , Energy and sea lanes of communication, *Journal of Indian Ocean Studies*, Vol.9, No.1, April 2001, p.65.
37. Klas Marklund, "Indonesia: Development Scenarios, 2020-2030", *Asia Paper*, September 2009, Institute for Security and Development Policy, Sweden, p. 39.
38. http://www.mindef.gov.sg/imindef/news_and_events/nr/2008/mar/29mar08_nr.html.
39. http://www.india-defence.com/reports-1387.
40. "India-Singapore Relations: An Overview - Vibhanshu Shekhar "(Special Report 41), http://www.ipcs.org/IPCS-Special-Report-

41.pdf.
41. Anushree Bhattacharyya, India's Joint Naval Exercises in the ASEAN Region, http://www.ipcs.org/whatsNewArticle11.jsp?action=showView&kValue=2361&status=article&mod=b.
42. http://indiannavy.nic.in/events2005.pdf.
43. Vibhanshu Sekhar, "India-Indonesia Relations-An Overview" (Special Report 38) http://www.ipcs.org/IPCS-Special-Report-38.pdf.
44. Annual Report, 2008-2009, Ministry of Defence, Government of India, p. 37.
45. http://www.hindu.com/2005/05/21/stories/2005052104421200.htm.
46. http://indiannavy.nic.in/events2005.pdf.
47. http://www.bangkokpost.com/News/27May2003_news12.html.
48. Phil Radford, "Big Boats, Little Punch in South China Sea", *Asia Times*, August 17, 2011, http://www.atimes.com/atimes/china/mh17ad02.html.
49. See n. 29.
50. http://articles.timesofindia.indiatimes.com/2008-05-03/india/27780957_1_joint-naval-exercise-naval-ships-indian-ships.
51. Navy checks out Malaysian Scorpene, June 21, 2010 http://www.stratpost.com/navy-checks-out-malaysian-scorpene.
52. *International Naval Symposium 2008*, Booklet.
53. Ibid.
54. Peter Lehr (et al.), *Panchayati Raj in the Indian Ocean: Towards Maritime Regime, Project Description*, see http://www.sai.uni-hiedelberg.de-abt-SAPOL-forsehung-forsehung-naval_security.html.
55. *The Hindu*, 15 February, 2008.
56. Bradford, p. 69.
57. 'Increase Asia-Pacific Cooperation for Maritime Security: Pranab', Singapore, June 03, 2006, http://news.webindia123.com/news/Articles/Asia/20060603/352994.html.
58. India ready to help protect Malacca strait.
59. C. Arasakumar, *Maritime Cooperation: The Mantra for Security*, Paper in the seminar "Maritime Security: Emerging Trends", University of Madras, December 2004.

60. Klas Marklund, ibid., p. 47.
61. Port opens to public.
62. Termed the 'String of pearls strategy', the location of the ports, signal facilities and other infrastructure development projects around India surely add fuel to this idea.
63. S.D. Muni, Creating Strategic Space: China and its New ASEAN Neighbours, *Occasional Papers on East Asia,* #4, Centre for East Asian Studies, Monash University, 2003, p. 1.
64. Security and Defence Relationship, http://www.indonesianembassy.in/index.php?option=com_content&view=article&id=146&Itemid=136&lang=en.
65. Indonesia May Have Role in India's Regional Plan, Defence News, May 15, 2009, http://www.defensenews.com/story.php?i=4090898.
66. India-Indonesia Relations, Ministry of External Affairs, Government of India, August 2010, http://www.mea.gov.in/meaxpsite/foreignrelation/indonesia.pdf.
67. Refer to the ASEAN website for full text, http://www.aseansec.org/16839.htm.
68. http://www.eastasiaforum.org/2010/10/19/admm-plus-cooperates-on-security-and-defence-issues/
69. Yang Razail Kassim, ADMM Plus: New Twists to Old security Issues, *RSIS Commentaries*, 19 October 2010, http://www.rsis.edu.sg/publications/Perspective/RSIS1332010.
70. Barry Desker, ADMM Plus Eight Defence Cooperation: Rise of a New Player, *RSIS Commentaries*, 15 October 2010 http://www.rsis.edu.sg/publications/Perspective/RSIS1322010
71. http://www.asean.org/25551.htm.
72. Singapore, Indian navies conduct bilateral maritime exercises, *Asia One News*, April 1, 2012, http://www.asiaone.com/News/Latest percent2BNews/Singapore/Story/A1Story20120401-337069.html.

9

Security Dimensions of Andaman and Nicobar Islands

Gopalji Malviya and K. Udhaya Kumar

For over a decade the strategic dimensions for Andaman and Nicobar (AN) Islands have come into focus in the larger discourse on maritime security aspects. Traditionally, as a maritime nation, India's oceanic vulnerability has increased many fold despite of technological advancements. The key to the security of Andaman and Nicobar Islands lies in the rapid infrastructure build-up facilitating growth, commerce, trade and economic benefits. In the overall security matrix with India's emerging status and its role in the region in consonance with its "Look East Policy", the role of Andaman and Nicobar Islands has been increased.

In addition to the need for harnessing its economic potential, these Islands face the challenges of military and non-military threats from immediate neighbours and also from growing maritime powers in the region, particularly China and Sino-Pak nexus. Increase in maritime trade activities, unstable littorals in the neighbourhood, illegal immigration, drug trafficking, poaching, piracy, natural disasters and small arms proliferation are some threats that need mention. The Andaman region faces a range of threats from micro security to macro-strategic threats. These threats could be categorized into traditional military threats and non-traditional security issues. This emerging trend and security environment in the maritime domain poses serious changes to India's national interests.

It is in this context, that the security development and governance of Andaman and Nicobar Islands could be visualized with India's emerging status and its role in the region in consonance with its "Look East Policy". The role of AN Islands increased many fold and requires special attention towards enhancing its economic potential and fine tuning the governance to meet a modern requirement.

The Overall development of AN Islands is the key for securing the region's prosperity that would also be integral to India's emerging regional power status. Therefore, the urgency requires the synergy between tri-services with true sense of jointness, civil administration and identifying economic potential of AN Island region. A robust security apparatus to control and dominate the region particularly oceanic sea bed keeping India's national security and interest in mind.

The AN region in India's far east has long been perceived as a key vulnerability particularly due to geographical distance from the main land and the history its repeatedly 'slipping away' syndrome from the Indian main land. Since the past decade, several measures have been taken to enhance its defence capability in the region and accordingly an integrated AN command was established in 2001. These steps were meant to translate India's geo-strategic vision that would enable AN command to play a vital role and security India's maritime interests in the region.

India's forward presence in the eastern IOR is enabled by Andaman Islands. The location and geography of these Islands impart them with immense strategic advantage. The propinquity of these Islands to the busy shipping lines is specially Malacca Straits not only opens up an opportunity for India in controlling and commanding this oceanic highway but also provides proximity to archipelago to the South East Asian neighbours. This provides excellent opportunity for trade, diplomacy and other maritime engagements.

The Andaman and Nicobar group of islands straddle the strategic seaway leading to the Malacca Straits. The Archipelago comprises of 572 islands, islets and rocks of which only 37 are inhabited. It accounts for 30 percent of country's EEZ, has vast marine resources and a potential reserve of natural oil and gas. Notwithstanding the distance of the AN Islands from the mainland, which is more than 1200 kms., these Islands have a close proximity to a number of littoral states. Apart from possessing the abundant natural resources, these Islands are our national assets for India's 'Look East Policy'. This policy fuels the engine that drives the functioning of the Andaman and Nicobar Command.

While the Andaman contributes large part of EEZ to India's total oceanic areas, various species, untapped marine life and high value seafood are located in and around this region. This region has potential for seafood export to Southeast Asian countries if appropriate infrastructure facilities and expertise are developed the port Blair could also be developed as an international trade centre and oil terminal and trans-shipment port to meet the increase of maritime activity.

The non-traditional threats to national security have emerged as a significant feature of the security calculus. Assessing the risk of threats to human and ecological security is a complex task. Today, states grapple with non obtrusive attacks on the core values and cultural systems without the faintest idea of how these threats can manifest themselves in a variety of national and regional sectors which stroke the embers of violent conflicts, large scale migration and social unrest. Even if these issues do not lead to violent conflicts, they can and do constitute a risk to regional stability and security. It is in this context the security of AN Islands needs to be analyzed. Continued maritime piracy and other oceanic crimes have now spilled over to Bay of Bengal region.

The rise of Islamic militancy and fundamentalism is causing considerable security concern, the thick forest is spread over 570 Islands, its terrain and topography makes it ideal place or perhaps a sanctuary for insurgents and terrorist groups operating in this region. Also it becomes an extremely difficult task for maritime security forces and law enforcement agencies to detect, destroy or eliminate such extensions and movements.

In the light of the foregoing, it is important for India, as a regional power and emerging global player, to make a risk assessment in its area of influence which at this point of time and in the midterm would be the Indian Ocean Region (IOR). In conceptualization of such a risk assessment, a multidisciplinary approach that identifies the challenges to each component of national power, which is diplomatic, informational, military and economic, is now a necessity. Assessing of risk is an intellectual process of constructing, communicating, accepting and even opposing particular geo-cultural and popular concepts of danger, hazards and security.

The process has both temporal and spatial dimensions. Risk assessment in accordance with one model envisaged risk to be a product of severity, probability and exposure. Risk management with respect to non-traditional threats to security in the region requires convergence of different elites at the levels of the individual, government, non-government and inter-state actors. A convergence of perceptions through social solidarities would go a long way in addressing these issues.

In the current strategic environment, probability of a conventional threat to these Islands from immediate neighbours appears remote. However, Chinese strategic threat looms large in the form of possible military interventions, influence, collaborative engagement through an adversary or any other form to destabilize the region. With the increase of its prowess the power projection efforts of the Chinese Navy has increased its activities in the IOR. Its non-military benign activities also need to be viewed through the prism of displaying 'strategic reach and sustenance' in the backyard of India.

Chinese military presence in AN Islands and Oceanic region around, its declared agenda, its military might clubbed with its collaborative strength has continued to be a cause of concern for Indian security establishment. The question thus arises about the actual Chinese designs in the Indian Ocean Region. China is currently working for great power status. The Chinese attempt to adopt a containment strategy against India, the 'string of pearls', encompasses the strategy to build leverage points in areas that lead to Indian Ocean and also to strategically surround India.

This region falls within the Chinese strategy and its focus. Chinese declaration of 'sting of pearls' strategy is one that needs to be countered appropriately. According to this strategy China seeks to setup bases at outposts across the region. Strategically located along its energy supply lines and also to monitor and safeguard its energy flows. Each 'pearl' in the string of pearls construct is a link of China's geopolitical influence and its maritime presence. In the IOR, the string passes through Myanmar and towards to Chittagong in Bangladesh and thereafter to Sri Lanka. The string further moves west into the continent of Africa via Gwadar deep sea port on Pakistan's Makaran coast. This ambitious plan exists to link the post with Karakorum highway thereby providing China with the gateway to the Arabian Sea.

India's rigorous diplomatic exercises in Southeast Asia can also be traced from the Chinese presence in the region. China has been developing a powerful nuclear submarine base in the Hainan Island in the South China Sea which is only 2,000 nautical miles from Andaman Islands. It also occupies the Paracel Islands seized from Vietnam and has built naval facilities. Its strings of pearls in the Coco Islands in Myanmar and the Gwadar Port in Pakistan add anxiety over the real intent of China.

While New Delhi must wait and watch, it cannot ignore the fact that both North Korea and Pakistan are the closest allies of China and going through unprecedented domestic challenges that could intensify concerns for neighbours in South Asia alike. Pakistan has been accused of giving North Korea crucial nuclear technology relating to North Korea.

The Sino-Pak-North Korea nuclear designs and its covert

missile proliferation agenda is well known to the strategic community all over. Any illicit trade of nuclear armament or technology from Pakistan to North Korea goes through these waters. Hence, AN island regions and its strategic command need to be strengthen for surveillance, intelligence gathering and have the capacity to intercept such delinquent ships in AN region. As far as Indian Strategic thinking is concerned, Beijing has promoted these two unstable regimes on its periphery to keep neighbours like Japan and India off balance. Their instability and uncertainty could revive old weapons and nuclear proliferation ties between Pyongyang and Islamabad that would have a direct bearing on India's security.

Traditionally a marine nation, India's coastal vulnerabilities have increased manifold despite of technological advances. The key to the security of these Islands in particular and the main land in general lies in the rapid infrastructural build up thereby facilitating growth of commerce and trade, the benefits of which will be reaped by the locals up to the grass root level and will ensure greater participation in the overall security matrix as their economic stakes grow. Overall development is the key to these challenges and is integral to India's emerging status as a regional power. For this, the need of the hour is to have synergy not only within the armed forces but also with the civil administration. Jointness is the quintessence of strength and the Andaman and Nicobar Command serves as a role model for jointmanship.

The geo-strategic importance of the Island underlines the threat that can manifest in the following forms:

1. Remote location from Indian mainland with large number of uninhabited island and inter/intra Island connectivity problems.
2. The Islands' location in the most challenging seismic-zones on the Earth.
3. Illegal immigration from the Littorals. The need to maintain cultural, ethnic and religious balance on the Islands.

4. Proximity to unstable littorals of which some have radical outlook amongst its populace. Proximity to the Golden Triangle that is prone to drugs/gun running and piracy.
5. Oceanic crimes/piracy and armed robbery.
6. Maritime terrorism.
7. Phantom ships.
8. Cargo fraud.
9. Smuggling of small arms.
10. Drug trafficking/gun running.
11. Illegal exploitation of marine resources.
12. Marine pollution.
13. Insurgency/illegal migration.
14. Natural disasters.
15. Illegal fishing and poaching.
16. Rebels from neighbouring countries occupying any Island as a safe haven.
17. Militant/rebel groups occupying an Islands with a view to subsequently stake their claim on the territory occupied.

With India's emerging status and its role in the region in consonance with its 'Look East Policy' the role of Andaman ana Nicobar Islands has increased manifold. In addition to the need for harnessing its economic potential, the Islands face the challenges of growing Chinese influence in the region, increase in maritime trade activities, unstable Littorals in the neighbouring, illegal immigration, drug peddling, poaching and piracy. India's diplomatic skill in Southeast Asia is particularly visible in the context of Malacca Straits. This sea lane carries major stake for India as a prominent share of ships pass through the Straits.

Almost 70 percent of the world's commercial traffic passes through this area. Development of south Eastern tip of Nicobar as a Trans-Shipment Port for Container handling, bunkering and refuelling of international/national ships would provide great economic and strategic potential. This port could provide an alternative to Singapore and Colombo and become a major strength for India. Such an initiative will also help the country in fulfilling our growing ambitions in the fields of regional co-operation with south East Asia and the issues of the National Look East Policy.

There is sufficient potential for industrial and socio-economic development by harnessing available resources on sustainable basis while having a balance between environmental concerns and the development requirements. This balanced growth would envisage without disturbing the ecosystem of the Islands. This Island chain is a vast store house of timber and its adjoining water contains various species of marine life. The Island would also become an attractive place for trade and investment and also tourist paradise. This may require sufficient infrastructure development with upgraded air and sea links currently the revenue generation largely depends or tourist. The handicraft industry could be encouraged to its optimum potential, this sector would be key to provide development and employment generation capacity. Private players could also be encouraged and there is sufficient place for these players to contribute towards economic development of these Islands.

Another thrust area for development of these Islands is guided by its potential to tap the natural resources, achieve agriculture, self reliance and creating modern facilities for preservation and export promotion for sea food. Improved means of communication and alternative source of power would provide value addition to the development of these Islands. The growing population and their aspirations require creation of modern infrastructure and development of new vistas in health care, sanitation and hygiene, due to possibility of biological threats, disease like malaria, cholera, dengue, HIV, and SARS etc. that could affect the population.

Primary and higher education requires serious attention to provide opportunity for information technology knowledge resource for the island population and to open up research activity for the scholars. This would further enhance the capacity building of youthful population and provide equal opportunity with their counter part in the mainland. The best option of governance of these tiny Islands would be the existing status of Union Territory, while the democratization of its local governance is essential and this could be reviewed to provide greater opportunity to the citizens with in the certain amount of autonomous status. However, any overambitious dream or short- sighted plan of statehood may prove to be disaster in the present context. Limits of growth in the AN Islands is strictly conditioned by the geographical and environmental factors.

While governance and development need concrete attention, it is the maritime dimension of the strategic interest in this far flung territory that needs special focus. The realization of this value of the island group led to the establishment of a separate strategic command called the Andaman and Nicobar command. Andaman and Nicobar Command (ANC) was created in October 2011 with its headquarters at Port Blair. This command functions under the direct control of Chief of Staff Committee. The board functions of ANC could be divided into three major categories i.e. military, diplomacy and policy. The military role involves maintaining deterrence through maritime domain, ensuring physical presence of the tri-service in this region, protection of India's interest and also conducting joint naval exercise with friendly neighbouring countries.

On diplomatic level, conducting naval exercises, initiatives like *MILAN* for the purpose of promoting regional cooperation and mutual understanding and addressing maritime issues and concerns are already underway. Policing functions primarily involve enforcement of the rule of law at sea, checking smuggling, collecting information, conducting low intensity maritime operations to prevent poaching, illegal migration, narcotics and arms smuggling in the region. Although the ANC charter did include protection of sea lanes and surveillance of EEZ, it is more oriented towards 'territorial defence' of the AN region.

Security of widely scattered islands of AN is always a difficult task. There are a number of constrains affecting the smooth operational logistics functioning at ANC. They could be addressed as short term, medium, long term strategies for a robust security approach in the region. The ANC could also be seen from the angle of India's acquisition of power projection capabilities. It would be better if ANC could be transformed into a theatre command. This could synergize the role of Navy, Coast Guard, Air force, and Army and theatre command would provide a robust security arrangement to deal with traditional and non-traditional threats in and around these waters.

The Islands could function as a 'springboard' for further engagement with Southeast Asia paralleling the efforts on the naval diplomacy side. Quick response to disasters by way of rapid deployment of naval and other assets to deliver relief has been amply illustrated during the 2004 tsunami. This would enable building political trust and reinforcing economic ties. The earlier suspicions due to India defence modernization programs have been assuaged after a series of confidence building measures like a series of naval exercises and the Indian Ocean Symposium that showcase India's desire to cooperate with a wide range of states in ensuring peace and stability in the maritime realm. Also, the concern about the rise of China as an important player in Asia-Pacific and its assertion regarding territorial claims increases the importance of India as possibly a balancer in the region.

Economic and non-traditional considerations are other reasons for keeping Andaman and Nicobar Islands on the national policy radar. The growing economic strength of India heightens the dependence on the maritime lanes for trade and energy transfer. Hence, the security of these vital routes will assume primacy. Related threats of maritime terrorism and piracy thus gain special significance. The anti-piracy activity undertaken by India on its western flank should also prepare her for any such eventuality in the eastern shores. Developing more marine infrastructures like energy prospects in off-shore gas and oil fields and the *Sethsamudram* canal by India, call for added vigilance against possible disruptions.

The remoteness of some of the Islands make them ideal grounds for nefarious activities. Separatist groups in other countries of the region could exploit this vulnerability. Therefore, island reconnaissance needs to be spruced up. Drug trafficking and small arms trade are rife in the adjoining region. The safety of the islands must ensure they are not used as conduit zones. Safety of the sea lanes can act as spur for multilateral cooperative mechanisms that keep the waters clear of all abovementioned threats. However, this must be supported by a military power that can effectively counter existing and new threats to the stability in the region while simultaneously augmenting India's strategic imprint in the area. This must be accomplished by factoring in the sensitivity of the states in the region with India's own long-term interests.

Considering various dimensions of micro and macro issues of security concerns there is a need for a change in India's attitude towards AN region. Instead of merely defending it, the Islands should be viewed as the first line of defence. The main objectives of India's security perspectives should be to assess the threats especially from China and Pakistan and evolve appropriate strategic apparatus to counter them. This would require highly efficient surveillance network to monitor non-conventional threats emanating in the region. The advance communication network would also have to be developed to carry out surveillance and monitoring. This will require skill and trained human resources and state of art equipments. The implications for policy and operation thus have become pertinent agenda for a comprehensive academic discourse on maritime security issues and concerns. An intense debate among the strategic fraternity would be fruitful for appropriate policy formulation at highest level of the country decision making establishment.

10

India's Energy Security Policy: A Review

Dharitri Parija and Mohanan B. Pillai

Introduction

The issue of energy security is not a new subject in India. It has been discussed ever since the first oil shock that took place during 1973-74. However, recent political developments around the globe indicate that energy security is the driving force of foreign policy decisions of any country and the concept of energy security is very much part of a larger socio-economic and political construct. Energy availability is one of the foremost requirements for any country to grow economically and to prosper. Thus energy security has become the primary concern to most of the countries in the world.

The Planning Commission of India provides a comprehensive definition of energy security. According to it, "the country is energy secure when it can supply lifeline energy to all its citizens as well as meet their effective demand for safe and convenient energy to satisfy various needs at affordable costs at all time with a prescribed confidence level considering shocks and disruptions that can be reasonably expected".

Economic reforms, population growth, urbanization, demographic transition, and a growing transport sector in India are contributing towards ever increasing demand for energy. India's rapid economic growth has made it the second fastest-growing energy market in the world. India's intensified search for energy security is likely to play a significant role in shaping Asia's future.

Through a rapidly growing economy and expanding diplomatic influence, India is emerging as a major regional and global power. However, low levels of energy production and per capita consumption are a major hurdle in the way of attaining that status. Many people in India still lack access to electricity for their basic needs. Energy security in India is linked to both growth and poverty. On the one hand, it has to provide enough commercial energy for growth and on the other hand it has to minimize the inequality gap between the urban and rural people's consumption level of energy.

So, a clear articulation of long term goal is essential for prioritizing short-term activities for building the path to a sustainable future. The long-term energy requirements must be both affordable and should be characterized by near zero emissions of both air pollutants and greenhouse gases. From a longer term perspective and keeping in mind the need to maximally develop domestic supply options as well as the need to diversify energy sources, renewables remain important to India's energy sector. Against this backdrop, the present paper makes an assessment of India's increasing energy demand. This paper also looks into the challenges, opportunities and success or otherwise of |India's attempts to gain access to alternative energy sources to sustain the already achieved growth rate.

In the light of the above, the study is divided into two sections. The first section provides an overview of India's energy mix and the increasing energy dependency in the present phase of India's economic growth. The second part deals with India's energy diplomacy in its regional and global dimensions.

India's Energy Security Scene: An Overview

In recent years, the Indian economy has emerged as one of the fastest growing economies in the world with a registered 7 to 8 percent GDP growth rate. With a population of 1.05 billion, India is the second most populated country in the world after China. As a result, India faces daunting challenges in meeting its energy needs to maintain its fast-growing economy as also to achieve the developmental goals of its rising population. In the past couple of decades, energy related issues and policy challenges have grown very prominent in India. Depending upon a number of driving factors such as economic development, population growth, lifestyle changes, rapidly growing automobile sector etc., energy consumption and its concomitant concerns have grown steadily.

At present, coal accounts for a predominant share in India's energy basket. But, being a signatory to the Kyoto Protocol, India's burgeoning energy needs of urbanisation, modernization and rapid growth in transportation will have to be catered through cleaner fuels. However, though fossil fuels are the source of most of India's commercial and primary energy supplies they are not a resource the country is particularly well endowed with. Furthermore, with respect to coal, the most abundant energy source in India, if production continues to grow at five percent per annum as it is doing now, proven extractable reserves are estimated to last for only about 40 years. Though 90 percent of India's commercial energy comes from fossil fuel, domestic reserves of crude oil are estimated to be sufficient for only about eight years worth of current consumption (33 years at current production levels). The situation is also not different in the case of natural gas, where proven reserves stand at about 1100 billion cubic meters and would last for about 32 years at the current level of production. (Nanda, 2009: 51)

Major Sources of Energy Consumed in India

According to the International Energy Agency (IEA), hydrocarbons account for a major share of India's energy use. Together, coal and oil represent about two-thirds of the total energy use. Natural gas now accounts for seven percent share. Combustible renewable and waste constitutes about one fourth of the Indian energy use which include traditional biomass sources such as firewood and dung, which are used by more than 800 million Indian households for cooking. Other renewable sources such as wind, geothermal, solar and hydroelectricity represent a 2 percent share of the Indian fuel mix and nuclear energy holds only one percent share. According to B.P. Statistical Review of World Energy, 2011, coal, oil, natural gas, nuclear power and hydroelectricity account for the bulk of the total primary commercial energy consumed within India. Therefore, the following sections try to analyze the five important primary sources of energy consumed in India.

Coal: Coal is the most important source of energy for India. As the third largest producer of coal in the world, India relies on coal for more than 40 percent of its total energy needs. About 70 percent of the total coal consumed is used for power generation. However, high ash content and low calorific value of Indian coal causes considerable environmental degradation. Therefore India is importing most of the coking coal it needs. India's coal consumption is growing by 10 percent every five years and simultaneously low productivity and high cost of coal production have made imported coal cheaper and more attractive. (Chellaney, 2005: 63)

Oil: The position of India in oil is not as comfortable as coal. India has limited oil resources and would have to import oil to meet the growing energy requirement. According to the CIA World Factbook, 2011, of the proven oil reserves estimate, India ranks 21 in the world. The proven oil resource with India is estimated to be 5.6 billion barrels. Oil, which contributes roughly 40 percent of India's energy need is very crucial to Indian economy and its secure and reliable supply at affordable price will shape up the over all economy. The statistics shows that the demand has been steadily increasing and is likely to rise in the time to come but the overall oil production is not growing along with the growth in demand. Thus, rising oil consumption and relatively flat production has left India increasingly dependent on imports to meet its petroleum demand. In 2010, India was the world's fifth largest net importer of oil, importing more than 2.2

million bbl/d, or about 70 percent of its consumption. (Sahu, 2010: 24)

Table 10.1: Resource Endowment: Proven Oil Reserves

Country	Oil Reserves(bbl)	Rank
Russia	60,000,000,000	8
US	20,680,000,000	13
China	20,350,000,000	14
India	5,682,000,000	21
Germany	276,000,000	57
Japan	44,120,000	80

Source: CIA World Factbook, 2011 (1st January estimates) accessed on 30-01-2012.

A majority of India's crude oil imports come from the Middle East, with Saudi Arabia and Iran supplying the largest shares. Africa adds 22 percent to Indian oil imports.

Table 10.2: Resource Enndowment: Proven Natural Gas Reserves

Country	Natural Gas Reserves (Cu m)	Rank
Russia	44,800,000,000,000	1
Iran	29,610,000,000,000	2
Qatar	25,370,000,000,000	3
Saudi Arabia	7,807,000,000,000	4
US	7,716,000,000,000	5
India	1,074,000,000,000	26
China	800,000,000,000	29
Germany	175,600,000,000	48
Japan	20,900,000,000	76

Source: CIA World Factbook, 2011 (1st January estimates) accessed on 30-01-2012.

Natural Gas: The situation in natural gas is not very different from the oil sector. India ranks 26th in world's proven natural gas reserves having an estimated gas reserve of 38 trillion cubic feet (TCF).

Though India's internal production of gas has increased substantially, the demand for gas, however, has increased much faster than the production. As a result, India has become an importer of gas. India's natural gas demand is driven by power and fertilizer sectors, which consume roughly three fourth of the total demand.Natural gas demand is expected to grow considerably, largely driven by demand in the power sector. Moreover, natural gas is expected to be an increasingly important component of energy consumption as the country pursues energy resource diversification and overall energy security. It is emerging as an alternative to oil in the transportation sector in the form of compressed natural gas (CNG) both for environmental reasons and to reduce India's increasing dependence on oil. (ibid)

Nuclear Power

Nuclear power accounts for a small portion of the total commercial primary energy consumed in India. Though nuclear power contributes a small amount, it has the potential to offer India a reliable source of energy. The future development of nuclear power within India is dependent on civil nuclear commercial engagementwith the international community. According to the India Energy Handbook, 2011, Indian nuclear market is estimated to be worth US$ 100 billion, and planners hope to build 40,000 mw of nuclear capacity by 2020. The GoI wants the share of nuclear in the overall fuel mix to increase from around 3 percent to 25 percent by 2050. The signing of the Indo-US nuclear deal in October 2006 has opened up opportunities for India in the field of civilian nuclear trade. (India Energy Handbook, 2011:14)

Hydro Power

Hydro electricity accounts for 5-6 percent of the total commercial primary energy consumption in India. In recent years, hydropower has contributed to 23 percent of the total electricity generation in India. The country is endowed with many large rivers and two close neighbours having enough hydro potential from which barely a quarter has been tapped yet. Controversies with regard to the hydal projects indicate that India faces serious ecological, social and political challenges in developing its hydel power. But hydroelectricity cooperation at the regional level in south Asia has important implications for India's energy security and foreign policy goals.

According to the report of the Ministry of New and Renewable Energy, India occupies 2.4 percent of the world's land area but supports 16.2 percent of the world's human popualtion with a GDP growth of average 8-9 percent annually which needs more and more energy to sustain the growth paradigm. It is the fourth largest energy consumer in the world after the US, China and Russian Federation. However, the per capita energy consumption in comparison with the other global powers is very low. Out of 72 percent of rural population, 45 percent of rural households are yet to be electrified and 14 percent of the population lives in unelectrified villages. (Maithani, 2011) Therefore, India needs an uninterrupted and secure supply of energy to meet its global power aspiration as well as to bridge the rich- poor gap. However, it needs to diversify the energy sources and develop and tap every possible alternative on a urgent basis. In this context, we are discussing India's renewed energy diplomacy and international engagement in the following section.

Energy Diplomacy: The Alternative Way Forward

Any number of important developments in the global scene have made the issue of energy security to be a dominant global agenda. The tight oil market, the crisis in Iraq, Iranian nuclear issue, Russia's reemergence as an energy superpower, political crisis in oil-rich countries outside the Middle East i.e Venezuela and Nigeria, the rising energy demand of emerging

China and India, the geopolitical competition among the world's major and emerging powers etc., have influenced the energy security aspect and international politics to a great extent.

There is a geographical mismatch between the major centres of oil and gas productions, primarily the Middle East, Central Asia and the Caucasus and the centres of consumption i.e. the US, Europe, China, Japan and India as the large consuming nations which are pursuing foreign and security policies in the energy rich regions with an aim of increasing their political, economic and military influence there. (Pardesi and Ganguly, 2009: 102) To meet the rapidly growing energy needs through imports from various nations having energy in surplus in some form or the other, involves diplomacy with the respective nation. Diplomacy becomes imperative because the energy exporting nations have the liberty of choosing from various buying nations and similarly they would see the best possible benefits from the buying country. Since energy relations are long lasting, they need to be throughly analysed and strategies have to be carefully framed in this respect.

As an emerging power, energy security has always been a foreign policy priority area for India as the country has been traditionally dependent on imports of energy. The hydrocarbons sector plays a vital role in the economic growth of the country. Therefore, in order to have a long-term policy for the hydrocarbons sector, which would facilitate meeting the future needs of the country, the Hydrocabon Vision, 2025 is an important step by the Government of India. The Hydrocarbons Vision, 2025 lays down the framework to guide the policies relating to the hydrocarbons sector for the next 25 years which reads as follows:

1. 100 percent exploration of unexplored domestic basins.
2. Ensure long-term supplies in countries and regions of high energy supplies (e.g. Russia, Central asia, Africa, Central America).
3. Pursue projects aimed at greater supplies of LPG (e.g.

Sakhalin, South Paras, Kazakhstan).

4. Maintain adequate strategic storage of crude and petroleum (strategic reserves e.g. ONGC Videsh Ltd. present in more than 20 countries).
5. Open national hydrocarbon market to private, public and global energy players (New Exploration and Licensing Policy, NCEP I,II,III etc.).
6. Rational pricing policy for affordable price to consumers.
7. Creating policy frameworks for clean and green fuel (National Energy Action Plan[NAP], June 2008). [1]

To put it in other words, India has reassessed its foreign policy objectives and energy strategies to address the issue of energy security in the following ways:

- diversification of suppliers;
- diversification of sources of energy;
- the purchase of equity stakes overseas;
- the security of its hydrocarbon supplies;
- ensuring adequate storage of energy; and
- cooperation with neighbouring countries within South Asia as well as outside South Asia. (ibid)

Regional Dimensions

The first pillar of India's search for energy security has to increase the domestic supply and then to increase the building of bilateral energy cooperation with neighbouring nations of South Asia to facilitate plans for regional natural gas and oil pipelines, including from Burma, Bangladesh, Iran and Turkmenistan and hydroelectricy from its Himalayan neighbours. Though India is actively trying to engage its Himalayan neighbours to harness hydroelectricity to reduce its dependence on fossil fuels for electricity generation, there are various domestic problems associated with it. Nepal and Bhutan curenly harness merely 1.2 and 2.6 percent of their total hydroelectricity potential respectively.

The financial and tecnological assistance from India in hydropower cooperation has become an important consideartion for both Nepal and Bhutan. At present, 15 joint hydroeletricity projects with four of its neighbouring countries i.e Bhutan, Nepal, Myanmar and Afghanistan are under discussion. But India's misinterpreted position as 'Big Brother' among the countries of South Asia has serious implications on this issue, which has created some kind of resentment in Indo-Nepal relations.

Moreover, the increasing anti-Indian sentiment in Nepal that India cheated Nepal in the Mahakali Treaty of 1960 as also the increasing involvement of China in Nepal's development programmes have fueled the fire. Therefore, it needs a careful reassessment of engaging Nepal through creating goodwill and cooperationin its hydroelectric sector. However, small hydropower projects having less environmental impact seems to be a viable alternative. By engaging Nepal and Bhutan in a more cooperative manner, India can counter the tilt towards China as well as assure of a sustainable source of energy.

In the case of the making of gas pipeline from Burma, the Burmese military junta's propopsal to start building a pipeline to India's North-East marked the potential of bilateral energy cooperation in Southern Asia. If materilised properly, Myanmar could become an important source of energy supply to India's eastern states. But unfortunately, India has been too slow and is not having a clear long term vision on how to engage Myanmar and to deal with Chinese influence there (Lall, 2008). India's pipeline plan was finally rejected by Myanmar after China's state owned company got theproject .

According to Sreeradha Datta (2008), as quoted by Panwar, "One ONGC official conceded that, 'China matched India's offer very aggressively and they made every effort to ensure that this gas project is wrapped up. We lacked that kind of aggressive strategy and also suffered from delays in decision-making". (Panwar, 2009: 14) Furthermore, the 'Look East Policy' has not added much to improve the relationship. The same is the case of Bangladesh. Bangladesh can not only earn substantial foreign exchange by selling natural gas to India, but also can earn large transit fees from a pipeline running across its territory from Burma to India's West Bengal. (Chellany, 2005: 75)

However, because of Bangladesh's unwillingness to export gas to India and India's unwillingness to link trade-related issues in its negotiation with Bangladesh, the cooperation is still not near. One fact is clear that India's energy diplomacy has been restricted by its conflicting interests which is hampering its energy expansion efforts. While it is engaged in more aggressive oil diplomacy with a few countries for acquisition of oil and gas assets abroad through the construction of pipelines, these attempts are hindered by some other strategic factors, including the US factor. India also seems to run into conflict of interests with the US when cooperating with potential energy suppliers like Myanmar, Sudan and Venezuela.

To make it more understandable, India's quest for energy supply is being influenced by its tense border relations with energy suppliers, energy transit countries and energy competitors. Unlike China,which has either resolved or shelved its border disputes, India has unsolved conflicts with almost all of its neighbouring states. India's sensitive relations with Pakistan is influencing negatively on the proposed gas pipeline from Turkmenistan or Iran to India, which will have to pass through Pakistani territory. Furthermore, India's poor relations with natural gas-rich Bangladesh and Myanmar who are very much China friendly have again hampered its energy quest inside South Asia. Thus, India has to deal with more serious geopolitical and security challenges before it can realize its overland pipeline dreams. (Hong, 2009) Moreover, China is always there as a strong competitor in the regional as well as global market.

Another most important factor affecting India's energy security is the absence of an institutional structure which could allow for an integrated energy policy. As mentioned,

India, now has seven or eight different ministries that are currently involved with energy. As a result, there will obviously be the absence of one holistic framework within which an integrated energy policy can be framed. (Mehta, 2011) Unlike China, which has a high level energy entity in charge of formulating and implementing its overall energy development strategy, India has a number of ministries and groups that are jointly responsible for policy making related to various energy sources.

In the year 2005, China established the Energy Leading Group which is a supra-ministerial coordinating body headed by Premier Wen Jiabao, and in March 2008, China established a national-level energy institution the National Energy Administration. All this shows China's increasing priority to strengthen its energy sector management by improving coordination between industries and ministries in promoting the formation, implementation and enforcement of energy policies and strategies. (Hong, 2009) Therefore, India needs an integrated energy adminisration structure and a coherent energy srategy in its regional as well as global engagement.

Global Dimensions

With unprecedented growth rates in recent years, India has become increasingly conscious about the importance of its energy security where interdependence and diversification of energy sources remain the fundamental starting principle for both oil and gas.The majority of oil and gas reserves are concentrated in the unstable Middle East and Persian Gulf, Central Asia and Russia. Over 70 percent of natural gas reserves are located in Russia, Iran and Qatar. In this new energy world order of intense competition between the developed and emerging countries, Iran, Russia and the energy resource rich Persian Gulf states have reclaimed their advantageous positions as popular energy suppliers where India and China have become the biggest consumers of Eurasian energy resources in general and Middle Eastern resources in particular. (Coşkun, 2011: 73)

Middle East

In recent years, India's policy towards the Middle East has often been assessed through the parameter of Indo-Iranian relations which have come under intense scrutiny. Not only did Pakistan sign a pipeline deal with Tehran, but India's competitor China also is trying to play a major role in the geopolitics by undertaking massive investments in the country and by becoming Iran's largest trading partner. Recent years have marked India's shrinking presence and China's growing engagement with Iran when firms such as Reliance Industries withdrew due to western pressure. Moreover, a number of important projects with Indian businesses and the Indian government have either been rejected by Iran or have yet to be finalized due to last minute changes in the terms and conditions by Tehran which shows the unreliability of Iran and the short-sighted diplomacy from the Indian side.

The nuclear issue is also equally complicated for this emerging Indian-Iranian relation. Iranwas not supportive of the Indian nuclear tests in 1998 and was in favour of the UN Security Council's resolution asking India to sign the NPT and CTBT. (Pant, 2011: 63,64) Moreover, the Iranian nuclear issue where US pressure on India was clearly visible in the case of I-P-I pipeline was also another reason of this undeveloped relation. However, India's support for the security of Afghanistan is a crucial point in Indo-Iranian relation where there is scope for positive development. While many contradictions and domestic constraints continue to remain and influence this relationship, India has to shape and foster its foreign policies giving attention to its changing priorities with an independent and pragmatic foreign policy.

At the same time, India also wants to secure energy supplies and consolidate economic and trade relations with the Gulf States i.e. Bahrain, Kuwait, Oman, Qatar, Saudi Arabia, and the UAE, or the members of the Gulf Cooperation

Council. India is now the fourth largest recipient of Saudi oil after China, the United States and Japan. Both India and Saudi Arabia are having their own strategic interest in themselves. Other than oil, India wants Saudi Arabia's partnership to counterweight its traditional ally Pakistan in the Islamic world. Having the third largest Muslim population in the world, India possesses an advantage. Likewise, the Iranian Islamic Revolution of 1979 which added a new phase of rivalry between Iran and Saudi Arabia, the relationship with India is having another advantage for Saudi Arabia.

Therefore, India must use the opportunity of engaging Saudi Arabia in a mutually beneficial manner. However, energy has become the major driving force in Gulf-Indian relations. The GCC countries supply 45 percent of India's petroleum out of which Saudi Arabia is exporting a quarter of those supplies and Kuwait, Oman, and the UAE are other major suppliers. Moreover, Qatar is the exclusive supplier of natural gas, annually supplying five million tons of LNG to India. India is also engaging with Israel bilaterally by becoming Israel's second largest trading partner of non-military goods and services in Asia. In essence, India is in a good position in its relationship with the Middle East.

The security consequences of a rising Iran in the Arab Gulf states, Tehran's nuclear drive, its interference in neighbouring Iraq, and President Ahmadinejad's aggressive rhetoric are raising anxieties in Arab states about a resurgent Iran, forcing them to reorient their diplomacy accordingly where an emerging India becomes a better option. (ibid) For India it is the 65 percent of Middle Eastern oil which has become the diplomatic priority. However, India also has to face China and the US as strong competitors in the Middle Eastern chessboard. China's ties with major Gulf States are on an upswing and this will be a major factor to determine India's regional policies in the long term. Moreover, India's aspirations to emerge as a major global power may also lead it to counter China's growing influence around the globe.

Therefore, India has to rearticulate a broader Middle East policy without relying upon the old outdated approach to meet the complex challenges of the future.

Central Asia and Russia

Central Asian and Russian oil and gas are another source where India can diversity its energy security thrust. However, India has not yet entered into any long term energy import agreement with the countries of Central Asia but it is trying to enhance its own political, economic and military influence there. The proposed gas pipeline from central Asia i.e. Turkmenistan-Afghanistan-Pakistan-India (TAPI), if successful, would be able to supply gas from Central Asia and the Caucasus region to India through an interlinked region connecting Turkmenistan. In addition to central Asian hydrocarbon, India is also trying to access hydroelectricity from Tajikistan and Kyrgyzstan to supply to its northern Indian states.

However, this path is also not free from any difficulty. India faces strategic competition from China and the US who is an old player in this part of Eurasia. (Blank, 2009: 302) China with its durable energy strategy has built its oil and natural gas pipelines from Central Asia faster than other countries. It has signed agreements with the central Asian countries with a long term vision. Through massive investments, Chinese influence and visibility is growing significantly in a positive way in the region.

However, China is not much comfortable with Russia where it will face strategic competition. (Pop, 2010) Russia's resurgence as a major energy power in the world stage has again changed the world politics. As an old ally, India assessed a better position for Russia to play a major role as a global power. At the same time, a rising India can play a great part for a multi-polar world ambition of Russia. So, in this new global system, it has become necessary to diversify their respective interest and engage each other in a mutually beneficial manner. India must have to frame a long term Central Asian energy vision to face a great deal of competition and to project itself as a major player in the region.

Africa

The energy resources in Africa have generated a great deal of interest all over the world including India. India opted to establish relations with more remote regions in order to secure its energy supplies, namely in Africa, Latin America and Australia. The African continent holds 9.4 percent of the world's oil reserves. Angolais is Africa's largest oil producer having superior grade oil with low sulphur content. The United States is the single largest buyer of Angolan crude followed by China, where Angola is the third largest source of Chinese imports.

Mozambican coal has attracted Indian companies and has seen growing investment. India's historical linkages and diplomatic relations brought these countries closer and helped in promoting investment. India and Mozambique have close diplomatic relations and in Mozambique, Indian companies have invested in coal. India also has invested in SaoTome and Principe and Indian companies have secured shares in oil blocks.

However, competition from international oil companies especially Chinese oil companies in Angola has kept India out of the oil sector. In 2004, the ONGC through its international arm ONGC Videsh Limited (OVL) made a bid to buy Shell's fifty percent share in Block 18 of Angola. The deal was important for India as it could have yielded about 5 million barrels of crude oil daily. But Chinese company's last minute intervention and much higher aid package made India lose the bid. (Sahu, 2010) Therefore, Indian decision makers should be prompt enough to deal with the competitive energy scenario and able to take a long term view of energy investment.

United States

In an article entitled 'Nuclear power is our gateway to a prosperous future' India's nuclear scientist and ex-President A.P.J Abdul Kalam has argued that India is blessed with a very rare and important nuclear fuel called Thorium which is considered to be the nuclear fuel of the future. Nuclear power, when compared with other sources of energy, provides a relatively clean, high-density source of reliable energy with an international presence. He further describes, "There is a need for better technology and more stable plant design across the world, but the occurrence of four failures in six decades cannot be made out as a case for completely disbanding the technology". He assures, "it is poor judgment and a deliberate act of spreading fear to compare a nuclear bomb with a nuclear plant. The bomb is designed to deliver a large amount of energy over a very short period of time, leading to explosions, firestorms and massive heat energy generated to obliterate every object in its path. That is what a bomb is supposed to do! Civilian nuclear applications in the form of a power plant, on the other hand, are designed to deliver small amounts of energy in a sustainable manner over a far larger time frame. It is designed with systems to control and cool the nuclear reaction. There are safety procedures and back-ups, and even in the event of failures, as in the 2011 disaster, the destructive might will never be even a fraction of what happens in the case of a nuclear bomb". Since July 2005, Indo-US relationship has accelerated a new point of strategic engagement. Nuclear power which is an affordable, clean and abundant energy source, if developed completely, can lead us to a healthy future. (Kalam and Singh, 2011)

To this end, the Indo-US Civil Nuclear Deal marked an end in India's nuclear isolation. The deal if unsuccessful will hamper India's energy security as well rising strategic profile. But this relationship is having its own rhetoric from both the sides which has to manage carefully by giving importance to each other's expectations.

Conclusion

Globalization and rapid economic development has added a new dimension to security discourses in the form of energy security, which has become the prime concern of every state in the international arena. Today's global world order, characterized by intense competition between the developed and the emerging world powers has created a paradigm shift in the foreign and strategic policy of any country for achieving energy security. In this complex scenario, India needs a very careful strategic move towards its regional neighbours as well as global friends. To achieve energy security and to fulfil the rising demands of its population as well as to sustain this rapid economic development, India needs to tap every possible alternative source. However, the path is not so easy.

There is strong competition from China in each sphere. Moreover, there will be the pressure of the US in areas where its interests are getting hampered by any strategic move from India. Therefore, with the diversification of energy sources, India needs to rearticulate its energy strategies and engage regional as well as global players through bi-lateral and multi-lateral mechanisms.

There is also a growing importance on the need for diplomatic and economic support for ways to curb the Middle East's influence by developing alternative supply sources and alternative energy routes from Central Asia and Africa by engaging them for a long term relationship. Furthermore, energy cooperation and proactive energy diplomacy in its South Asian neighbourhood would allow India to transform into an important global player who could shape its regional environment.

By emerging as a secured country in its energy sector, India can retain its dominant position in South Asia. Moreover, well-planned pragmatic energy diplomacy towards Central Asia, limited but healthy relationship with China and strategic relations with the US would enable India to emerge as a major player in international politics.

End Note

1. Lecture delivered by Ambassador K Srinivasan , IFS, Former Foreign Secretary, Ministry of External Affairs, Government of India in his inaugural address in a National Seminar on India's Security Policy in Pondicherry University, 2012.

References

Energy Outlook 2030, *BP Statistical Review 2011*, London, January 2011.

India Energy Handbook, 2011, *International Energy Consulting Corporation (IECC)*, PSI Media Inc., Las Vegas, Nevada (USA) www.iecc-us.com.

Road map for up scaling and mainstreaming renewables, *DIREC 2010 Report*, Ministry of New and Renewable Energy, Government of India.

Energy Information Administration, *Country Analysis Briefs*, www.eia.doe.gov.

Misra, Kishlaya (2012), "Energy Diplomacy for Energy Security" *Ninth AIMS International Conference on Management*.

Kalam, A.P.J. Abdul and Srijan Pal Singh (2011), "Nuclear power is our gateway to a prosperous future", Special Essay, *The Hindu*, Sunday, November 6.

Chellaney, Brahma (2005), India's Future Security Challenge: Energy Security in India as a New Global Leader", The Foreign Policy Centre.

Maithani, P.C. (2011), "The private sector and climate change: Opportunities and Challenges in emerging economies", *Renewable Energy in India-A Policy Perspective*, Ministry of New and Renewable Energy, Government of India.

Sahu, Manendra (2010), "Energy Resources in Lusophone Africa and India's Energy Demand", *African Current*, Volume XXX No. 46.

Lall, Marie (2008), "India-Myanmar Relations-Geopolitics and Energy in Light of the New Balance of Power in Asia", *ISAS Working paper*, No. 29.

Pant, Harsh V. (2011), "India's Relations with Iran: Much Ado about Nothing", *The Washington Quarterly*, No. 34:1, pp. 61-74.

Coşkun, Bezen Balamir (2010), "Energizing the Middle East: Iran, Turkey and Persian Gulf States", *Turkish Policy Quarterly*, Vol. 9, No. 2, pp. 71-80.

Mehta Vikram (2011), "India's Energy Options: New Sources, Innovations and Areas of Cooperation", Remarks at the Centre for Strategic the International Studies (CSIS) B1 Conference Centre.

Hong, Zhao (2009), "China and India: The Energy Policies", *EAI Background Brief No. 462.*

Pop, Irina Ionela (2010), "China's Energy Strategy in Central Asia: Interactions with Russia, India and Japan", UNISCI Discussion Papers, No. 24 (October).

Pardesi, Manjeet S. and Sumit Ganguly (2009), "India and Energy Security: A Foreign Policy Priority" in Harsh V. Pant (ed.), *Indian Foreign Policy in a Unipolar World,* Routledge, pp. 99-127.

Blank, Stephen (2009), "India and Central Asia: Part of the New Great Game" in Harsh V. Pant (ed.), *Indian Foreign Policy in a Unipolar World,* Routledge, pp. 277-304.

Panwar, Namrata (2009), "India and China Competing over Myanmar Energy resources", *Working Draft for BISA Conference*, University of Leicester, Leicester.

11

Euro-Asian Maritime, Trade and Security Issues and the West Asian/Gulf Factor

A.K. Pasha

Section I

The Asian continent has been home to great civilizations like the Indus Valley, Achamenian, Sassanian, Chinese, Mesopotamia, Dilmun and many others. Some also flourished in present day Oman, Syria and many other parts of Asia. Throughout history there has been vigorous interaction among the peoples of Asia leading to trade and cultural links. Indian influence extended to much of present day South-East Asia to what is known as 'Greater India'. Buddhism played a leading role in this field which is still visible through temples and cultural influences. Similarly to the Western part of Asia, Indian influence at one time extended to the entire area inhabited by the Kurds, Central Asia and the Gulf Region.

Before accepting Islam, the Kurds were followers of Buddhism. The Nabateans who established a powerful empire in much of West Asia from Petra now in Jordan are referred to as vegetarians thought to have migrated from India. The Gulf region has seen continuous maritime contacts with Gujarat and the West Coast of India. Navigators from both sides benefited with exchange of goods & ideas thereby enriching their culture and society. Many traders and peoples from both areas especially settled (in both the regions).

With the spread of Islam, Arab traders and Sufi Saints from the Gulf region added to this relationship and ties were consolidated. Many Indians converted to Islam, Christianity and Syrian Christians and monks settled in Kerala, the West

Coast and other parts of India. Many Jews who could escape persecution from the Romans in West Asia also settled in Kerala and along the West Coast of India. Large numbers of Indians regularly visit religious places in the West Asian/Gulf Region like Mecca, Medina, Jerusalem, Bethlehem, Najaf, Karbala, Mashed so on. The discovery of direct sea route from Europe by the Portuguese sailor Vasco da Gamma to Calicut in Kerala in 1498 and the subsequent European colonialism disrupted the close interaction India had with the Gulf region.

After defeating Haider Ali's son Tipu Sultan in 1799 (the last Indian ruler who seriously challenged them) at Mysore, the British consolidated their rule in India. From Bombay with the assistance of Indian soldiers and administrative staff the British controlled bulk of the Gulf region (present day GCC states). Large segments of the Gulf population who thrived on lucrative trade with India and beyond were now virtually dependent on the British dominated trade and maritime links.

They Gulf Arabs reverted to pearl fishing and the British transported their principal day to day requirements mostly from India. Many Indian families especially from Sind, Kutch and Gujarat settled in the entire Gulf region. People in the Gulf region now saw Indians as collaborators with British imperialism. The British deported undesirable people from the Gulf region to India. Also some Gulf merchants settled in India, mostly in Bombay.

The British who promised independence to the Arabs before and during the First World War, failed to keep up their promise. The Sheriff Hussein of Mecca who was promised a United Arab Kingdom over the liberated Arab lands from the Ottoman rule found British and French rule over Palestine, Iraq, Syria and Lebanon under the mandate's rule of the League of Nations. The Sheriffs two sons were installed as Kings of Iraq and Jordan. The Jews were also promised a homeland in Palestine through the Balfour Declaration. The Mufti of Jerusalem accused the British of having a design to settle in Iraq "many million Hindus from British India".

Hundreds and thousands of Indian soldiers died suppressing the Arabs who were opposed to imposition of monarchies, mandated rule and direct British/French occupation. Elsewhere in West Asia thousands of Indian soldiers died fighting with the British during and after the war. The article makes an attempt to capture the deeper significance of the interdependent nature of history, and the linkages between military, societal, economic and political foundations of history. It focuses on Egypt as a link between Europe and Asia especially in relation to the spice trade which formed the basis for interaction. Ottoman Turkey has also been an important link as it had become a Eurasian power which is studied as the basis of historical analysis. The military conquest and colonization of India and major parts of Asia by the Europeans was a consequence of superior technology. India's advantage at the moment in IT is fast changing its image around the world. India's present economic progress is linked to its past and a combination of new technology, family values, commitment to democracy and multicultural secular society.

Section II

Throughout history Egypt has been an important link between India and Europe for trade, political, cultural and other relations. India and Egypt have had close political, economic and cultural relations. Contacts have been through land and sea. The oldest recorded maritime contacts have been between India and Egypt. It is remarkable that both the countries despite having suffered several invasions and attacks have maintained their civilizations. The Nile and Indus valley civilizations and cultures have produced outstanding things in all fields and shared with the rest of the world.

Many civilizations like the Dilmun, Magan, Summerian and many others have flourished in West Asia but it is the Egyptian civilization that has managed as the only civilization continuum in the world along with Indian. The Egyptian Pharanoic civilization has been historically linked with

Hinduism in India especially in religion and culture. It is remarkable that the ancient Egyptians worshipped the same Gods as Indians. There is unique resemblance in the building of temples and their architecture. Painting and sculpture are very similar. Both appear to have shared a long history of vibrant interaction and such ties between the two peoples have unmistakably continued into the modern period. Indian textiles were familiar in Egypt.

During the Roman period, Egypt was an important link and India prospered due export of spices and other products. There was outflow of gold from Rome to India which became a matter of concern to the Romans. The colonial domination of the Indian Ocean since 1500 affected both the countries that came under British domination. These were the 'lost five centuries' and due to its impact both lagged behind. It was natural that after independence both established close ties in all fields. Whereas Egypt had to face Western-Israeli hostility, India was saddled with partition of the country and attacks from China and Pakistan. Both the countries have faced similar number of wars and have been struggling to regain the stability and prosperity.

Nehru recognized the importance of Egypt and established close ties and Nasser reciprocated. Whereas Egypt drifted since 1973 and established close ties with the US due to peace with Israel, India managed to retain autonomy in its foreign policy. Since 1991 India has also been striving to have close ties with the USA along with economic liberalization. Both have been working to strengthen their bilateral ties and the levels of political exchanges have increased giving a new dimension to their ties. Economic cooperation has increased in a number of fields and Indian investments in Egypt are also increasing. But bilateral relations cannot be based only on political and economic relations without strong cultural people to people bond. Given their long historical links the relationship in future can be built on the strong foundation which already exists. This article makes a modest attempt to analyze in a historical context political, economic and cultural relations between India and Egypt who can contribute as major powers in their respective regions to peace, security and stability.

The oldest known civilization identified by historian's world wide is without doubt the Nile based followed by the Indus and Mesopotamian civilizations. Both the Nile and Indus Valley civilizations were in constant contact through land with each other through the Tigris and Euphrates based civilization as also through maritime contacts directly. According to historians from the time immemorial there existed peculiar and deeper relations between India and Egypt. "The Indus civilization was built upon the same primary inventions and discoveries as the Nilotic and the Mesopotamian. Its authors may even have included men of the same racial types". [1] Dr. M.A. Murray says: "The type of men of Punt, as depicted by Hatshepsut's artists, suggests an Asiatic rather than an African race; and the sweet-smelling woods point to India as the land of their origin. A voyage from Egypt to India by coasting vessels would be quite feasible, and undoubtedly ports for the Indian trade existed along the south coast of Arabia". [2] India's recorded interaction with Egypt started since the third millennium before Jesus Christ.

In ancient Egypt, perfumes utilizing various Indian aromatics played an important role in worship, which in turn led to brisk trade. The Ishmaelites who bought Joseph from his brothers were en route to Egypt with an unspecified range of spices: They saw some Ishmaelite on their way coming from Galaad, with their camels, carrying spices, and balm, and myrrh to Egypt. [3]

The Egyptians were fond of aromatics and they procured it from a semi mythical place known as "Punt". To get aromatics the Egyptians sent the first recorded merchant fleet to Punt which continued to supply to the temples and God-kings of the Nile Pharaohs for thousands of years. The first known maritime trip to Punt took place during Pharaoh Sahure

[2491-2477 BC]. Not only had the Egyptians had close trade relations it is well known that Egyptian mummies were reportedly wrapped in Bengal Muslin cloth. Some writers have tried to establish a close link between Egypt and parts of Bengal in India. These similarities led historians to conclude that there was a conquest of Bengal by the heretic kings of Egypt of the XVIII dynasty who were driven out of Egypt by the orthodox school of Amon worshippers sometime between 1358 and 1355 BC. [4]

Around 1500 BC the famous Egyptian Queen Hatshepsut sent a great naval expedition to Punt. This is visible still on the walls of the temple of Dier al-Bahri carved at the orders of Queen Hatshepsut around 1495 BC. A fleet of five ships with mariners on top of ships, rowers, steersmen passing through a huge water body is depicted. These ancient sailors brought back to Egypt from the land of Punt, "all goodly fragrant woods of God's-land, heaps of myrrh resin, with fresh myrrh trees, with ebony, and pure ivory, with green gold of Emu, with cinnamon wood, kheyst wood, with ihmut-incense, sonter-incense, eye-cosmetic, with apes, monkeys, dogs, and with skins of the southern panther, with natives and their children". [5] The mariners also brought fragrant plants for the temple gardens. She also sent the mission to India perhaps seeking to establish commercial and diplomatic ties between India and Egypt.

Not only this initiative from the Egyptian Queen led to the direct maritime communications between India and Egypt several centuries before Christ but more significantly it showed that Egyptian sailors were able to navigate the Red Sea in appropriate time to make use of the Arabian Sea monsoons to reach India and Sri Lanka and maybe perhaps beyond. From modern Somalia the ancient Egyptians continued a voyage of more than two thousand miles south ward. The Egyptian ships also took Indian products like silk, perfumes, spices, medicines, rare fruits, sandal wood, incense and other items not available in the Nile valley. It is mentioned that the

Egyptian sailors must have observed the Indian festival of lights–Diwali–because Egypt also has a similar state festival of lights celebrated for nine days.

According to Hassan El Zayyat, this unique interaction is a proof "that the ships sailing to India did not serve the purpose of commerce only but also carriers of Indian culture." [6] Ramses III also sent an expedition to Punt. That Indian spices were an important link with Egypt is clear by the discovery of dhania (the umbelliferous fruit of the coriander plant) in the tombs of the Pharaohs especially Ramses. Its identity was confirmed in 1975-76 at Musee de L' Houmme in Paris, after long years of research that the spices came from the south of India. The Pharaoh's were obsessed with eternal life and in order to preserve the body from decomposition they used pepper as a preservative. "It was in all likelihood the supreme metaphysical importance of this end that accounts for the Egyptians extraordinary efforts to obtain a spice all the way from India". [7] Pepper was not only inserted in the nose of the Pharaoh but researchers also found traces of the spice in his abdominal cavity. Clearly this spice from India was familiar to ancient Egyptians. According to archaeological evidence, there was resemblance between a number of methods used in certain activities such as fishing, boat construction, measuring and weighing in both civilizations.

Between 200 BC and 200 AD, an Indian colony existed in Alexandria which was intellectually capable of influencing the Hellenistic scholars and philosophers of Alexandria. Ashoka the Great sent an Indian diplomatic mission to the Ptolemaic court in Alexandria. In the 6th century BC, the Achaemenians who ruled from Iran controlled Egypt and Sind and to improve the communications built a canal linking the Nile with the Red Sea which was beneficial to trade between India and Egypt. Trade between India and Egypt under the Pharonic rulers or otherwise greatly influenced both the societies.

As we have seen earlier it carried the culture from one civilization to another. When people move from place to place along the trade routes they carry ideas, philosophy, religions, customs, traditions, rituals as also books, handicrafts and artistic items which familiarize people in different societies. Due to the long sea coast both India and Egypt derived considerable revenues from trade in ancient times. As during the modern period, in ancient times also culture and civilization aspects followed trade and commerce between India and Egypt.

Along with the maritime contacts referred to between India and Egypt, there existed considerable trade through the land route via Iran, Babylon, Oman, Aden, and Palestine and onto Egypt. For the ancient period, one has to rely upon direct archeological evidence like seals made of ivory, stone, terracotta used in those lands or the use of Indian or Egyptian names for such items. In the second century BC an Indian sailor offered to show the Romans (who were ruling Egypt) the shortest direct sea route to India. Ptolemy Euergetes II (145-116 BC) the Roman ruler of Egypt welcomed the proposal and directed Eudoxus, a Greek [Cyzicus] explorer, to set out with the Indian across the high seas to India.

The Greek made two trips to India to buy spices and other eastern luxuries which Ptolemy seized. [8] This was a turning point in ancient Indo-Egyptian maritime links as it heralded direct trade contacts under the Greco-Egyptian dynasty of the Ptolemy's which declined with the demise of Cleopatra. The previous maritime contacts were not regular because the sea journey was long and arduous as the small ships had to sail along the coasts and hence target of pirates. When the Roman Emperor Augustus annexed Egypt in 30 BC he built new ports on the Red Sea and dug wells along the caravan routes crossing the desert from the Nile to the Red Sea. The Romans soon subjugated the Nabateans and the Hadhramauti merchants who had dominated the spice trade especially in the Red sea area. King Kaniskha was familiar with Rome.

The description of India by one Roman Apuleiu's [124 AD] is interesting: "The Indians are a people of great population and vast territories situated far to our east, by the Ocean's ebb, where the stars first rise at the ends of the earth, beyond the learned Egyptians and the superstitious Jews, Nabataean merchants and flowing-robed Parthians, past the Iruraeans [Palestine] with their meagre crops and the Arabs rich in perfumes-wherefore I do not so much wonder at the Indians mountains of ivory, harvests of pepper, stockpiles of cinnamon, tempered iron, mines of silver and smelted streams of gold: nor the Ganges, the greatest of all rivers and the King of the waters of the Dawn, running in a hundred streams...". [9]

During the second half of first century AD a Greek sailor, living in Egypt sailed to India through the Red Sea and along the coasts of Arabian Sea and recorded his experiences in a book called "*The Periplus of the Erythraean Sea*". The book is a pilot's guide to sailing in the Indian Ocean telling each step of the long and perilous sea journey also highlighting the ports and harbours to halt and what goods to acquire and sell over there. The water body between Red Sea, Persian Gulf and the Indian Ocean and beyond is called as the Erythraean Sea. The Romans who controlled Egypt sent ocean going ships to India. One Greek sailor named Hippalus found out the annual cycle of monsoon which was the secret of navigation in the Indian Ocean. The Romans apparently called at any one of the 19 Indian ports in which, in the words of the Periplus, "great ships sail...due to the vast quantities of pepper and malabathron".

It clearly reveals the extensive trade ties between India and Egypt as Roman and Indian ships sailed to coasts all along Oman, Yemen and to the Red Sea [Horn of Africa known in ancient period as Cape Guardafui or Cape of Spices] carrying among other things sugar, pearls, precious stones, spices, unguents, and cotton clothes—Muslin all of which were in great demand. In many of these ports/harbours on the sea coast Indians had settled for trade and that Aden and the Socootra Island had a colony of Indian merchants. [10] Many Indian Kings especially from South India, the Pandyas sent trade missions to Rome to the Emperor Augustus around 26 BC as also during subsequent period. Indian goods were carried by sea up to the Red Sea Coast and from there to Alexandria. The Gangas of Talakad in South India had flourishing trade with the Roman Empire as this is corroborated by the recent discovery of a large number of Roman coins in the temple town of Muduktherai on the banks of Kaveri which must have been sent for Indian goods shipped to Alexandria as similar coins were discovered over there. Thus, both India and Egypt not only had direct trade ties but Egypt especially Alexandria became the entreport for Indian goods to Europe.

The Romans through the Egyptians exported to India glassware, works of art, tin and Mediterranean coral-much prized in India for its imputed magical properties and bullion. They brought back from India ivory, pearls, tortoiseshells, diamonds, onyx, agate, crystal, amethyst, opal, beryl, sapphire, ruby, garnet, bloodstone, emerald, carnelian, linen, textiles, wheat grains, handicrafts and many hand made art products. Silk from China was also brought via India. Animals from India like parrots, tigers, rhinoceroses, elephants were also brought. But it was clearly the Indian spices which were the main attraction along with costus, nard and cloves as well.

The ancient Egyptians visited India frequently not only for the goods they needed but also to sell Egyptian products in the vast Indian market. It is recorded that Ptolemy II [ruled 285-246 BC] exchanged ambassadors with the Mauryan Emperors Chandragupta II [321-297 BC] and Ashoka [232 BC]. Alexandria in Egypt, ruled by Ptolemaic and Roman rulers being cosmopolitan city, was not only a major trading centre but far ahead of Rome and Athens culturally. Alexandria became the chief port of the Nile delta. The route from Alexandria to Rome was the most heavily trafficked trade route of the ancient world. Within weeks of sail brought prized goods including much sought after spices to Rome's great port at Ostia at the mouth of the Tiber. The distance was about 5000 miles from India.

Thus, Alexandria was not only a place where traders from all parts of the world met, but the cosmopolitan city also attracted scholars from all over the world especially from India who interacted with their Egyptian counterparts. Apart from the trade ties between India and Egypt, the Egyptian mind was also influenced by Indian mysticism, especially the doctrine of rebirth. The ties in historical period were further intensified during the Roman period. As more and more Persians began to take interest in commercial activities, direct Indo-Egyptian trade relations in the second and third century AD declined.

Although the discovery of monsoon winds in AD 44 had changed the maritime contacts between the two countries and the volume of trade had increased in first AD with every year around 120 ships travelled to India for various products, but the contacts decreased subsequently due to decline in Roman power in the aftermath of the invasions by barbarians [Franks, Visigiths and Alamannis] shattered the prosperity and order on which trade with India depended. The Gothic invaders who dismembered the Western Roman Empire dealt a severe blow to trade with India. This decline persisted for about 1000 years but sporadic demand for Indian goods remained despite invasions and disruptions. During the period of Pliny the Elder [23-79 AD] Rome's cosmopolitan tastes had reached such a pitch that he talk of the flavours of Egypt and India appearing in Roman kitchens. [11]

Egypt and India greatly benefited from trade with the Roman Empire, and as one writer said: "the money flowed out to foreigners". Gold and silver Roman coins reached India in great quantities as visible in the vast archaeological discoveries in South India particularly. Pliny the Elder apparently "complained that India swallowed up the colossal sum of 50 million sesterces per annum—all for the sake of pepper and other "effeminate" eastern fripperies. India and its luxuries were turning Rome into a city of wimps". India and its pepper became almost paradigmatic. To Pliny the Elder, the voyage to India was no more than a grubby quest for loot, "and so India is brought near by a lust for gain". [12]

After the reign of Caracalla [211-217] roman coins declined in India. Soon the Roman Empire suffered one disaster after another affecting the eastern traffic. Moreover, the Red Sea littoral passed under the control of the Blemmyes, a hostile African tribe, and Rome's direct trade route via Egypt was disrupted. But the Byzantine state maintained even in the sixth century a customs official at Clysma on the Gulf of Suez and a famous Greek-Egyptian monk Cosmas Indicopleustes travelled to India around 550 AD. The transformation was already visible as Syrian, Latin and Hebrew were the languages used by the merchants all along the spice routes. Socootra Island situated at the Bab el Mandeb near Yemen was an important link in Indo-Egyptian contacts. The memory of this trade still survives in western India especially among the people of coastal Gujarat who worship a goddess called Sakotri Mata, named after Socootra Island. [13]

The spread of Islam under Amr-ibn-al-As in major parts of Egypt brought Arabs from the heart of Arabian Peninsula to a country where idolatry, temples existed. Pharonic culture was widespread despite the growth of Christianity, but modest trade especially Egyptian imports of Indian textiles continued. Fragments of fabric were found at Al Fustat near Cairo which functioned as a major trading centre in Egypt. Initially the direct maritime trade contacts appear to have declined since the rise of Islam between India and Egypt as the Arabs from Oman, Yemen and others like Persians began to interact with Indians on a bigger scale converting the Indian Ocean as a Muslim lake. Muslim merchants especially Arabs were now firmly established from Malacca, Malabar to Maghreb to China.

The Arabs traders and mariners [Muslims] now controlled land and sea routes and used camels and ships to transport goods. The Jews now were also active with the Muslims. But Indian goods especially spices continued to reach Cairo in modest quantities for onward transmission to Europe in return for furs and amber from the Baltic's; slaves, timber and metals from the Alps and the Balkans. To one writer "pepper has perhaps been the oldest continuous link between India and Egypt and also between Asia and Europe and one that has survived, battered but intact, ever since". [14] Under these circumstances, Alexandria became once again the terminus of transcontinental trade as it had become famous earlier during the Romans. Trade ties between India and Egypt were revived through the Red Sea and once again there was brisk trade.

During this period, the "Syrian" i.e. Byzantine merchants [Constantinople still remained the capital of the Eastern Roman empire until 1453 when the Turks took over] and the Jewish traders also began to play an important in the trade between India and Egypt. The Jews were uniquely placed as a link between the Christians and Muslims. Many writers refer to a loose alliance of Jewish merchants known as the Rhadanites whose name appears in the Book of Routes composed around 850 by Ibn Khordabeh, Director of Posts to the Caliphs at Baghdad. The Jews were present all along the old silk route from Gaul to China. Interestingly the arrival of Muslims [Islam] at the gates of Arles and Marseilles [France] and at Saint Peter's Basilica in 846 propelled the Jews to prominence as even Charlemagne and his Frankish nobles were forced to rely on Jewish merchants for their luxuries.

Due to their new role, Christian persecution of Jews virtually stopped as also forced conversions common during the Frankish Dynasty Merovingians dynasty [476-750] in Europe. It must be noted that one of the oldest surviving decrees of the Venetian Senate forbade Jews from travelling in Venetian ships. [15] The Jewish presence was noticeable due to the Fatimid Dynasty's [969-1171] connections with Maghreb areas. Like the Romans the Fatimids encouraged trade through the Red Sea by maintaining a strong navy and providing security to merchants from all over the world.

According to one writer: "Cairo was then embarking on the period of its greatest commercial splendour, drawing commerce, merchants, and travellers like filings to a magnet. Alexandria regained the position it had occupied in classical antiquity as Europe's chief point of access to the exotic goods of the East". [16] In 996, a traveller to Cairo counted 160 merchants from Amalfi alone. Nahray ibn Nissim, a Tunisian Jew settled in Egypt, was dealing in products as diverse as Spanish tin and coral, Moroccan antimony, Indian spices, Armenian clothes, rhubarb from Tibet and spikenard from Nepal. The Jewish trade connections came to light from the remarkable collection of business papers, belonging to Jewish merchants, discovered in a Synagogue of Old Cairo.

The documents, letters, etc. cover the period 1000 to 1250. The commercial contacts of the Genizah (Cairo) Jewish merchants under the trading guild known as the Karimis existed through their agents from China through India to Morocco and were an important link between India and Egypt. The intermediaries in most cases were Jews themselves. According to K.N. Chaudhri, "Business was done by consigning goods to friends and relatives in Fustat or Aden, which the principal remained in India. It is significant from the point of view of commercial organization that the leading Jewish merchants of the period with business connections in distant countries did not find it necessary to travel with their own goods." [17]

The major items imported from India were spices but also included sandalwood, camphor, cloves, nutmegs, cubebs, coconuts, flaxen and cotton fabrics and ivory, pepper, lead, Kutla drug, bamboo, cane precious stones, cardamom, cinnamon, aloes, marjoram, myrrh, galangal, mastic, vermilion, parrots, saffron, mustard, cassia, garlic, musk, ginger, pearls, crystals and Sanbazaj (used for polishing stones). Wine and scents were imported from Egypt.

Many Arab Egyptian merchants settled on India's western coast like Gujarat, Konkan and on the Coromandel Coast. Jeddah now became an important link for trade between India and Egypt due to the trade being in Arab hands and also due to its proximity to Mecca–the pilgrimage centre for Muslims from all over the world. Large number of Indian scholars visited parts of the Arab world especially to Baghdad the capital of the Abbasid Empire taking with them their works in Sanskrit on astronomy, mathematics and medicine which were translated into Arabic and Greek. Gradually Islam began to influence India first through Arab traders in the coastal areas and later from Sind, Persia and Central Asia.

During the Fatimid period in 10th century AD, the Egyptian merchants were famous as El Karemia who traded mostly in Indian spices. Very often these merchants stayed in India for long periods and often married with Indian women. They also played in important role in spreading Islam in India. These Egyptian spice merchants came to be known as Bohras (apparently from bahar-spices or bahar (outside). The Bohras still are a very important Indian trading community in Egypt—Cairo in the business as well as a link between the two countries.

According to Sahar Abdel Aziz Salem, the Fatimid zeal to spread Islam in India indicates their desire to preside over the trade of the Indian Ocean. This could strengthen the economy of the Fatimid Caliphate in Egypt while at the same time weaken that of the Abbasids (at Baghdad). [18] He also argues that many Indian traders also visited Egypt as "Indian penetration into the Red Sea might have also taken place in the Fatimid period when relations between Egypt and India were very close and friendly, since they combined both commercial and spiritual interests". It appears Mohammed bin Tughluk Shah (who was known as the Sultan of India but also of Sind, Makran, Mogadishu and Sri Lanka) sent a ship to the Egyptian Mamluk Sultan Al Naser ibn Qalaun full of precious presents and diamonds, but it could not reach Cairo as the King of Yemen looted it. This clearly reveals that Indian ships were famous in Red Sea, Aden and along the Arabian coast. Egypt under the Fatimids flourished due to the brisk trade with India.

Indian influence is seen in Egyptian mosques, especially

design of the minaret as large number of Indian ships carried Moslems for Hajj and other Holy places. Egypt under the Fatimids continued to the extent possible interaction with India in trade and other fields. Since the entire Gulf region, Arabian Peninsula and North Africa including Egypt was undergoing rapid transformation under Islamic rulers this naturally affected the cultural relations as the Indian society was also undergoing similar changes in pockets of India under Muslim rulers both in north and South India.

The Spanish Rabbi Benjamin of Tudela visited Alexandria in 1160 and found European merchants like Italians, Catalans, Frenchmen, English and Germans rubbing shoulders with merchants from all over the world. This is interesting in the background of fierce religious wars in Europe. The Fatimids encouraged trade as they needed customs duties. Egypt also continued to be the link to the extent possible between India and Europe and interaction with India was very lucrative especially in spice trade and other fields.

During 1170-1260, the Fatimids in Egypt were replaced by the Ayyubid rulers under whom the total volume of trade declined as the European traders began to take active interest and increase their share. Moreover, the sea route to India became vulnerable to pirates and growing incidence of taxation. Some wealthy Egyptian merchants began to buy protection from rulers in the coastal regions to protect their ships from the menace of pirates. The role of Jewish merchants/agents (who could speak many languages) increased all along the routes from Alexandria, Jeddah, Aden, Muscat, Basra, and Bushier and to the Indian Coast.

This may also have partly increased the European volume of trade with the East and hence partly contributed to decline in Indo-Egyptian trade. Egypt soon came to be ruled by the Mamluks (1260-1517) and the devastation of the region from Persia to Palestine and the downfall of the Abbasids in Baghdad (1258) due to the Mongol invasion enhanced the importance of Cairo in the trade through the Red Sea area. The crusade attacks and the prominent role of Saladin in defeating the Crusaders led him to contain the growing role of Frankish merchants from gaining direct access to the Red Sea and limited their interaction to the North African and Mediterranean ports. Despite restrictions placed by the Pope on Christian traders for their purchases from Muslim countries, merchants from Genoa and Venetian did trade through Alexandria.

The Egyptians conducted trade through "safe conduct passes". The Mamluk rulers assured security to merchants, property and goods etc. It appears during the fourteenth century Egypt and the surrounding areas went through a difficult period due to economic disruptions and consequent decline in trade mainly due to the Black Death in Egypt in 1347. Religion again came as a hindrance in Indo-Egyptian trade as in 1322, the Pope excommunicated many leading citizens of Venice for their dealings with Muslim rulers and for some time a papal ban prevailed which slowed trade with Egypt with its repercussion on trade with India. The trade simply passed into the hands of Armenians merchants from Turkey to Persia to India and the Armenian port of Lajazzo became the link for Europe reducing Egypt's importance.

Despite restrictions placed by the Pope on Christian traders for their purchases from Muslim countries, some merchants from Geneo and Venetian did trade through Alexandria. The Black Death in Egypt in 1347-8, [bubonic plague-Rattus rattus] which divested agriculture and adversely affected the Egyptian population scarcd the foreign traders. This disease always started at thc coast, and from there went up into the interior wrote Procopius. Every freighter and galley shuttling from India to Egypt and from Alexandria to Byzantium was, potentially, a "death ship". [19] According to one writer, "the exact relationship between these events and the rhythm of long distance trade through the Red Sea is not quite clear but the Cairo-Alexandria trade network however, remained open", although it did not see the brisk trade it was used to in earlier periods.

It is interesting to know how an Egyptian scholar (historian) of the fifteenth century AD called Al-Qalqashandi appreciates India with these words. "India is a big and wide country having enormous wealth. The king lives with pomp and glory. Its ocean is full of pearls, its earth with gold and its mountains with rubies and emeralds. Its valleys have fragrance of sandal wood and camphor. The people are bestowed with wisdom. Peace and justice can be seen in the entire country". Another modern Egyptian scholar, Abu Zohra, in his book *Mohaderat Fi Muqarinat al Adyan* opines about ancient Indian religions and says: "Indians have a glorious history. They were possessed of civilization and culture in older days. The history of their civilization is so old that one remains unable to trace its origin". [20] Soon the crucial areas through which trade between India and Egypt was to pass came under the Ottoman Empire and this led to disruption in commercial transactions due to political troubles especially in Egypt.

But the most significant development came in the Indian Ocean with the discovery of a direct sea route from Europe to India by the Portuguese when Vasco da Gamma with the help of an Arab pilot landed at Calicut, on May 21, 1498 in Kerala. The arrival of Europeans in South India drastically changed the entire scene concerning trade, politics and control of colonies. The Portuguese met two stunned resident Tunisian merchants who spoke Genose and Castilian. Da Gamma also met Italian merchants who had reached Calicut by land route. On March 8, 1500 Portuguese Admiral Pedro Alvares Cabral came to Calicut with 13 huge ships and thousand strong crew.

Soon Cabral demanded the expulsion of all Muslim merchants, [Arabs, Persians, Indian Muslim merchants from Gujarat so on]. When the ruler Zamorin refused, Cabral seized a large and heavily laden Arab ship preparing to sail to Egypt through the Red Sea. He ordered two day heavy bombardment of Calicut destroying most ships and the port. "The Portuguese seized or sank all Muslim shipping they lay their hands on;

Muslim merchants were hung from the rigging and burned alive in view of their families ashore...Calicut's fate was just a taste of things to come. In the years that followed, similar treatment was revisited on the city and other Malabar ports... All to the strategic end of establishing a royal monopoly over trade in the Indian Ocean".

The new rulers of the Indian Ocean henceforth ordered traders of all nations to require a permit to sail waters they had freely sailed for time immemorial. "The goal was nothing less than to make the Indian Ocean a Portuguese lake. All competition would be taxed or blown out of water". [21] Soon they began to take over the spice trade in the entire Indian Ocean region. The Portuguese King Mauuel crowned himself as "Lord of Guinea, and of the Conquest, the Navigation and Commerce of Ethiopia, Arabia, Persia and India". The new masters of seas now ordered Venetian merchants to buy spices at Lisbon. Soon there was drastic reduction in the supply of spices to Cairo and Alexandria the traditional markets to which Indian traders supplied via Aden and Red Sea.

Since the Turks were also at war with major parts of Europe, this led to rise in the price of spices due to shortage of supply. All this greatly undermined the traditional Indo-Egyptian trade contacts and hence impacted on the cultural and other ties as well. The Portuguese discovered that the price of a quintal [128 lb] of pepper in Lisbon was a fraction of that paid in Alexandria for a like amount brought from the Indian Ocean by the traditional route, in Red Sea dhows and on the backs of camels. Even though the treasury of King Manuel was short of money, he enlisted the financial help from Lisbon's wealthy merchants who saw immense profits from direct spice trade with India. Vasco da Gamma again sailed to India in the middle of 1502 now with 25 ships, the ten largest containing 'much beautiful artillery, with plenty of munitions and weapons, all in great abundance.' Thirteen of the ships belonged to wealthy Portuguese merchants. Earlier he had come with three small vessels only. Six of the ships were sent to the Red Sea to put an end to Arab trade ships playing up to the Egyptian ports with spices.

On his way to Calicut Vasco intercepted an Arab ship with cargo and hajj pilgrims returning from Mecca. The rich cargo was seized and all 700 passengers were killed in sea 'until the sea is red'. The owner of the ship was the richest Arab in Calicut, a man related to the Sultan of Egypt. De Gamma proceeded to "conquer…the Indian seas and shores of Asia, killing, destroying and burning the Moors of Cairo, of Arabia and of Mecca, and other inhabitants of the same India, together with their fleet, by which for over 800 years they have controlled their trade in precious stones, pearls and spices". On reaching the Indian coast he devastated Calicut upon refusal by the Zamorin to surrender. King Manuel called the destruction of Calicut as 'inestimable damage' and he was told earlier by his spies that the India spice city Calicut was 'bigger than Lisbon'.

Not only many people including trader were killed but their ships were also burnt especially of the Arabs. In Calicut one rich Arab merchant Coja Mehmed Markar who traded throughout the Red Sea and much of East Africa and who lived in Cairo was taken prisoner by da Gamma's captain and almost beaten to death and killed. Coja became an enemy of the Portuguese like many other Muslim merchants who not only stayed in Egypt and traded with Calicut and other parts of India but mobilized others to persuade the Ottoman Turks to fight the Portuguese and put an end to their domination of the traditional trade routes in the Red Sea, Gulf and the Indian Ocean areas. Tired of deliberate policy of the Portuguese to obstruct Egypt's trade with India and the spice trade through the Red sea especially which had seriously undermined his finances, the Sultan of Egypt Qansuhah al-Gawri threatened to expel all Christians and destroy the holy places in Jerusalem if Portuguese ships went on interrupting trade between India and Egypt. The Egyptian emissary to Lisbon was a Christian priest from St Catherine's monastery on Mount Sinai.

The Portuguese King showed his imperious spirit and issued his own threat: "let the Sultan be warned that Portugal intended to do its Christian duty by entering the Red Sea, laying waste to Mecca, destroying the tomb of the 'false prophet Muhammad' and carrying away his remains". Soon King Manuel appointed Dom Francisco de Al Meida as the Viceroy with orders to plunder seize and destroy any ship-especially any Muslim ship-caught on high seas without a Portuguese passport [cartazes]. He ordered the mouth of the Red sea to be closed with a fort to stop any spices being sent to Europe by that route, and to "persuade all the people of India to put aside the fantasy that they can ever again trade with any but ourselves".

The Mauluk Sultan of Egypt and the Ottoman Sultan in Istanbul decided to respond to the formidable challenge posed by the Portuguese in the Red Sea and the Indian Ocean. The Turks with the help of the Venetian decided to build a fleet in the Gulf of Suez, Sinai port of Tor. There was a mutual interest in driving the Portuguese out of the spice trade of Indian Ocean and destroying the Portuguese 'floating fortresses. It is interesting to note that the Venetian "had at one stage thought of urging the Egyptians to dig a canal through the Suez peninsula as the easiest way to put ships into the Indian Ocean. They withdrew the idea, fearing that the Sultan would suspect them of wanting to open a route for their own trade."

By early 1507, the Egyptians, Turks and the Venetian had completed the building of twelve huge warships. Amir Hussein was made the admiral in charge and he left Tor, Sinai, with his heavily laden warships with 1500 fighting men and their weapons, as well as the best cannons transported in cargo boats across the Mediterranean to Egypt from Turkey "because the Mamluk military caste which ruled Egypt made guns designed only for defensive use on land". It took 8 months for Amir Hussein to reach Diu where Malik Ayyaz, a Russian Christian converted to Islam by the Turks, was waiting to welcome Hussein's fleet. At the same time the Zamorin of

Calicut who had also suffered immensely at the hands of the Portuguese sent 100 light vessels armed with cannons made by two Portuguese renegades. These ships were carrying food for the Egyptian naval armada at Diu. They would also give support when battle was joined.

The unprecedented Portuguese and later European challenge at the sea to two very ancient states, cultures and civilizations led to the formation of a unique strategic alliance between India and Egypt not only to checkmate the growing threat to their trade and commerce but to safeguard their interests. In this first known Asian Solidarity Alliance in the modern period—Egyptians, Turks, Kurds and Indians came together to contain the formidable Portuguese challenge at sea. The Muslim ruler of Gujarat, Mahmud [I] Begarha, [1458-1511] came to establish a vast empire from Sind to Deccan. Malik Ayaz [died in1522] a Turk, who had found employment in the court of Gujarat, was made Governor of Diu who made the Gujarati coastal city a prosperous place replacing Cambay as the great transshipment centre and mart of Gujarat. Diu under Malik Ayaz's rule had impressive fortifications. Ayaz consistently rejected Portuguese demands for a factory and trade concessions. He also controlled Sawarath, Patan, Gogha, Surat, and Rander among other areas. The Governor commanded large influence at Mahmud's court and maintained a huge military and a strong naval fleet.

His ships sailed far and wide mainly trading with Gulf, Red Sea and East Africa. His navy is said to have comprised at least 100 fustas, each one with 25 pairs of oars, one heavy cannon, and two lighter pieces. He also had larger war vessels, and many armed merchant ships. Mahmud Bergha in alliance with Qwansauh-al-Ghauri, Mamluk Sultan of Egypt, tried to check the rising power of the Portuguese in the Indian seas. The customs revenue of Egypt had been seriously affected by Portuguese attacks on ships carrying spices from India to the Red Sea. As seen before, the Egyptian Sultan sent a naval fleet, under the command of Amir Hussein, the Kurd,

Governor of Jeddah, to drive the Portuguese out of the area. The Egyptians had heavier and powerful ships with artillery. The Indian contingent, under the command of Malik Ayaz, had 34 fustas. The historic naval battle between the Portuguese, Egyptians and the Indians took place near Chaul.

The combined fleet defeated the Portuguese squadron commanded by Dom Lourenco d' Almeida, son of the Portuguese Viceroy, Francesco de Alameda, near Chaul, South of Bombay, in 1508. The flagship in which Dom Lourenco commanded sank with the rest retreating south. The Portuguese lost at least 140 men dead and many scores were taken prisoners. Malik Ayaz was supported by the Egyptians and ships from Calicut. This victory was short-lived. Soon Dom Lourenco's father Francisco de Almeida, the Portuguese Viceroy on learning about the defeat and death of this son began to plan his revenge attack on Diu and especially the Egyptian naval fleet. He also began contacting Malik Ayyaz to change sides who remained noncommittal.

The Portuguese Viceroy D. Francisco d'Almeida on 2 February 1509 reached Diu with a large naval fleet from Goa, and found the Egyptian naval fleet lined up at anchor, ordered firing mercilessly at the Egyptian ships and the "answering fire never matched this onslaught". The Portuguese ships some carrying as many as 40 guns, stood higher out of the water, so that their cannonballs hurtled and inflicted defeat on the Egyptian-Turkish fleet. The Governor of Diu Malik Ayyaz according to one source "was a passive onlooker, never firing a shot against the Portuguese attack and keeping his ships well out of range". When Admiral Amir Hussein returned to Istanbul he told the Ottoman Sultan how the naval battle at Diu had been lost, and he is reported to have said: "he was betrayed at the crucial hour by the Governor of Diu, who had been born a Christian".

The Portuguese intoxicated by their naval victory went about destroying any Muslim ships, ports, harbours, burning cities and killing captains, traders, and looting and plundering anything of value in their way of death and destruction. The Portuguese had a new naval commander as Almeida successor, Afonso de Albuquerque, who became the real founder of Estado da India. He was 'fervent in his desire to kill Muslims' and had spent a lifetime of fighting in North Africa before making his first visit at 50, to the Indian Ocean. He "dreamed of using Ethiopia as a base for destroying Mecca, and talked of bringing engineers from Madeira to work on the absurd scheme for diverting the Nile into the Red Sea and so starving Egypt into submission". Failing this his first move was to mount an attack on the powerful fortress of Aden, at the entrance of Red Sea because, "it had always been Portugal's ambition to take Aden, for then there could be a virtual blockade against any Muslim ship trying to carry spices on to Egypt". The attack was a complete failure and the Portuguese suffered heavy losses and the only satisfaction they had was in setting fire to all Arab merchant ships in the Aden harbour and in collecting reports that the Egyptians and Turks had not yet started building another naval fleet at Suez.

According to other sources Malik Ayyaz continued to resist the Portuguese demands for a fort at Diu during his lifetime. Mahmud Begarha died on November 23, 1511 The Portuguese position strategically was weak because with no base nearer than Goa or Hormouz in the Gulf, they were unable to lie off Diu for long in the face of ships fron Malik Ayaz's fleet. Unable to take Diu, the Portuguese continued to raid, sack and burn Surat, Rander, Gogha, Mangrol, Somnath, Bassein and many other Gujarati ports thereby crippling trade with the Gulf and the Red Sea. Subsequently the Portuguese were granted a site for a factory at Diu by Bahadur Shah. This was mainly to stop Portuguese seizures of Gujarati ships trading with the Gulf and Red Sea including ships carrying Hajjes on pilgrimage to Mecca.

The Gujarati ruler in order to ward off the growing threat from the Mughal ruler Humayun gave the Portuguese permission to build a fort at Diu in return for their help against the Mughals. The Portuguese even after this concession continued to prohibit Indian trade with the Red Sea. In December 1534 and October 1535, Mahmud Bergha's successor Bahadur Shah signed a peace treaty with the Portuguese Governor Nuno da Cunha whereby the Portuguese were given the port of Bassein and its nearby lands and permission to build a fort in Diu. All Indian ships bound for Red Sea from Gujarat were to pass through Bassein and also return through this port under Portuguese control.

The Portuguese who had seen the naval power of the Gujarati rulers now imposed a complete ban on building of warships, nor could they use they already had. Ultimately the Portuguese killed Bahadur Shah treacherously mainly because he was very much interested in sea trade and building a powerful navy. According to one writer: "He travelled frequently by sea, and pursued an active policy go building ships for both commercial and military purposes. These ships were admired by the Portuguese themselves, and were apparently as large in number of oars as contemporary Turkish vessels Bahadur Shah had a fleet of 160 sail at his death in 1537".

He had also been in continuous touch with the Ottoman Sultan "with the object of driving the Portuguese out, not only from Diu but also from India and the Red Sea". The Ottoman Sultan more than once sent ships and artillery of the Ottoman naval fleet to help the Gujarati ruler Bahadur Shah and this was quite effective. After they took over Constantinople in 1453, the Ottomans lost naval supremacy in the Mediterranean in 1571, when they were defeated at Lepanto. The Europeans began to dominate trade in the Indian Ocean and Arab *Mudarabah* or speculative trade declined, as the former came to dominate the territories as well.

The Ottoman Sultans found they were unable to control the growing Portuguese take over of vital trading areas in India, Gulf, Red Sea and even in the Mediterranean areas (Ports). At this stage it is necessary to briefly assess the

Ottoman Empire's position which was under mounting challenge from the European powers. After they took over Constantinople in 1453 and renamed it as Istanbul, the Ottoman's were undisputed naval power in the Mediterranean. They had achieved unprecedented growth mainly due to their skill in facilitating the transport of the products from the East after taking over the traditional silk routes in Central and West Asia, such as cotton, spices, silk and agricultural produce to Europe in exchange for weapons, ships and manufactured goods. The unprecedented and truly revolutionary geographical discoveries by the Portuguese, Spaniards, Dutch, French, British and others and the direct sea route especially to India led to importation of gold and silver from the new colonies and the almost takeover of Orient trade adversely affecting the Ottomans.

Soon the Ottomans were to suffer a terrible defeat in 1571 at the hands of Italians when they were defeated in a naval battle at Lepanto in East Mediterranean. This was seen as a "watershed in the history of East-West Relations". According to one writer: "Once the Ottomans were stopped at Leponto, the continued long-term autonomy of the Western Mediterranean would never again be in doubt. Leponto ensured that the growing Atlantic trade with the Americas would continue as Europeans not only became enticed by the New World treasure but found the Ottoman Empire increasingly irrelevant to their growing commercial interests in the Orient via routes around the Horn of Africa." Not only European control and hegemony over the Eastern Mediterranean was restored but the with the rise of the Europeans, the Arab-Islamic lakes as the Indian Ocean, Gulf, and Red Sea were known, came to be dominated first by the Portuguese, then by the Dutch, French and soon the British became undisputed masters over the area.

The secret was due the fact that the Europeans possessed large number of sophisticated ships with powerful guns than the Ottomans. This also led to the shift in focus from the

Mediterranean Sea to the Indian Ocean and the Atlantic. Clearly this marked a new era in which powerful guns, cannons with ships using sophisticated technology proved to be decisive and a real strategic shift. The Ottoman advantage with cavalry was now in changed circumstances not much of an asset compared to ships owned by small states like Portugal or Venice. The Ottomans saw rapid drying of capital with the highly lucrative maritime trade carried by the Europeans with India and the East in general. In 1580 Emir Mehmet ibn Emir es Su'udi wrote: "*The Europeans have discovered the secret of Oceanic travel. They are Lords of the new world and of the gates to India...The people of Islam are without the latest information in the science of geography and do not understand the menace of the capture of the sea trade by the Europeans*". [22]

These momentous developments pioneered at sea by the Europeans sent the crucial spice trade shipping from Egyptian/Arab and Persian merchants as the price of spices went up due to war, scarcity of supplies and dislocation of the regular shipping between Malabar, Gulf and the Red Sea. Along with the Egyptian merchants, the Red Sea route was also busy with Persian traders from the Gulf and also the seafaring Omani Arabs. "After a few disrupted decades as the shock of the early Portuguese conquests reverberated back down the spice routes, Alexandria and Venice staged a comeback. In the 1560s, there were so many spices for sale at Alexandria that a Portuguese spy suggested that a Portuguese should abandon the Cape route altogether and ship their spices via the Levant in order to cut costs.

Such great was the flow of illicit spices through the Portuguese blockade that there was speculation that the Portuguese viceroy was in tacit revolt against the King". [23] The religious bigotry and excessive violence earned the Portuguese many enemies. Other Europeans followed the Portuguese in their quest for spices, colonies, slaves and wealth. But Egypt regained its place as the prime intermediary between Europe, India and the Far East as prime supplier of spice. "By unknown means and ferried by unknown hands... spices arrived...in the souks of Cairo and Alexandria and thence to the markets of Europe like so much cosmic driftwood. Arab dhows conveyed them across the Indian Ocean to the Persian Gulf or the Red Sea. At any one of a number of ancient ports-Basra, Jeddah, Muscat or Aquaba- the spices were transferred onto one of the huge caravans that fanned out across the deserts to the markets of Arabia and on to Alexandria and the Levant". [24]

Since Napoleon's invasion of Egypt in 1798, Britain took keen interest in the West Asian region as it was then establishing its grip over India and feared a French invasion by way of Egypt. It must be pointed out here that the south Indian ruler of Mysore, Tipu Sultan looked for French help against the British during the latter part of 18th century. After defeating Tipu in 1799 the British with the help of Indians took over much of the Arab world. In 1839, the British occupied Aden in Yemen and subsequently in 1882 they brought Egypt under their control basically to protect the communication lines between London and India.

British desire to strengthen her grip over India was facilitated by her control over Egypt. [25] The Suez Canal which is in Egyptian territory and opened for traffic in 1869 was an important link in the British Communication/transport lines. The Canal since then has proved to be a vital link between India and Egypt, although the British tried to reduce the relations between two ancient civilizations.

Section III

Even since Haider Ali became the *de facto* ruler of Mysore between 1761-1782 with control over a large chunk of South India, the British perceived him as a mortal enemy and relations had been strained. Under his son Tipu Sultan they reached a nadir primarily due to determined British efforts to isolate him and bring about his downfall. The British challenge to Haider Ali and Tipu Sultan which the former saw as a great hindrance to their interests in India and neighbouring areas was one of the most formidable an Indian ruler had to face in the second half of 18th century, and in self-defence both the Indian rulers had been compelled to take a series of bold measures. In the Gulf region European rivalry was common, especially British attempts to bring it under its control. It is pertinent to note that the French had already conceded defeat to the British and were confined to few pockets in insignificant areas.

Having curtailed the trade and profits of the Arabs especially those belonging to the Omanis they could easily be manipulated and eventually subjugated by the British. The Ottoman Sultan due to determined attempts by the Russian Czars and mounting challenges from the Europeans had come to acknowledge British supremacy in the Gulf region in numerous ways. The Persians were busy fighting amongst themselves while it was easy for the British to foment trouble for the Afghan rulers in view of the tribal factor in Afghan politics. From all this, it is abundantly clear that the room to manoeuvre for Tipu Sultan internationally was extremely limited given the British naval supremacy and superior technology which enabled them to have the global reach and paramountacy. [26]

The British challenge to Tipu was formidable, it prompted him to respond with equally forcible, bold and prompt measures to tackle it. Most remarkable was his attempt to seek friendship with the Ottoman Sultan, Oman, France, Persia, Afghanistan, and other Gulf countries, who were also, equally at the same time under intense pressure and vulnerable to British power. Despite his forced involvement in British inspired wars and the huge burden of war reparations, whenever his economic and political position improved, Tipu Sultan, sent embassies abroad as he strongly believed in close cooperation with the Ottoman Sultan, Oman and other Gulf countries in order to contain the formidable threat posed by the

British to his regime. Towards this end, he began to offer numerous concessions in order to induce them to support him. To the Ruler of Oman, Tipu sent a diplomatic mission headed by Mir Abdul Rahman and Mir Iyantullah.

They were accompanied by Mirza Karim Beg Tabrizi the Persian envoy to Mysore. Like on previous such missions, Tipu Sultan sent valuable gifts to the Ruler of Muscat. These included jewels, elephants, khillats, sandalwood, ivory, pepper and cardamoms. It must be mentioned that Haider Ali had also maintained close ties with the Ruler of Muscat and also had an establishment at Muscat but this special arrangement lapsed as was customary with his death in 1782. Tipu's intense diplomatic activity with Oman which had essentially political, economic and military consideration only showed his desire to keep up contacts with influential and powerful rulers but also to continuously seek allies in his ceaseless quest for partners to withstand the British challenge.

Thus, the guiding principles of Tipu's diplomacy were to neutralize his enemies and maintain the integrity of his Kingdom and to contain British imperialism as also their expansionism. It is significant to note, that the French also maintained close ties with the Ruler of Oman but Tipu's and the Omani ruler's relations with the French appear to have been complementary but independent. With France plunged into turmoil and instability whatever little hope Tipu Sultan had from France were dashed. This explains his decision to send a high level delegation to the Ottoman Caliph with three goals: (a) to gain recognition as an independent monarch of Mysore; (b) to seek military assistance; and (c) to explore the possibility of establishing close economic and trade relations. [27]

At this stage it is necessary to briefly assess the Ottoman Empire's position which was under mounting challenge from the European powers. After they took over Constantinople in 1453 the Ottoman's were undisputed naval powers in the Mediterranean. They had achieved unprecedented growth mainly due to their skill in facilitating the transport of the products from the East such as cotton, spices, silk and agricultural produce to Europe in exchange for weapons, ships and manufactured goods. The geographical discoveries by the Portuguese, Spaniards, Dutch, French, British and others and the direct sea route especially to India led to importation of gold and silver from the new colonies and takeover of orient trade adversely affecting the Ottomans. Soon the Ottomans were to suffer a terrible defeat in 1571 at the hands Italians when they were defeated in a naval battle at Lepanto. This was seen as a " watershed in the history of East-West Relations."

According to one writer: "Once the Ottomans were stopped at Leponto, the continued long-term autonomy of the Western Mediterranean would never again be in doubt. Leponto ensured that the growing Atlantic trade with the Americas would continue as Europeans not only became enticed by the New World treasure but found the Ottoman Empire increasingly irrelevant to their growing commercial interests in the orient via routes around the Horn of Africa." Not only European control and hegemony over the Eastern Mediterranean was restored but the with the rise of the Europeans, the Arab-Islamic lake as the Indian Ocean was known, came to be dominated first by the Portuguese, then by the Dutch, French and soon the British became undisputed masters over the area.

The secret was due the fact that the Europeans possessed large number of sophisticated ships with powerful guns than the Ottomans. This also led to the shift in focus from the Mediterranean Sea to the Indian Ocean and the Atlantic. Clearly this marked a new era in which powerful guns, cannons and ships proved to be decisive and a real strategic sense. Ottoman advantage with cavalry was not much of an asset compared to ships owned by small states like Portugal or Venice. The Ottomans saw rapid drying of capital with the highly lucrative maritime trade carried by the Europeans with India and the east in general. Bernard Lewis quotes from Umar

Talib, one of the Turkish elite, who complained in 1625 that: "The Europeans have become acquainted with the whole world, sending their ships everywhere and seizing the harbours. The goods from India, Sind and China previously came to Suez and were distributed by the Muslims to the whole world. Now, however, these goods are transported by the Portuguese, the Dutch and the English to the Frankish countries, from whence they distribute them to the world. The goods that they don't need, they bring to Istanbul and the Islamic countries selling them at five times their value, thus reaping great profit. For the reason both gold and silver have become scarce in Islamic countries". [28]

But Tipu Sultan still perceived the Ottoman Empire as strong and hence thought of seeking assistance. As early as 1784 Tipu had sent an exploratory mission to the Sublime Porte to find out whether an Embassy there would be productive. When he was told about the efficacy of having a mission at the Porte, Tipu decided to send a large mission consisting of 900 people on November 17, 1785. The leader of the delegation was Ghulam Ali Khan and included Nurullah Khan, Lutf Ali Khan and Jaffar Khan among others. The delegation after a long and difficult sea and land journey via Muscat, Bushier, Basra, Baghdad and other places reached Constantinople on September 25, 1787. It was only on November 5, 1787 the Ottoman Sultan Salim-III received Tipu's emissaries with honour and decorated them.

The Sultan accorded permission to Tipu to assume the title of an independent monarch and the right to strike coins and to have the Khutbha read in his name. The envoys were also given for Tipu friendly letters, Khillats, a sword and a shield studded with precious stones by the caliph and his Grand Wazir. With this, one of the major objectives of the mission had been accomplished. [29] Tipu also sought military assistance from the Ottoman Caliph to put an end to the British menace in India. In order to impress upon the Ottoman Sultan the gravity of the situation and urgency of his demand Tipu sought to arouse the religious sentiments of the Caliph by highlighting to him the subversive and deceitful manner in which the British had become overlords of large parts of territories which actually belonged to the Mughals and other Indian rulers.

More significantly in order to make sure his mission would succeed, Tipu also impressed upon the Ottoman Sultan that the British were humiliating the Muslims in India by forcibly converting them to Christianity and changing the mosques to Churches. The Ottoman Sultan found it easy to recognize as an independent King but saw his request for military assistance hard to entertain, because he himself was preoccupied with defending his possessions under challenge from the Russians, Austrians and others. He politely but firmly turned down Tipu's request for a body of Turkish soldiers to be sent to Mysore to fight against the British. Actually Tipu wanted the Ottoman Sultan to send him a body of troops whose expenses would be borne by him and they would be sent back to the Porte at his expense whenever they would be required by the Caliph. In the end, the Sultan declined to provide any tangible military help to Tipu.

It must be repeated that the Ottoman Sultan facing outside threats could not expect help from France due to the turmoil there leading to the revolution. In fact, Britain was busy mediating peace between Turkey and her enemies- Russia and Austria. The Ottoman Sultan therefore, was in no mood to help Tipu and lose British friendship. [30] Tipu had also urged the members of the delegation to secure trade privileges with the Ottoman Empire on a reciprocal basis; he wanted facilities in Basra in exchange for Mangalore. He also wanted Turkey to help him in establishing various factories in Mysore and by sending technicians specialized in the art of making muskets, guns, glass, chinaware and other military hardware or spares and in return Tipu would send workers required by the Ottoman Sultan. The delegation carried large quantities of goods produced in Mysore with them to be sold at various ports of call so that wide publicity is given to the products and hence exports boosted.

The mission costed Tipu more than 20 lakh of rupees and out of about 900 men only a handful returned to Calicut on 29 December 1789. [31] Tipu also wanted the Ottoman Caliph to mediate in settling his differences with the British. In early 1799 Caliph Salim III addressed a letter to Tipu describing the French invasion of Egypt and their plan to conquer Arabia, divide it into republics and extirpate Islam. He also wrote that the French also wanted to conquer India and deprive its people of their religion, life and property. He advised Tipu to refrain from any hostile activities against the English at French instigation and offered to adjust satisfactorily any cause of complaint that he might have against them. [32]

Although the British had succeeded in frustrating Tipu's attempt to get recognition from the Mughul Emperor in Delhi despite their influential presence and machinations at the Ottoman court, Tipu did succeed in gaining recognition for his independent status as a King. Even though the British were quite concerned for a variety of reasons at the recognition of Tipu, but their rapidly growing influence in India and in the vast Indian Ocean region gave them comfort and confidence about ultimately their ability to encircle and crush Tipu. It must be mentioned that the British were apprehensive of Tipu's growing contacts with the Muslim rulers both in India and abroad. His extensive links with Afghanistan, Persia, Oman, Ottoman Empire and other smaller states, his strategy aimed at intensifying political and economic cooperation particularly setting up of factories, state to state trade ignoring the Europeans, establishing military cooperation all were considered too dangerous and revolutionary ideas which if implemented could undermine their position in the area and ultimately dash their hopes of establishing an empire where the Sun would never sets.

Moreover the Nizam of Hyderabad was equally disturbed at Tipu's recognition by Turkey which was a *coup de grace*.

Since the Ottoman Sultan still enjoyed great prestige as the most dominant Muslim power relegating the Mughul Emperor to the background, the Nizam felt out manoeuvred as he could no longer claim to be legally superior because "the Sultan of Mysore had a better title to his Kingdom than the Viceroy of the Deccan to his Viceroyalty". No wonder the Nizam wanted the British to wipe out Tipu for which he provided all assistance. Many of Tipu's enemies were also concerned at Tipu's not inconsiderable achievements at Constantinople and other places which brought name and fame from abroad and ended his isolation throwing his enemies in confusion. The British correctly analyzed Tipu's comfortable and secure position at home which propelled him to seek outside recognition and success; hence they did everything to pull him down from within using his enemies and their manipulative skills. [33]

Tipu's ambassadors on their way to Turkey stayed in Oman for about three months, from early April to late June 1786 and a journal was kept of their dealings there. The secretary credited with having written the Persian journal was Khwaja Abdul Qadir. Keeping in view the crucial role-played by the Gulf region from all dimensions, which would enable Tipu Sultan to better understand the prevailing conditions there because of its direct bearing on his Kingdom. The delegation carried large quantities of goods produced in Mysore with them to be sold at various ports of call so that wider publicity was given to the products and hence exports boosted. Tipu Sultan encouraged Omani, Arab, Persian and Armenian merchants among others to come and settle in Mysore and gave them special privileges as they were seen as successful businessmen.

Even though no treaty resulted between Mysore and Oman but an extensive report on Muscati trade and opportunities was sent back to Mysore by Tipu's Ambassadors to Turkey. One of the crucial reasons why Mysore was prosperous was due to the state monopoly of trade. Tipu Sultan naturally placed severe restrictions on European trading companies especially the English. Even the French could not trade freely in Mysore. The British in order to circumvent Tipu's restrictions, used to send other merchants disguised as Muscati traders to make cheaper purchases from Mysore. Through his alert and vigilant intelligence, Tipu Sultan learnt about British cheating and he promptly instructed that only genuine merchants who had valid passports or authorized certificates from his officials in Muscat could engage in trade at Mysore. Tipu urged foreign rulers especially the Ottoman Sultan and the Ruler of Oman, to send him skilled people and technicians who would assist his government in the setting up of modern industries.

This was possible due to his wide knowledge of the advanced countries in the West, extensive foreign trading contacts and familiarity with foreign goods apart from foreign languages. Thousands of foreign skilled workers were brought in and among them Turks, Arabs, (especially Omani) Persians, Afghans were also present. They not only brought their technical skills but by their interaction with locals a new vision of modern world was projected. According to one writer, "No other sovereign in Indian history had given such an impetus to industrial production with foreign collaboration". [34]

Thus, he undertook the role of an international trader, manufacturer, banker and moneychanger. In most of these areas, Tipu was close to Mohammed Ali, the founder of modern Egypt. Tipu's tremendous interest in international trade and other foreign economic matters in the midst of battles, challenges from the British and other threats, reveals his far sightedness and realization that promotion of commerce and industry was the true strength of his Kingdom. According to one writer, "If Tipu Sultan had been allowed to rule Mysore peacefully for a few more decades, there is little doubt that he would have brought about an economic revolution of the first magnitude. The seeds which he sowed did however bear fruit after his death and the state of Mysore, long before the era of planning, was in the vanguard of industrial progress and public welfare in India." It was due to Tipu's efforts that Mysore which is now called Karnataka has become India's leading silk producing state.

Silk industry was developed in Mysore by obtaining silk worms from Muscat and by encouraging the plantation of mulberry trees. It was also due to Tipu's efforts that a huge quantity of sandalwood was sold in the Omani markets. Tipu Sultan gave all the incentives to grow sandalwood and saw to it that the wood and oil were exported to foreign countries especially to Oman where there was large demand. Mysore owes an immense debt of gratitude to Tipu Sultan to this day, sandal wood and oil is exported to Oman and other parts of the Gulf region. Tipu's foreign economic diplomacy, which primarily aimed at increasing My sore's exports through state trading even though fell short of his hopes, but was largely successful in trade with Muscat due to his pragmatic plans.

This has to be considered Tipu Sultan's most significant commercial success. The British viewed Tipu Sultan as a dangerous competitor and their goal was to put an end to all his trading activities and imaginative enterprises. Tipu's factories and Agency at Muscat that was intended to improve trade between the two states was closed down after his death in May 1799. [35] The ruler of Muscat did not endear himself to the English by his friendly dealings with Tipu Sultan. After Tipu's defeat, the British ordered the Imam of Oman to stop the French and Dutch ships from trading to and from Muscat, as this was not only a threat to their own trade but in fact they were actually at war with the British during this entire period.

Tipu Sultan's relations with Oman charted new and unprecedented course except for Haider Ali's limited initiative in this field. His embassies/missions to Oman and other Gulf countries not only gave him legitimacy to his rule (which was denied by his neighbouring Indian rulers and the British, but with other countries even though he could not get the help he anticipated) but had flourishing trade with them like Muscat, Aden, Persia, Afghanistan. These were undoubtedly bold and courageous initiatives, basically a response to the massive challenge from the British, taken by a shrewd and ambitious ruler who had a clear global vision. Undoubtedly, Tipu's shrewd diplomatic initiatives in the Gulf region especially his ties with Oman were bold, imaginative and he was largely successful. Unfortunately, his skilful diplomacy pushed the British to redouble their efforts to neutralize Tipu's diplomatic initiatives, friendships and achievements.

The British due to their worldwide contacts and modern means of transport and communication net works were able to reach out to places where Tipu Sultan intended to send his envoys, much faster and take effective and tangible steps to neutralize in advance his initiatives. Since the other Europeans including the French, had already been elbowed out by the English effectively from the Gulf region, it was far easier for them to frustrate Tipu's energetic diplomatic moves. The room to manoeuvre for Tipu Sultan was extremely limited as the British concentrated all their power, skills and resources to bring about his downfall. It must be mentioned that Tipu Sultan was ready for a conditional compromise or reconciliation with the British which would allow him to rule as an independent ruler and not as a subordinate ruler while other Indian rulers had submitted meekly to the British; but all his [Tipu's] overtures were spurned by the British and he was repeatedly rebuffed because they considered him an adversary and his ideas too dangerous and hence they decided to eliminate him.

It must be recalled that since Napoleon's invasion of Egypt in 1798 Britain took keen interest in the entire West Asian region as it was then establishing its grip over India and feared a French invasion by way of Egypt. After defeating Tipu, the British with the help of Indians soldiers and resources took over much of the Arab world. In 1839, the British occupied Aden in Yemen and subsequently in 1882 they brought Egypt [little earlier Sudan] under their control basically to protect the communication lines between London and India. British desire to strengthen her grip over India was facilitated by her control over Egypt. The Suez Canal which is in Egyptian territory and opened for traffic in 1869 was an important link in the British Communication/transport lines. The Canal since then has proved to be a vital link between India and Egypt, although the British tried to reduce the relations between the two ancient civilizations. [36]

To sum up, in the final analysis Tipu Sultan should be seen as India's first serious freedom fighter who clearly saw British evil intentions of subjugating India. It's unfortunate that other Indian rulers instead of supporting his efforts opposed him and became collaborators with the British. It must also be mentioned that Tipu's historical stature is guaranteed by two great qualities that he showed through his state craft: his ability to take innumerable diplomatic initiatives that transcend the force of circumstance and his ability/willingness to take enormous risk even in the face of setbacks and formidable forces. In the ultimate analysis, all of Tipu Sultan's intricate, complex international manoeuvring, risks, initiatives, friendships, and negotiations were primarily aimed at upliftment, prosperity, providing security and improving the life of the people, and making Mysore a truly developed state like Britain or France were at that time.

The British dominated India fully only in the 19th century, Holland had pockets of influence in South East Asian islands, European domination in West Asia and North Africa is mainly after First World War and China was never colonized like India. Despite all the attempts made by the Europeans to dominate ancient cultures and civilizations and stunt their development, Egypt and India are once again on the road to all round progress and are showing their vibrancy in all fields. The ancient civilizations like Egypt, India, Iran, China and others are regaining the development initiative in their hands much to the discomfort of the West. Asian economies are once again booming and the shift in power towards Asia is irreversible.

End Notes

1. Childe, *The Most Ancient East,* p. 208, cited in Sudhansu Kumar Ray, *Prehistoric India and Ancient Egypt* (New Delhi: Cambridge Book and Stationary Store, 1956) p. 39.
2. Shereen Ratnagar, *Encounters: The Westerly Trade of the Harappan Civilization* (London : OUP, 1980).
3. Jack Turner, *The History of a Temptation* [New York : Vintage Books, 2005], p. 204.
4. A. Murray, *The Splendour that was Egypt* (New Delhi: Cambridge Book and Stationary Store, 1956), p. xxi.
5. Maqbul Ahmad, *Indo-Arab Relations: An Account of India's Relations with the Arab World from Ancient up to Modern Times* (New Delhi : ICCR, 1969); Turner, n. 3, pp. 238-239.
6. Ray n.1, pp. 7-12; Shereen Ratnagar, *Understanding Harappa Civilization in the Greater Indus Valley* (New Delhi: Tulika, 2001).
7. Mohammed Hasan el Zayyat, *India and Egypt: Modern Relations between two Ancient Nations* (New Delhi: ICCR, 1984) p. 12; Turner, n. 3, p.147; Turner, n. 3, p. 147.
8. See also Abdullah el Madani, *Arabian Gulf during the British Era: The Impact of India,* in N.N. Vohra (ed.), History, Culture and Society in India and West Asia [New Delhi: Shipra, IIC, 2003] p. 109; Turner, n.3, p. 62.
9. Saryu Doshi, Influences and Interactions, in *India and Egypt: Influences and Interactions* (New Delhi: Marg Publications, ICCR, 1993) p. xiii; and Sir George Watt, *The Commercial Products of India* (London: 1908); Turner, n. 3, pp. 63-64.
10. Zayyat, n. 4, p. 14.
11. Ray, n. 1, p. 38; Turner, n. 3, pp. 238-239.
12. Ibid, p. 11 and 13; S. Maqbul Ahmad, *India and the Neighbouring Territories* (Leiden: 1960); Turner, n. 3, p. 82.
13. S.M. cl Mansouri, *Art and Culture of India and Egypt* [Calcutta: K.L. Mukhopadhyay, 1959], p. 46.
14. Ibid. p. 48; M. A. Saleem Khan, *Early Muslim Perception of India and Hinduism* (New Delhi: South Asian Publishers, 1997), Turner, n. 3, p. 66.
15. Ibid, p. 49; N.A. Faruqi, *Early Muslim Historiography: A Study of Early Transmitters of Arab History from the Rise of Islam to the end of Umayyad Period, 612-750* (Delhi: 1979), Turner, pp. 96-97.

16. M.K. Dhavalikar, Early Contacts, in Doshi, n. 4, p. 50. See also S. Maqbul Ahmad, *Indo-Arab Relations* (Bombay: Popular Prakashan, 1969).Turner, n., p. 104.
17. K.N. Chaudhuri, *Trade and Civilization in the Indian Ocean: An Economic History from the Rise of Islam to 1750* (New Delhi: Munshiram Manoharlal Publishers, 1985) p. 59.
18. Doshi, n. 4, p. xiv; see also Sahar Abdel Aziz Salem, *Commerce and One Faith*, in Doshi, n. 4, p. 96.
19. Salem Khan, n. 8, p. 102; Tara Chand, *Influences of Islam on Indian Culture* (Allahabad: The Indian Press, 1965); Turner, n. 3, pp. 180-181.
20. Andre Wink, *Al Hind: The Making of the Indo-Islamic World*, Vol. I, (New Delhi: OUP, 1999).
21. Chaudhuri, n.11, p. 59-60; Turner, n. 3, pp. 20.
22. V.D. Hanson, *Carnage and Culture*, [New York: Anchor Books, 2002] pp. 265-269; Quoted from Bernard Lewis, *Some Reflections on the Decline of the Ottoman Empire*, Studies Islamica, 9, 1959, p. 118 ; A.K. Pasha, *India and West Asia: Continuity and Change*, [Delhi : Gyan Sagar, 1999], pp. 7-15; Ibid., p. 67; See also Mawlana Syed Sulaiman Nadwi, *Indo-Arab Relations: An English Rendering* (Hyderabad: The Institute of Indo-Middle East Cultural Studies, 1962); Turner, n. 3, pp.22, 42, 45-47; *National Herald* (Delhi), 28th September 1992.
23. Riyaz Punjabi and A.K. Pasha (ed.), *India and the Islamic World* (New Delhi: Radiant Publishers, 1998) p. 97; M.S. Agwani, *India and the Arab World*, in B.R. Nanda (ed.), *Indian Foreign Policy: The Nehru Years* (New Delhi: 1976), pp. 72-73.
24. A.K. Pasha, "Indo-Egyptian Cultural Relations: Retrospect and Prospects", in Zohurul Bari, Ed, Modern Egypt: Culture, Religion and Politics, (New Delhi: Shipra Publications, 2003) p. 199; see also Saryu Doshi (ed.); India and Egypt: Influences and Interactions (New Delhi: Garg Publications, ICCR, 1993); A.K. Pasha, "Tipu and the Ottoman Empire", in B. Sheik Ali (ed.), Tipu Sultan: A Great Martyr (Bangalore: Prasaranga, Bangalore University, 1993) pp. 219-232; Mohibul Hassan, History of Tipu Sultan (Delhi: Aakar Books, 2005), pp. 128-138.
25. A.K. Pasha, "Tipu Sultan's Relations with the Ottoman Empire" Détente, [New Delhi], Vol. X, Nos. 4 and 5, January-April, 1992, pp. 6-11; I.H. Qureshi, "The purpose of Tipu Sultan's Embassy to Constantinople", Journal of India History, Vol. 24,

1945, pp. 77-85.

26. Quoted from Bernard "Lewis, "Some reflections on the decline of the Ottoman Empire", Studies Islamica, No. 9, 1959, p. 118; see also K.N. Chandhari, Trade and Civilization in the Indian Ocean: An Economic History from the Rise of Islam to 1750 {Cambridge: 1985); and The Trading World of Asia and the English East India Company 1600-1760 (Cambridge: 1987); Patricia Rico, Oman and Muscat: An early Modern History (London: Croom Helm, 1986).
27. Virendra Verma, "Tipu Sultan's embassies to Constantinople and Kabul," Journal of Historical Research, Vol. XVI, No. 1, August 15, 1973, pp. 51-56; Mohibul Hassan ed, Waqai-I, Manzil-i.Rum-Tipu Sultan's Mission to Constantinople (Delhi: Aakar Books, 2005), pp. ix-xiii; pp. 1-4, pp. 61-63; A.K. Pasha, (ed.), Perspectives on India and the Gulf States (New Delhi: Detente Publications, 1999) pp. 1-23 and pp. 210-211; Azmi Ozan, Pan-Islamism: Indian Muslims, the Ottomans and Britain, 1877-1924 [Leiden: E.J. Brill, 1997], pp. 11-12.
28. Iqbal Hussein, "The Diplomatic Vision of Tipu Sultan: Briefs for embassies to Turkey and France, 1785-86" (Translation" in Irfan Habib (ed.) State and Diplomacy under Tipu Sultan Documents and Essays (New Delhi: Tulika Books, 2001) pp. 19-65. See also Khaldoun Hasan al Naqueeb, State and society in the Gulf and Arab Peninsula: A Different Perspective (London: Routledge, 1990), pp. 31-42; A.K. Pasha, India and West Asia: Continuity and Change, (Delhi: Gyan Sagar, 1999) pp. 1-15. I. Hussein Qureshi, "Tipu Sultan's Embassy to Constantinople, 1787" in Irfan Habib (ed.), Resistance and Modernization under Haidar Ali and Tipu Sultan (New Delhi: Tulika, 1999) pp.69-78.
29. Pasha, n.1, p. 229, see also Aniruddha Roy, (ed.); Tipu Sultan and his Age: A Collection of Seminar Papers (Kolkata: The Asiatic Society, 2002); A.K. Pasha, Tipu Sultan Diplomacy in the Gulf Region, GSP, Working Paper No. 10, CWAAS, SIS, JNU, 1997.
30. Pasha, n. 2, p. 9; see also K.M. Pannikar, Asia and Western Domination (London: Unwin and Allen, 1953) and Malabar and the Dutch (Bombay: 1931); M. Redha Ehacker, Trade and Empire in Muscat and Zanzibar; Roots of British Domination (London: Routledge, 1992) pp. 34-35.
31. Sheik Ali, History of Tipu Sultan (New Delhi: NBT, 1972) and

Tipu Sultan : A Study in Diplomacy and Confrontation [Mysore: Rao and Raghavan, 1982); see also A.K. Pasha, (ed.); India and Oman: History, State, Economy and Foreign Policy (Delhi: Gyan Sagar, 1999), pp. 1-21; see also A.K. Pasha "South India and the Gulf: Trade and Diplomacy during the late 18th Century", in N.N. Vohra, (ed.), History, Culture and Society in India and West Asia (New Delhi: Shipra, 2003), pp. 237-249. See also Akhtarul Wasey "Turkey and Evolution of Indian Culture, "Islam and Modern Age", Vol. XXXIII, No. 4, November, 2002. pp. 87-94; See also R.L. Shukla, Britain, India and the Turkish Empire, 1853-1882, (New Delhi: People's Publishing House, 1973), B.R. Nanda, Gandhi: Pan Islamism, Imperialism and Nationalism in India (New Delhi: Oxford University Press, 2002); Najma Heptullah, Indo-West Asian Relations: The Nehru Era (New Delhi: Allied Publishers, 1991); A.K. Pasha, "Nehru and the Crises in West Asia", *Detente*, Vol. IX, No. 1, May-June 1990, pp. 4-9; Prithvi Ram Mudiam, India and the Middle East (London: British Academic Press, 1994); and Saad Bin Zia, Turkish Freedom Movement and the Role of Al Hillal of Maulana Azad (1912-14) M. Phil. dissertation (CWAAS, SIS, JNU, New Delhi, 2005).

32. See also Aniruddha Roy, (ed.), *Tipu Sultan and his Age: A Collection of Seminar Papers* (Kolkata: The Asiatic Society, 2002); A.K. Pasha, "Tipu Sultan Diplomacy in the Gulf Region", Gulf Studies Programme, Working Paper No. 10, CWAAS, SIS, JNU, New Delhi, February 1997; "Tipu Sultan's Relations with the Ottoman Empire", *Detente*, Vol. 4 and 5, January-April 1992, pp.6-11; see also Wrike Freitag and William G. Clarence Smith (ed.), Hadhrami Traders, Scholars and Statesmen in the Indian Ocean, 1750's-1960's (Leiden: E.J. Brill, 1997); V.D. Hanson, Carnage and Culture, [New York: Anchor Books, 2002], pp. 265-269; Richard Hall, *Empires of the Monsoon: A History of the Indian Ocean and its Invaders,* [London: Harper Collins,1998], pp. 195-224; B.R. Nanda, Gandhi : Pan Islamism, Imperialism and Nationalism in India (New Delhi: Oxford University Press, 2002); V.D. Hanson, Carnage and Culture [New York: Anchor Books, 2002], pp. 267-269; Richard Hall, Empires of the Monsoons: A History of the Indian Ocean and its Invaders [London: Harper Collins, 1998]; Allen Calvin, *Sayyids, Shets and Sultans: Politics and Trade in*

Masqat under the Al Abu Said 1785-1914, Ph.D. Thesis University of Washington, (Seattle), 1978; and Pamela Nightingale, Trade and Empire in Western India 1784-1806 (Cambridge: CUP, 1970); Denys Lombard, Jean Aubin, (eds.), Asian Merchants and Businessmen in the Indian Ocean and the China Sea, [New Delhi: OUP, 2000]; John Jeay, The Spice Route: A History, [London: John Murray, 2005]; Martin, *Dispatches, Minutes Correspondence of Wellesley,* Vol. 1, pp. 307-308, cited in Ibid, p. 55; *Forrest,* No.7, p. 244; Sultan, Muhammad Al Qasimi, *The Myth of Arab Piracy in the Gulf* (London: 1988), pp. 22-28; A.K. Pasha, "Tipu Sultan and Saddam Hussein: Regime Change-History Repeats Itself", paper presented in a National Seminar on *Contemporary Oman and Emerging Indo-Omani Relations,* 25-26 October, 2005, organized by Gulf Studies Programme, Centre for West Asia and African Studies, School of International Studies, Jawaharlal Nehru University, New Delhi; see the text of Treaty of Friendship and Culture Agreement in A.K. Pasha, India and Turkey: Past and Emerging Relations [Delhi: Academic Excellence, 2006] pp. 159-161; see also Mushirul Hasan and Margaret Pearson, (ed.), Regionalizing Pan Islamism; Documents on the Khilafat Movement (New Delhi, Manohar, 2005); Sanjay Subrahmanyam, Explorations in Connected History: Mughals and Franks, [New Delhi: Oxford University Press, 2005]; A.K. Pasha, "India and West Asia: Continuity and Changes", in Nalini Kant Jha, (ed.), Indian Foreign Policy in a Changing World (New Delhi: South Asian Publishers, 2000), pp. 240-269; A.K. Pasha, "India's Cultural Diplomacy in West Asia", in A.K. Sinha and A.K. Singh (eds.), Udayana: New Horizons in History, Classics and Inter-Cultural Studies, [Delhi: Amanika Publications, 2007], pp. 295-310.

33. See also Mawlana Syed Suleiman Nadwi, *Indo-Arab Relations: An English Rendering* (Hyderabad: The Institute of Indo-Middle East Cultural Studies, 1962); For details see R.C. Majumdar et al., An Advanced History of India (Delhi: Macmillan, 1978), p. 346. See also M.N. Pearson, *Merchants and Rulers in Gujarat: The Response to the Portuguese in the 16th Century,* [New Delhi: Munshiram Manoharlal Publisher, 1976] pp. 67-85; see also Saryu Doshi, (ed.); *India and Egypt: Influences and Interactions* (New Delhi: Garg Publications, ICCR, 1993);

Rennell J., *Memoirs: Marches of the British Armies in India during the Campaign of 1790 and 1791* (London: 1972); P.C XXXIX cited in Mohibbul Hassan, *History of Tipu Sultan* (Calcutta: 1971) pp. 392-393; B.S. Gidwani., *The Sword of Tipu Sultan* (New Delhi: 1989), pp. 239-240; Roger M. Savory, "The History of the Persian Gulf 600-1800", in Alvin Cottrell, (ed.), The Persian Gulf States-A General Survey (Baltimore, MD: 1980), pp. 38-39;Vikram Sampath, Splendours of Royal Mysore: The Untold Story of the Wodeyars [New Delhi: Rupa and Co., 2008]; Sultan Muhammad al Qasimi, *The Myth of Arab Piracy in the Gulf* (London: 1988) pp. 26-28; Praxy Fernandez, *Storm over Seringapatam: The In crucible Story of Hayder Ali and Tipu Sultan* (Bombay: 1969), pp. 163 and 211; A.D. Gupta, *Malabar in Asian Trade 1740-1800* (Cambridge: 1967); A. Leevis, "Maritime Skills in the Indian Ocean, 1500-1968", *Journal of the Economic and Social History of the Orient,* Vol. 6, 1973; see also B.J Hamilton, "The Role of Monopoly in the Overseas Expansion and Colonial Trade of Europe before 1800", *American Economic Review,* Vol. 38, 1948; and A. Das Gupta, *India Merchants and the Decline of Surat* (Wiesbaden: 1979); and A.H. Abu Hakima, *History of Eastern Arabia, 1750-1800* (Beirut: 1965); Edward Simpson and Kai Kresse, (eds.), Struggling with History: Islam and Cosmopolitanism in the Western Indian Ocean, [New Delhi: Hurst and Co., Foundation Books, 2007].

34. See also Denys Forrest, *Tiger of Mysore :The Life and Death of Tipu Sultan* (New Delhi: 1970), p. 117; Sanjay Subrahmanyam, *Explorations in Connected History: From the Tagus to the Ganges*, [New Delhi: Oxford University Press, 2005]; Muzaffar Alam and Sanjay Subrahmanyam, (eds.), *Indo-Persian Travels in the Age of Discoveries, 1400-1800*, [New Delhi: CUP, 2007]; see also K.M. Pannikar, *Asia and Western Domination* (London: Unwin and Allen, 1953); —and *Malabar and the Dutch* (Bombay: 1931); M. Redha Bhacker, *Trade and Empire in Muscat and Zanzibar: Roots of British Domination* (London: Routledge 1992), pp. 34-35; Marie Francoise Boussac, Jean-Francois Salles, *A Gate Way from the Eastern Mediterranean to India: The Red Sea in Antiquity* [New Delhi: Manohar, 2005] ; *—Athens, Aden, Arikamedu: Essays on the interrelations between India, Arabia and the Eastern Mediterranean,* [New

Delhi: Manohar, 2005] ; Himanshu Prabha Ray, *Archaeology of Sea Faring: The Indian Ocean in the Ancient Period* [New Delhi: ICHR, 1999]; B. Sheik Ali, *History of Tipu Sultan* (New Delhi: NBT, 1972) and *Tipu Sultan: A Study in Diplomacy and Confrontation* [Mysore: Rao and Raghavan, 1982); see also A.K. Pasha, (ed.); *India and Oman: History, State, Economy and Foreign Policy* (Delhi: Gyan Sagar, 1999), pp. 1-21; see also A.K. Pasha "South India and the Gulf: Trade and Diplomacy during the Late 18th Century", in N.N. Vohra, (ed.), *History, Culture and Society in India and West Asia* (New Delhi: Shipra, 2003), pp. 237-249; See also Akhtarul Wasey, "Turkey and Evolution of Indian Culture," *Islam and Modern Age,* Vol. XXXIII, No. 4, November, 2002. pp. 87-94; see also R.L. Shukla, *Britain, India and the Turkish Empire, 1853-1882.* (New Delhi: People's Publishing House, 1973).

35. F.C. Danvers, *The Portuguese in India* [New Delhi: Asian Educational Services, 1992]; See also K.M. Mathew, *History of the Portuguese Navigation in India, 1497-1600* [Delhi: Mittal Publications, 1985]; See also Y. Subhi Labib, "Karimi" in *Encyclopaedia of Islam*, Vol. 4, [Leiden: EJ Brill, 1990], pp. 640- 643; Pius Malekandathil, *Maritime India: Trade, Religion and Polity in the Indian Ocean* [Delhi: Primus Books, 2010]; — and "From Merchant Capitalists to Corsairs: The Role of Muslim Merchants in Portuguese Maritime Trade", *Portuguese Studies Review*, 12, 1 2004; see also E. Ashtor, "The Venetian Supremacy in Levantine Trade: Monopoly of Pre-Colonialism", *Journal of European Economic History*, 3, 1974; Tara Chand, *Influences of Islam on Indian Culture* (Allahabad: The Indian Press, 1965); Turner, n. 3, pp. 180-181; W.J. Fischel, "The Spice Trade in Mamluk Egypt", *Journal of the Economic and Social History of the Orient*, 1, 1958; Andre Wink, *Al Hind: The Making of the Indo-Islamic World,* Vol. 1 (New Delhi: OUP, 1999); see also Hugh Bibbs, *The Islamic Foundation of the Renaissance*, [British Columbia; Canada: Northwest and Pacific Publishing; 1999].

36. Abbas Hamdani, "An Islamic Background to the Voyages of Discovery", in Salma Khadra Jayyusi, (ed.), *The Legacy of Muslim Spain*, [Leiden: E.J. Brill, 1994], pp. 273-306; G.W.F. Stripling, *The Ottoman Turks and the Arabs, 1511-1574*, [Urbana: University of Illinois Press, 1977], p. 35; W.H.

Moreland, *India at the Death of Akbar* [London: Macmillan, 1974], p. 25; See also W L Wright, [tr] *Ottoman Statecraft: The Book of Counsel for Viziers and Governors* [Princeton: Princeton University Press, 1935]; Palmira Brummet, *Ottoman Sea power and Levantine Diplomacy in the age of Discovery,*[New York: State University Press, 1994]; For the Mughals see A.C. Roy, *A History of Mughal Navy and Naval warfare,* [Calcutta: World Press, 1972]; V.D. Hanson, *Carnage and Culture*, [New York: Anchor Books, 2002] pp. 265-269; G.F. Hourani, *Arab Seafaring in the Indian Ocean in Ancient and Early Medieval Times,* [Princeton, 1951]; See also Mawlana Syed Suleiman Nadwi, *Indo-Arab Relations: An English Rendering* (Hyderabad : The Institute of Indo-Middle East Cultural Studies, 1962) ; Murat Cizakca cited in A.A. Islahi, " Mercantilism and the Muslim States: Lessons from the History", *Quarterly Journal of the Pakistan Historical Society,* July-September 2009, Vol. LVII, No. 3, pp. 7-26; Bernard Lewis, *The Emergence of Modern Turkey*, [Oxford: OUP, 1968], pp. 24-25; A.K. Pasha, "Byzantine Trade and India," *Yavanika,* no. 13, 2010, pp. 3-36; see also, Kemal H. Karpat, (ed.), *The Ottoman State and its Place in World History,* [Leiden: E.J. Brill, 1974], pp. 79-98; J. Raja Mohammad, *Maritime History of the Coromandel Muslims* [Chennai: Government Museum, 2004]; Metin I. Kunt, "The Later Muslim Empires: Ottomans, Safavids, Mughals", in Marjorie Kelly, (ed.)., *Islam: The Religious and Political Life of a World Community*, [New York: Praeger, 1984,], pp. 113- 136; Pius Malekandathil, Winds of Change and Links of Continuity, *JESHO,* Vol. 50, No. 2-3, 2007, pp. 259-286; Marshall G.S. Hodgson, *The Venture of Islam: The Gunpowder Empires and Modern Times,* [Chicago: The University of Chicago Press, 1974], Vol. 3, pp. 134-222; see also Stewart Gordon, *When Asia was the World*, [Philadelphia, P.A; Da Capo Press, 2008], p. 191.

References

Energy Outlook 2030, *BP Statistical Review 2011*, London January 2011.

India Energy Handbook, 2011, *International Energy consulting Corporation(IECC)*, PSI Media Inc., Las Vegas, Nevada (USA) www.iecc-us.com.

Roadmap for Upscaling and Mainstreaming Renewables, *DIREC 2010 Report*, Ministry of New and Renewable Energy, Government of India.

Misra, Kishlaya (2012), "Energy Diplomacy for Energy Security" *Ninth AIMS International Conference on Management.*

Kalam, A.P.J. Abdul and Srijan Pal Singh (2011), "Nuclear power is our gateway to a prosperous future", Special Essay, *The Hindu*, Sunday, November 6.

Maithani, P.C. (2011), "The private sector and climate change: Opportunities and Challenges in emerging economies", *Renewable Energy in India-A Policy Perspective*, Ministry of New and Renewable Energy, Government of India.

Lall, Marie (2008), "India-Myanmar relations: Geo-politics and Energy in Light of the New Balance of Power in Asia", *ISAS Working Paper*, No. 29.

Pant, Harsh V. (2011), "India's Relations with Iran: Much Ado about Nothing", *The Washington Quarterly*, No. 34:1, pp. 61-74.

Coşkun, BezenBalamir (2010), "Energizing the Middle East: Iran, Turkey and Persian Gulf States", *Turkish Policy Quarterly*, Vol. 9, No. 2, pp. 71-80.

Mehta, Vikram (2011), "India's energy options: New sources, innovations and areas of cooperation" Remarks at the Centre for Strategic & International Studies (CSIS) B1 Conference Centre.

Hong, Zhao (2009), "China and India: The Energy Policies", *EAI Background Brief No. 462.*

Pop, Irina Ionela (2010), "China's Energy Strategy in Central Asia: Interactions with Russia, India and Japan", UNISCI *Discussion Papers*, No. 24 (October).

Pardesi, Manjeet S. and Sumit Ganguly (2009), "India and Energy Security: A Foreign Policy Priority" in Harsh V. Pant (ed.), *Indian Foreign Policy in a Unipolar World,* Routledge, pp. 99-127.

Blank, Stephen (2009), "India and Central Asia: Part of the New Great Game" in Harsh V. Pant (ed.), *Indian Foreign Policy in a Unipolar World,* Routledge, pp. 277-304.

Panwar, Namrata (2009), "India and China Competing over Myanmar Energy Resources", *Working Draft for BISA Conference*, University of Leicester, Leicester.

12

Indo-US Nuclear Deal: Implications for India's Foreign Policy and National Security

K.S. Pavithran

Introduction

India and United States historically had and continue to have very different conceptions of the global order, determined in part by their position in the international system. During the Cold War, the disjuncture between hope and reality of Indo-US relations was often widened by the pressure of strategic imperatives. However, as India tries to carve its place in the New Global Order, its relationship with the United States has undergone major shifts. The opening of Indian economy, globalization, India's acquisition of nuclear weapons, and the war on terror seem to set a new world stage upon which to reappraise the relationship. In this respect one of the major initiatives of the Congress led United Progressive Alliance (UPA) government has been to put India's relations with the United States of America on a new footing. [Bajpai, 2005:3577]

Consequently, on June 28, 2005, the defence minister Pranab Mukharjee and the US defence secretary Donald Rumsfeld signed an agreement titled "New Framework for the US-India Defence Relationship" [1] and on July 18, 2005 during Prime Minister Manmohan Singh's visit to the US, the two countries issued a document called the "India-US Joint Statement". These are the two basic documents that will govern India-US relations in the changing global scenario.

The July 18 Joint Statement between India and the United

States will be seen as one of the decisive movements in world politics. There is bound to be a contentious debate on the matter of nuclear energy cooperation between India and USA, that is the most substantive part of the joint statement. Unfortunately this complex and problematical deal, like so much else in the realm of strategic affairs and foreign policy formulations in recent years, including the Indo-US Defence Framework Agreement, has been sprung on the people of India —forsaking the method of democratic discussion and consensus—building in advance rather than after the deal is done. This essay seeks to analyse the impact of Indo-US nuclear cooperation on India's nuclear policy, independent foreign policy and on its national security.

Indo-US Joint Statement

It is obvious that President George Bush had broken away from the long term US non-proliferation policy towards India. Recognizing India as "a responsible state with advanced nuclear technology" he has committed himself to working to achieve "full civil nuclear energy cooperation with India as it realizes its goals of promoting nuclear power and achieving energy security". Towards this end, he did seek an agreement from the US Congress to adjust domestic laws and policies. He said that he work with allies to adjust restrictive international regimes so that India can benefit from "full civil nuclear energy cooperation and trade". The policy relaxation has factored in expeditious consideration of fuel supplies for safeguarded nuclear reactors at Tharapur. [http:// www.whitehouse: 2005]

The UPA government accepted a formidable list of conditionalities but some of them must be recognized as the product of the interminable Jaswant Singh-Strobe Talbott dialogue [2] during the Bharathiya Janata Party (BJP) led National Democratic Alliance (NDA) regime. The conditionalities include:

1. Identifying and separating civilian and military nuclear

facilities and programmes "in a phased manner" and placing all the civilian nuclear facilities voluntarily under the safeguards regime of the International Atomic Energy Agency (IAEA);
2. Signing and adhering to additional protocol with respect to civilian nuclear facilities;
3. Continuing unilateral moratorium on nuclear testing;
4. Working with the US to help conclude a Multilateral Fissile Material Cut-off Treaty (FMCT);
5. Putting in place, comprehensive export controls on sensitive goods and technologies; and
6. Harmonisation and adherence to Missile Technology Control Regime (MTCR) and Nuclear Suppliers Group (NSG) guidelines. [Ramachandran, 2005: 7]

Indian Compulsions

What are the 'compulsions' to opening up for international inspection of all the civilian nuclear facilities and limiting the countries nuclear options? The Planning Commission in its Mid-Term Appraisal of the Tenth Plan noted in June 2005, that the load factor achieved by the nuclear power plants had come down primarily due to the unavailability of nuclear fuel because the development of domestic mines has not kept pace with addition of generating capacity. [Venugopal, 2005] It is perhaps the first official acknowledgement that the pipeline is running thin and may not be adequate to feed the existing power plants, let alone new ones. The Department of Atomic Energy (DAE) may only be producing about 300 tonnes of uranium a year.

This falls well short of the fuelling requirements. DAE has been able to continue to operate its reactors by using stockpiled uranium from earlier days when the nuclear capacity was much smaller. Estimates are that this stockpile would be exhausted by 2007. [Mian and Ramana, 2005: 3809] The DAE has been desperately trying to open new uranium mines in the country. But it has been met with stiff public resistance everywhere. [3] The Planning Commission believes that nuclear energy remains an important tool for "de-carbonising the Indian energy sector". As indigenous uranium resources are limited, it says India must seek at least about 20,000 MW of additional nuclear capacity on a turn key basis, based on a comprehensive power tariff. That implies putting out a global tender.

For India, nuclear energy has become critical in meeting its needs in the medium term. Right now, the country is heavily dependent on oil imported from West Asia and the increased use of coal would run up against the issue of green house gases and global warming. It would need to expand its nuclear energy programme from a target of 10,000 MW from nuclear energy with a restrictive regime, it would be possible under the new agreement to get 40,000 MW to meet the energy needs in the medium term. Suppliers of nuclear fuel from outside have become critical to India to meet the needs of the expansion programme.

Nuclear Power and National Security Concerns

The US law as well as the rules of the Nuclear Suppliers Group (NSG) [4] that it leads bar any nuclear fuel or other supplies to India so long as some of its nuclear facilities including the indigenously built power reactors and test reactors and fuel processing facilities remain outside IAEA safeguards. By keeping the wraps on the civilian nuclear plants all those years, India had the option to divert some of the spent uranium fuel for reprocessing into weapons–grade plutonium. Once these plants were thrown open to international inspection the capacity to produce weapon–grade plutonium would be restricted to the research deterrence. For the many that have had but a dim view of the deterrent effect of nuclear weapons, it would indeed be a virtuous turn of events. [Ramana et al., 2005:1767] One possible move could be to provide fuel for the US supplied reactors at Tarapur. That should be possible without an amendment of the law. Built with US assistance in the early 1960s the 400 MWe plant is well past what was initially thought to be its life span.

The fact is that, ever since India's "peaceful nuclear explosion" at Pokhran in 1974, the US has been extremely wary of supplying nuclear fuel and equipment as well as dual use high technology, even getting out of the contractual obligation to provide fuel supply during the entire life span for the US built reactors at Tarapur. The restrictive regime was further tightened after Pokhran II in 1998, when sanctions became oppressive with even visits of top scientists to America barred. After a period of intense engagement, when futility of the sanctions became apparent and they were seen as a major hurdle to normal relations, they were eased gradually.

An important issue raised by experts in India in this regard is that the agreement would cap nuclear weapons at the current levels and that it would hamper research. Allowing international inspectors access to all civilian nuclear plants would seriously hamper ongoing research work on the fast breeder reactor (FBR) programme and compromise India's long-term energy security. Pointing to the importance of the indigenous FBR programme, A.N. Prasad, former Director of the Bhabha Atomic Research Centre (BARC) pointed out that the suggestion of allowing safeguards "goes against the national interest".

Since FBRs will be the main stay of India's nuclear power programme for sometime and since there is a lot to be established for the first time and improved upon to achicvc a level of maturity required to make it a succcss, bringing in safeguards at this stage just because they are civil nuclear facilities will seriously hamper our efforts and cut into our freedom to pursue the development of the programme". Dr. Prasad also stated that no point should compromise the basic inherent strength so relentlessly built over the years under heavy odds. [The Hindu, 2005] According to P.R. Chari of the Institute of Peace and Conflict Studies, the BARC reactors that produce weapon-grade plutonium also facilitate a significant amount of civilian research and activity, such as the production of radio isotopes.

Fire walling military and civilian nuclear activities would mean denying scientists from University departments across the country access to BARC's research facilities. Further allowing IAEA inspectors and signing the Additional Protocol means throwing open not just your reactors but the entire chain, the whole fuel cycle. The decision would make the military programme very expensive and that it would cap the fissile material available for weapons. [Gopalakrishnan, 2005: 3573]

The US Strategy

Following India's nuclear tests in 1998, the US had two options:

1. Continuing to believe Indian nuclear genie could be put back; or
2. Harnessing India's evident strategic weight for its own geo-political aims before that power grows too immense or is harnessed by others like Europe or China.

Thus US has chosen the latter option and joint statement released by President Bush and Prime Minister Manmohan Singh was the most dramatic textual manifestation of what America is attempting to do. While large number of factors induced the Bush administration to accept the nuclear bargain, it is clear that Asian geo-politics including concern about the rise of China must have influenced the American decision for a joint statement. Geo-politically, India and Pakistan serve non-substitutable US interests. This means India cannot turn the US against Pakistan in a serious way [Kapur, 2003: 202] and in fact has bad to accommodate itself to the US perspective which aims to utilize alliances with both countries separately and not to take permanent sides with one against the other.

India too had a choice. It could use its nuclear weapons as a lever to push for a multi-polar world system as well as for global restraints on the development of weapons of mass destruction. It could also use its status as an instrument to help perpetuate an order based on the production of insecurity and violence in which it eventually hoped to be accommodated as a junior partner. By walking away from forty years of non-proliferation policy, India must understand the tectonic shift that is taking place in the bilateral relationship as a result of increasing fears in the US business and strategic circles about China giving India anything less or insisting that it cap or scrap its nuclear weapons, is seen by Washington's neo-conservatives as tantamount to strengthening China in the emerging balance of power in Asia.

From a strategic and security perspective, one of the most puzzling aspects of the joint statement was the inclusion of a reiteration by India of its unilateral moratorium on nuclear testing without the US making an explicit reciprocal commitment to abide by its own 1992 moratorium. The United States has no altruistic notions of its foreign policy. It will expect a price for "building" Indian power. However, both India and US have abandoned positions that were until recently, virtual articles of faith for their respective establishments. The US says it is now in favour of "full civil nuclear energy cooperation with India, which it describes as "a responsible state with advanced nuclear technology". In return India has agreed to "separate its civilian and military nuclear facilities and programmes in a phased manner" and place its "civilian nuclear facilities under IAEA safeguards".

No matter how important a position India has come to occupy in US strategic thinking, Washington will be careful not to do anything that will weaken the non-proliferation initiatives announced by President Bush in February 2003. The American embargo on the supply of civilian nuclear equipment to India is linked to both its domestic laws and its membership of the NSG. Though domestic law can be waved and adherence to the NSG guidelines is voluntary, the question of whether or not America will reverse itself on the supply of civilian nuclear equipment will depend on its assessment of how this would impact on its wider counter-proliferation initiatives. Making an exception for India-without India granting something in return would likely make its task of tightening the NPT-plus regime harder. [Varadrajan, 2005]

Foreign Policy Implications

The replacement of the BJP led NDA regime with the congress led UPA I and II governments; no significant change has taken place in neo-liberal economic policies and foreign policy behaviour. The present leadership in the congress has few foreign policy differences with the BJP. The ideological fervour that lay behind BJP's desire for alignment with Israel is missing but the commitment of the congress to strategic partnership with United States and to sustaining the relationship with Israel remains intact, despite Left pressure. [5]

India's decision to vote against Iran at the IAEA meeting on 24th September is an instance of the fact that the India-US civil nuclear deal has altered New Delhi's foreign perceptions. India which has championed Non-aligned cause for long, did not find itself in the company of South Africa and Malaysia at the IAEA governing board meeting in Vienna. [6] There seems little doubt that India's eagerness to get a membership in the UN Security Council and the civilian nuclear deal between India and the US has begun transform New Delhi's 'independent' foreign policy".

The Iran vote underlies the fact that Indian foreign policy suffers from insecurity, a poor understanding of the realities of the international situation, a lack of confidence in the nation's strategic weight, and an absence of belief in, or commitment to, genuine independence and non-alignment. The downward trajectory initiated by the NDA government in dealings with the United States, signalled by support of all things to 'star wars' has hit a new low. In fact some influential policy makers in the present government are of the view that that NDA government's cosying up with Washington and Tel Aviv when it was in power was only a continuation of the foreign policy initiated by the congress in the 1990's after the end of the Cold War. [Cherian, 2005: 14]

The new defence agreement and nuclear accord are proof enough of that. With the vote against Iran on September 24, the UPA government has taken a major step which adversely affects India's independent foreign policy and its status in the Non-aligned movement. This proves that India cannot expect to be a beneficiary of the nuclear agreement unless it meets the US concerns about Iran and China. The irony of the Indian capitulation on Iran is that its display of political weakness comes at a time when the US has finally become aware of India's strategic weight and significance and is attempting desperately to harness these for its own ends.

It is evident that unipolar domination is what the US imperial project is all about. Ceasing, post-9/11 to disguise its hegemonic intent is an "emollient cream of tact", divisions between the sole superpower and a world that doesn't recognize its manifest destiny are emerging". [Hobsbawn, 2004:9] The American ambition is not the creation of a global equilibrium through power balancing but the establishment of its global hegemony through a world wide system of alliances that would accept its undisputed and indisputable leadership. Behind the rhetoric of wanting to help India become 'a major power in the world' lied this crystal clear ambition. [Vanaik, 2005:3583]

Energy security and National security are two sides of the nuclear coin. India's sense of vulnerability began with the Chinese atomic test in 1964. India's neighbourhood also became increasingly dangerous, with Pakistan acquiring nuclear and missile technology from China and North Korea. On the other side, it was no secret that Bush administration regarded China as a long term threat to the US and India appeared as a possible counterweight or balancer. [Cohen, 2005: 117] India's geopolitical importance for the US lies southwards and eastwards towards Indian Ocean and as a junior partner in strategic perspectives concerning the possible containment of China. While India should not be reluctant to accept Americans support to become a major player in Asia and beyond, it needs to ensure that it retains the space to be able to carve out its own equation with China, Iran and other countries.

The UPA's common minimum programme commits the government to pursue an independent foreign policy–"the policy will seek to promote multipolarity in world relations and oppose all attempts at multilaterism". Such a framework also goes against the grain of foreign policy initiatives such as the Russia-China-India-Brazil-South Africa forum. The emergence of multipolarity therefore requires a very substantial political and strategic weakening of the United States. The US needs to be politically defeated in places like Iraq, in Central and West Asian, and elsewhere, e.g., in Latin America where resistance to neo liberalism is strongest and where Venezuela is proving to be a growing irritant.

However, right up to October 2012, more than seven years later, the Indo-US nuclear deal had yet to become a 'done deal'. In between the American Congress passed the Hyde Act in December 2006, giving a 'free pass' to India. Later in March 2007, the 123 Agreement was finalized. P.R. Chari points out that three further hurdles needed to be crossed: India had to negotiate an India-Specific Safeguards Agreement with the IAEA; the US had to persuade the NSG to amend its guidelines and make India an exception to its mandate, and finally, the US Congress had to pass the 123 Agreement to incorporate the IAEA and NSG requirements. [Chari, 2009:1]

Conclusion

In the present environment, there are four possible strategic perspectives that a state can pursue through appropriate diplomacy and statecraft when faced with an aspiring hegemonic like the US. It can seek to balance against it. It can bandwagon on it. It cannot hide i.e., be neutral. It can try to transcend i.e., insist on abiding by international laws so as to excuse, itself from not aligning with the hegemony. [Vanaik, 2005: 3583] What the Indian state is currently doing is precisely bandwagoning and therefore exactly what the United States wants. But India is also pretending to itself that this is in its national interest and for energy security. The end result is that India merely pays lip service to the striving for multi-polarity and does not at all see the contradiction in what it is doing and in what it says it ultimately wants.

With so many forecasts of a multi-polar world, it should have been clear that India would have a significant place in it. But little analytical work has been done on the emerging poles and even less on the potential relations among them. [Delph, 1998-99: 57] There is a profound disjunction at the level of diplomacy and foreign policy behaviour between the claimed strategic goal that it believes it must pursue because it would give it greatest relative autonomy and authority in the system of nation-states–promoting multi-polarity–and its actual practice of statecraft as embodied in the policies and diplomatic stances it pursues and adopts.

With the July 18 agreement, India has become something more than a 'major non-NATO ally' of America. It has joined the 'free world'. It has gone from being a victim of nuclear discrimination to a 'beneficiary'. By allying so closely with the United States, the UPA has ensured that terms such as "multipolarity" and "democratization of international relations" spouted often by Indian leaders in the past, have little or no meaning left. Dr. Singh has raised the political stakes, preferred the 'economic advantages' over the military, and even sold a bit of national pride. In short, while 'non-proliferation' concerns figure in 'the Joint Statement, the UPA government has regrettably failed to show the slightest interest in returning to India's traditional policy of promoting nuclear disarmament on the world stage. There remains the unsolved question of how under the globalist agenda to avoid the hegemony and domination of a strongest power over the rest of the world.

End Notes

1. The new defence framework will chart military relations between India and the United States until 2015. Obligating India to a defence relationship some of whose provisions go against the tenets of India's foreign policy. These clauses include the intention to "collaborate in multinational operations", "expand collaboration relating to missile defence" and "assist in building worldwide capacity to conduct successful peace keeping operations" [for details see Dikshit, 2005].
2. As early as 19685, Rajiv Gandhi visited the US and created a greater interest in defence co-operation between India and the US emerged. With the end of the Cold War, Narasimha Rao had to rethink India's diplomatic and security options and began a dialogue on nuclear issues. It was Jaswanth Singh-Strobe Talbott talks that were held from 1999 to 2001 took it forward.
3. What is increasingly becoming critical is access to fuel–both natural uranium for the indigenous PHWRs as well as enriched uranium (with 2-3 percent U-235) for the twin US built light water reactors (LWRs) at Tarapur. Particularly the former, essentially because uranium ore from the currently operational mines at Jaduguda in Jharkand is of very poor quality and is depleting as well. Mining operations at other potential uranium deposits in Nalgonda district of Andra Pradesh and Domiasat in Meghalaya have not taken off on environmental grounds.
4. The guidelines of the 44 member NSG-which forms an essential component of the current non-proliferation regime built on the tenets of the NPT—require the application of full-scope safeguards (FSS) of the IAEA on all current and future 'peaceful' nuclear activities of a non-nuclear weapon state (NNWS) for transfer of items on the NSG's Trigger list, which include equipment material and technology directly related to the nuclear fission fuel cycle. This includes the source of the fissionable material, namely uranium ore or the processed yellow cake, as well.
5. The Left Parties cautioned the Manmohan Singh government against accepting the defence framework agreement on US-India defence relations saying it would have serious consequences for the countries strategic and security interests. They alleged that the UPA government had taken a major step in trying up with the US to serve its strategic goals in Asia. The Left viewed it as

a violation of the Common Minimum Programme of the UPA. According to them the Joint Statement was a continuation of the pro US shift in India's foreign policy and it displays the anxiety of India to align with the United States at a time when the superpower has become notorious for its unilateralist and anti-democratic activities.

6. The IAEA resolution finds Iran in "non compliance in the context of Art.XII.C (which mandate referral of the matter to the Security Council of UN) of the Agencies statute specifically, it recalls Irans alleged "failures in a number of instances" as a party to Nuclear Non-proliferation Treaty, "to meet its obligations under its NPT safeguards agreement and its alleged "policy of concealment".

References

Bajpai, Kanti (2005), 'Where are India and US heading', *Economic and Political Weekly*, Vol. XL, No. 32, August 6-12.

Cherian, John (2005), 'A Document of Deviation', *Frontline*, Vol. 22, No. 16, August 2.

Cohen, Stephen P. (2005), 'The US and South Asia', *Seminar*, No. 545, January.

Delpech, Therese (1998-99), 'Nuclear Weapons and the New World Order: Early Warning from Asia?", *IISS, Winter.*

Dikshit, Sandeep (2005), 'Decoding the India-US Defence Tie up', *The Hindu*, July 5.

Gopalakrishnan, A. (2005), Indo-US Nuclear Co-operation: A Non Starter?, *Economic and Political Weekly*, Vol. XL, No. 27, July 2.

Hobsbawn, Eric (2004), 'Uncontrollable and Irrational Government in Washington Endangers World Peace', *Mainstream*, December 25.

Joint Statement between President George Bush and Prime Minister Manmohan Singh, released by the Office of the White House Press Secretary, July 18, 2005 Kapur, Ashok, *Pokhran and Beyond: India's Nuclear Behaviour,* New Delhi: Oxford University Press.

Malhotra, Vinay Kumar and Sergounin, Alexander A. (2001), *Theories and Approaches to International Relations,* New Delhi: Anmol Publications.

Mian, Zia and Ramana M.V. (2005) 'Feeding the Nuclear Fire',

Economic and Political Weekly, Vol. XL, No. 35, August 27-September 2.

Ramachandran, R. (2005), Behind the Bargain', *Frontline*, Vol. 22, No. 16, August 12.

Ramana, M.U., Antonette D'sa and Amulya, Reddy K.N., 'Economics of Nuclear Power from Heavy Water Reactors', *Economic and Political Weekly*, Vol. XL, No. 17, April 23.

Vanaik, Achin, 'Significance of Framework Agreement on Defence' *Economic and Political Weekly*, Vol. XL, No. 32, August 6.

Venugopal, K.,'Swallowing some pride to win the Nuclear Game', *The Hindu*, July 22.

13

India's Foreign Policy: Need for Democratization

Biju B.L.

Introduction

Conventional studies in International Politics and Political Science on democracy focus on different arenas and actors. In the former, the global arena is the location of power struggle and the nation states are conceived as the participants while in Political Science interest finds with the domestic structure of power and actors. Norms, procedure and values of democracy in domestic politics are traditionally different from those in international politics. [1] Most notable is the difference in obligation of an actor while performing domestic political functions and international performance. Such a separation is greatly challenged in the contemporary times, and the statesmen had to pay due attention to both external reactions and domestic compulsions while formulating foreign policy. Foreign policy is a connector between domestic politics and international environment. However, there is a disagreement on whether the domestic sources or the external factors are the chief determinants in shaping the forcign policy behaviour.

Morton Halperin suggests: 'Conventional analyses of foreign policy usually assume that the actions of other nations (the international environment) are the major stimuli for foreign policy decisions...they are only one source of stimulation, and not even the more frequent source. Decisions are responses to domestic pressures, and the actions of other nations often figure merely as devices for argument'. [2] But those who criticise conventional studies for their negligence to domestic compulsions in foreign policy making do not adequately explain several factors/actors which cannot be strictly called as domestic or international, for instance capital; especially finance capital and the transnational capitalist class in the contemporary times of globalisation. Thus, recent analyses of foreign policy, mainly the critical political economy and sociological studies, try to understand the interconnections between national and international sources of foreign policy for better comprehension. [3]

In the post-Second World War period, debates among the liberal idealists on the problems of democratic substance in the foreign policy were mainly confined to explain the external implications. Arguments were surrounding the international means and factors to maintain accountability of the national government's foreign policy to international peace. The degree of democracy inside the state was considered as only having a complementary role in maintaining democratic foreign policy. It gave the impression that democracy in foreign policy was imposed from above out of international compulsions, not as a result of demands from the domestic politics. Therefore, in international politics accountability of foreign policy to international community, which stands in contrast to the meaning of accountability in the domestic politics, is generally conceived as essential to make the foreign policy more democratic. It leads to two contrasting views predominating the meaning of democracy in foreign policy, which were based on the differences between external and internal definitions of democracy. [4]

Certainly, political leaders manipulated the ambiguities of democracy in foreign policy behaviour to avert regime crises. To contradict the allegations about anti-national factors in foreign policy they cited international obligations as a reason, and to tactfully evade from international pressure they pointed out domestic political compulsions as an excuse.

The discipline international politics hardly evolves a sound theoretical framework to examine domestic sources of foreign policy except a few like 'linkage politics', 'pre-theory' and 'two-level analysis' (Rosenau), 'rational actor, organisational and bureaucratic framework' (Allison), 'decision-making unit analysis' (Hermann and Hagen) and 'cross-level linkages' (Peter Gourevitch). [5]

Most of the other studies during the Cold War were preoccupied by the view that the chief determinants of democratic behaviour through foreign policy are the international events and the order. They have a tendency to hide the variety of actors and interactions involved in the 'black box' of decision making. The discourses were awash with simplified metaphors, for instance, national interest; political expediency etc. which is a general problem of theory builders belonging to conservative and liberal schools in any discipline. [6]

Marxian tools of analysis might have been a help to give a structured explanation, but the dominant schools in International Politics are not in tune with this. Putnam's attempts were a motivation to build up frameworks of research on the interactions of various factors in foreign policy making, but his concept of polyarchy is neither helpful to find out the reasons behind the highly irreconcilable conflicts in international politics nor adequate to reveal the substance of metaphors like national interest. [7]

Analysis based on the dichotomy between national interest and international commitment does not fully explain the conflicting interests in foreign policy. Conventional division between national and international is more an intellectual fantasy than a reality. [8]

Each source of foreign policy is not homogenous; they shall be subdivided into multiple interests held by different stakeholders. Presumably, certain dominant elements of each source largely collude to shape the foreign policy.

Therefore, the foreign policy is likely to deprive democracy to the subaltern groups though they numerically constitute the unspeaking majority in both global and domestic politics. Negligence to their perspectives by describing them as either undemocratic or as petty inexpert voices results in further elitisation of our discussions of foreign policy. Andrew Moravscik suggests that models integrating three levels of analysis—society, political system and international environment–are required to understand foreign policy. [9]

It is more essential to understand democracy and security dimensions of foreign policy.

Democracy and Security: Cold War and Post-Cold War Politics

The vision of a democratic world order in the mid-twentieth century was characterised by increasing concerns for security, stability and non-aggressive foreign relations of the governments. The UNO and its feeder organizations aimed at partially increasing the scope of security by incorporating more additional infrastructure that is essential to maintain durable peace based on collective endeavours. However, the dream of liberal idealists failed to reach at climax because of the 'menace' of the Cold War. Each rival group in the Cold War put forward contrasting definitions of democracy and security. The threat of extinction as a result of the possible damages by a total war compelled them to legitimise the subjective definitions of democracy and security by means of propaganda. Debates were triggered by the Marxist intelligentsia and the Soviet bloc about the democratic credentials of the capitalist economic production, which was the chief mode and a determinant of the US led states' public policies. It indirectly points out that the contesting ideologies, which were the derivatives of the social conflicts, had implications on the discussions in international politics. [10]

Each power bloc aimed at security outside the means of UNO and claimed that it was essential to preserve their versions of democracy. Each of these security mechanisations were pledged to either Marxian or liberal democratic version of democracy, though it was demagogic on several instances. Both the regional security devices and the multilateral institutions played the role of deterrents to avert open war during the cold war. They were more concerned about the international dimensions of security and peace. The security arrangements aimed at maintaining the status quo based on deterrence. Democracy in different subjective meanings was used to justify the security arrangements. It indirectly shows that the argument for democracy by means of cold war security arrangements in result produced stability rather than change. Dominant definitions of democracy and security shared conservative meaning rather than radical one in most of the cases. It resembles the view of conservative form of liberalism, which is more concerned about the stable, orderly relationship between nations, like one that it envisages between the citizens in the case of domestic politics. [11]

This view of international politics has many drawbacks especially when we attempt to discuss security and democracy in the foreign policy. Democracy in the western bloc's security arrangements and foreign policy became a catchphrase aiming at democratisation of domestic politics by the last decade of the Cold War. [12]

The 'democratic peace theory' has become one of the tasks of the US foreign policy after the break-up of communist bloc and it has been transformed and practically applied in the process of aiding democratisation, promoting democratic consolidation and the enlargement of 'democracy's protector' international institutions, such as the NATO. [13]

The famous post-Cold War formulation that the democracies would not engage in war with each other was a derivative of the faulty assumptions propagated by the pro-establishment intelligentsia in international politics. They seldom try to explain the reasons for the liberal democracies to be compliant to each other in bilateral relations. Significantly, the liberal minded intellectuals gloss over structural similarities of their economic systems in the global capitalist economy. In result, the democratic peace theory remains as a vestige of the cold war syndrome, rather than having any therapeutic effect on the threats to democracy in international politics. In several instances, the definition of democratic behaviour and the typology of regimes in international politics were ideology-driven and subjective. The subjective meanings and the resulting conflicts had had caused to dissolution of consensus about democracy during the cold war. Construction of security mechanisms by each group was mainly based on the antagonism rather than on any collective definition of democracy. [14]

After the end of the Cold War, the US group, which became a unipolar entity for every political and ideological purpose in international politics, is exercising monopolistic clout in the production of meanings attached to security and democracy in such a way that it ensures their military's transnational dominance and serves the transnational economic interest of the capitalist classes. Compared to the defensive mood of arguments for democracy during the cold war period, current arguments for democratisation is unrestrained and predatory. Therefore, the post-Cold War democracy in international politics is clubbed with imperialism and expansion of capitalism. By the end of Cold War, wider consensus has been prevailing among the nation states except a few 'rough' states about security and democracy. [15]

Neo-liberal economic policies have been a reference used by the capitalist states to describe their democratic project.

The impact of globalisation on the debates of democracy in international politics has substituted the poles of previous debates represented by democracy and state's sovereignty with democracy and the market. From this, two inferences are possible. First, the sovereign state has declined in discussions of democracy in international politics. Second, the globalisation promoted direct negotiation and conflict between the democracy and the market. Third, inference partially opposite to the first one but elaborate the second inference is that the sovereignty is reformulated in times of globalisation so as to suit the democracy which in turn is determined by the global free market, a neo-liberal theoretical utopia.

Since sovereignty faced erosion in theoretical discussions on democracy in international politics, it was substituted by free market. This polar opposition between market and democracy is hidden in the hyper globalists' view compared to its preponderance in the view of the critics of neo-liberalism. On the other hand, the globalists refer to the market friendliness as universal criteria to evaluate the state's democratic character and they suggest global capitalism and free market as a democratic system. But the ephemeral existence of the state in the globalisation process is a hindrance to criticise that globalisation changed the previous contradiction in international politics between the state's sovereignty and democracy into another contradiction between the market and the democracy and that the sovereignty is of no relevance in the current global settings.

Therefore, criticism of the plight of democracy in neo-liberal globalisation needs a subtle revision which demands for a theoretical construction in which the neo-liberal state and free market constitute one pole and the democracy and the people rejected and exploited by the market the other. Then only the debate about the contradictions between democracy and free market is possible for evaluation of democracy in foreign policy. Theoretically speaking, the neo-liberal state, which scarcely bear 'sovereign' as the usual adjective in the contemporary international politics, is considered as the facilitator of democracy by the globalists and as a deterrent by the critics. Sovereignty of the state has been reduced in the neo-liberal theorizations, but the state power is still important due to its significance for the globalists who have advanced globalisation as a theoretical utopia and political project. [16]

However, the value of state power to reorient the economic and foreign policies is limited to the purpose of neo-liberalism. For the facilitation of neo-liberalism, sovereignty and state power are still have operational significance to the neo-liberal globalists. In other words, democracy is the pretext for the neo-liberal policy changes. Truly, it becomes a constraint for the anti-globalists who are attacking globalisation on the basis of political programmes that derives energy from nationalism. The retention of sovereignty in international politics in discussions and governance is a tool for implementation of neo-liberal policies. Neo-liberal definition of sovereignty is not based on the requirement of any particular class of the national population but it is a tool more amenable to the needs of the globalising capital to overcome its crisis and to accomplish accumulation and legitimation.

There is a change in view of imperial states about state power in the post-9/11 scenario. While the freedom from the state was highlighted by the neo-liberals in the beginning of accelerated globalisation the current scenario shows that this was replaced by another notion 'freedom by the state'. Transition of the role of capitalist state from one of maintaining passivity over globalisation to activism over the war on terror can be seen as the neo-liberal state apparatus is consolidated with extreme force and coercion in the name of security. [17]

At the ideological level it legitimises the coercive power of the neo-liberal state. The diminishing capacity of the state regarding regulation of capital accumulation and execution of welfare policies was compensated by increasing state capacity for protection of capital.

Globalisation and Democratization of Security

Which form of security, the state-centred on non-state, is prominent in the international politics today? The state-centred security perceptions have not been ceased to influence the corpus of security in the international politics. If state-centred security still attracts majority of the security debates, does it have the same meaning and substance compared to the cold war time? Prior to the propaganda for war on terror the capitalist states and their intellectual support system presented the security issues of the excluded, exploited and oppressed sections of the world population under the term of 'risk', but soon after the 9/11, Islamic terrorism was identified as a 'threat' to the patron states of world capitalism. Comprehension of security as vulnerable to various 'risks' actually intended to give a democratic and inclusive outlook to the unfolding neo-liberalism by including many a contentious issue of social security, for instance, poverty, human rights violation, income disparity, environmental cost etc.

Democracy, as defined in a neo-liberal fashion, has become an appendage to the security of dominant states and supportive classes across the geographical boundaries in the post-cold war global politics. [18] However, it seldom means that democracy enforces only a single meaning for all the participants. In fact democratisation through globalisation is a complex process that involves non-state actors as the emerging participants in the dialogue. And issues concerning security are more in number than that during the time of the cold war. Post-cold war debates on security show that it is more democratic than the old paradigm because now a large number of issues appear in security dialogue and it has multiplied the ideological frameworks used to describe security.

Certainly, the diversification of security issues is of positive impact on debates on democracy. But to grasp the reality, one has to clearly take stock of effectiveness and ineffectiveness of the arguments on the basis of its influence vis-à-vis the practices in international politics. The unipolar world, in terms of both military and economic indicators, poses threats to the anti-imperialist and anti-neo-liberal groups, while it maintains the dominance of the capitalist states and classes much stronger than ever before. In short the quantitative increase in the items and discussions do not produce a qualitative shift in security and democracy in international politics. Here the practice of the dialogue and the mode of incorporation of newer issues into the debates are relevant for analysis.

Moreover, compared to the period of cold war, because of the absence of a political consolidation of the critical perceptions, the critical perspectives are largely bypassed or cunningly co-opted by the establishment in practice. In short though the contemporary discussions of security are wider than the previous period in scope, it is not politically strong. In the view of this paper, the political strength of criticisms against the dominant views and practices is a yardstick of the substance of democracy. In the new devices of security as well as in many of the modified versions of the cold war security devices, democracy became an ingredient. The enlargement of security devices in the post-cold war, mainly by the US and European powers, is under the pretension that security is necessary for democracy. They hardly approve that democracy is necessary for security or both are complementing each other. Security in the view of the dominant players is supportive of the leading dynamics of international politics and political economy. Therefore, the concept of democracy has to be revisited in international security, providing it with a critical spirit.

In the prolonged unhappy marriage between democracy and security a paramour is involved in the post-Cold War the benefactor. The 1990s saw a deluge of talks about globalisation in the discussions of international politics. Deepening of capitalism into the interior spaces of nations and individual lives with the sole purpose of accumulation and legitimation is a characteristic feature of globalisation to its critics. They are worried about the neo-liberal dimensions of globalisation. Neo-liberal globalization changed the context, the structure, and the institutions of the nation-state and drastically altered the objectives of public policies. It envisages greater prospects of democracy for the international system. The hyper globalists are increasing concerned with the international democracy than the national one. [19]

The neo-liberal definitions of democracy replace the primacy of political in sustaining democracy with preponderance to free market. The globalized competition of states for the allocation of private companies gives the latter enormous bargaining power that permits them to some extent to dictate conditions unilaterally, to the detriment of the democracy. Even the traditional core area of public security is being affected, and rationalities from business and the market are being introduced to the security field. [20]

More precariously the majoritarian element of democracy, which is a check on the state's decisions in globalisation, is effectively tackled by neo-liberal globalists in theoretical arguments. They recommend market economy for the undemocratic states by envisaging a spill over effect of the liberal component in the economic sphere to the political after opening the economy for competition and private investment. [21] The argument is following the normative view of classical liberalism that the market (often it is not termed as capitalist market in the neo-liberal texts) is democratic. They prescribe the same criteria of choices in market as the criteria of people's choice in democracy and state's decisions making. [22] Foreign policies of the nation states, which are traditionally considered as the chord that links the domestic politics with the international politics, are formulated under the compulsions of globalisation, mainly its thrust for facilitation of the market. The changing perception of state about security is related to the gaining currency of neo-liberal rules in its public policy making. Higgott says that the foreign policy of the hegemonic states in globalisation gives importance to securitisation of globalisation. He remarks:

"From a reading of (US) policy in the contemporary era, we can say that a unipolar moment does indeed appear to have tempted the hegemon to integrate economic and security policy more closely than under conditions of multi-polarity. It has done so in a manner in which economic policy has become an arm of security policy. Economic policy, rather than being a mere instrument of economic relations and statecraft becomes a part of the armoury of influence that the hegemon uses to develop a strategy towards potential challengers". [23]

In the post-Cold War, the US is cautious to forge security partnership with the global competitors of the capitalist bloc, for instance EU, Japan and the East Asian countries. [24]

Necessarily, security in today's foreign policy making has a fresh dimension. It leaves a question for much concern. Does the imperial power interest of the States or their supportive class's economic interest and the economic system is a determinant of the security dimension in their international relations and foreign policy?

In the post-Cold War, the attempts to make security as necessary condition for liberal economic policy under the pretext of democracy did not face any serious constraint till the 9/11 episode. In the post-9/11 scenario, the security centred policy making and alliances, which were earlier offered to 'democratise' the erstwhile socialist and the US-sponsored authoritarian states, appeared in a new form. Challenging the claims of any hardcore globalist, the police and imperial power of the state assumed dramatic return in the domestic and international politics. Military and state power as a means to security damaged the legitimacy of the post-Cold War neo-liberal formula which bound together market, civil society and democracy. The formation of international coalitions against terrorism serves as a pretext for the governments to extend and intensify the use of national security laws to suppress movements for democracy and expression of dissent. [25] It gives international consent to coercive regimes, provided the states remain as the constituents of the neo-liberal imperialist bloc.

The turn of events was actually a setback to those who predicted stability and order in the 21st century. It was also a setback to liberal internationalism which was under way in 1990s in the form of creating regional organisations and debates on governance at the initiative of global funding agencies. [26]

The US-led group of states and their international

institutions lacked legitimacy to bridge democracy and security in international politics. It was simultaneous to the spread of local and transnational movements against imperialist globalisation. The civil society groups, which were criticised by the wooden Marxists as the puppets of international lending agencies and charitable organisations of the capitalists, and a large number of new social movements fight the combination of militarised security and neo-liberal market in different planes. Emergence of radical forces from the civil society in the democracies in transition, for instance, Latin America led to anti-neo-liberal and anti-American governments coming to power with alternative foreign policy options.

Hence it is not untenable to say that the contemporary security regime of the neo-liberal and imperialist powers is facing severe challenges for sustenance from these parallel lines of resistance. Trends in the contemporary world order can only be understood by an examination of the changing nature of security under the conditions of economic globalisation. [27] Neo-liberal policies propagate false and myopic notions about security. In their understanding security of capital and the state protection to smooth functioning of the free market summarize the agenda of security and those political conditions which shall sustain these practices constitute democracy. It shortens the agenda of foreign policy by squeezing many vital issues of security out of it. Significant still, the neo-liberal policies and transnational capitalist practices not only aggravate the existing problems of insecurity but also it generates new forms of security threats.

Democratization is the only way to guarantee an inclusive agenda of security. But such a possibility has to be sought for keeping in mind the fact that those who demand for enlargement of the security agenda are those groupings which contravene the establishment at several instances in their political struggle. Threats to capital and the threat of capital dominate the security perceptions of the neo-liberals and their opponents respectively. However, the resistance movements of various hues and shades that critically oppose the oppressive state and exploitative market at different planes of our societal space actually kindle the flames of hope about democratization. To understand this, one should properly discern the inner dynamics of globalization. [28] In a deeper analysis, globalization involves three streams:

1. International relations (between nation-states) which are the vestiges of the classical international system. It gives more importance to the territorial and geopolitical dimensions of security. This, coupled with the current transnational capitalist practices, constitutes the most powerful stream of globalization.
2. The transnational movements of resistance against imperialist state structures and the transnational capitalism represent the second stream. [29] This is the most organised form available to the dissidents of neo-liberalism and imperialism.
3. Numerous scattered groupings that fight against oppression, exploitation and exclusion at national, regional and local levels form the last stream.

The culmination of this process may end up in utter disaster or a more liveable world. Geographical differences of the resistance show that some states stand as exception, mainly in the developing world. Examination of the interplay of international and domestic factors may reveal the reason. Certain states which remain out of the epicentre of the international developments naturally keep out of the process. India is the best example. In spite of the growing divergence due to ethnic divisions and related political changes, India's political society shows greater convergence of opinion in the economic policies and foreign policy options. [30] This paper examines the domestic sources of foreign policy making in India in the settings of imperialist globalisation. Thus it brings out the drawback cf democracy in substance and procedure of foreign policy making.

Indian Foreign Policy: Elites vs. the Masses

India, under the leadership of Jawaharlal Nehru, joined the idealist bandwagon of international politics of that time and liberal idealism was lodged into the nation's foreign policy establishment. However, the ideology of independent India's foreign policy was not a revelation of the leadership as it is commonly understood. On the contrary, it was evolved in the specific historical juncture of the post-World War settings, which was characterized by manifold interactions between various socio-economic, developmental and political factors. The economic backwardness of the infant state naturally forced it to keep out of wars and turmoil and seek for economic aid and assistance from both the rival blocs of the Cold War. [31] Even though it is condemned as idealistic, the policy was the most pragmatic given its compliance with the developmental demands of the Indian masses as well as the global poor.

A review of India's foreign policy shows that in the objectives it was more democratic in the initial years of independence even though the procedure of policy formulation was dominated by the bureaucracy and encircled by the charismatic leadership of Nehru. Liberal idealism in spite of its elitist nature was conducive for proposing some humanitarian objectives at the international level by India. Critics may also remark that the ambivalent post-colonial leadership pursued idealism in the foreign policy to legitimize the power of the state among the masses. [32] In fact, two hidden objectives underlie the urge for idealism, firstly, the ambition of India to build up its image at the international level as a benevolent democratic state in order to seeking for legitimacy to its global interventions; and secondly, its aspiration to become the leader of the third world and a regional super-power in South Asia. However, the principles of the idealist foreign policy mirrored the democratic ethos of the domestic economic policy to a great extent. Notably, the state had been considerate to the aspirations of the masses, at least in rhetoric.

At present, both substance-wise and process-wise the policy is in short of democratic component. A transformation from '*elitist idealism*' into '*elitist pragmatism*' best illustrates the ideological and historical trajectory of independent India's foreign policy. After the Nehru era India's foreign policy oscillated between idealism and opportunistic realism. Ironically, there was no sincere effort from the ruling parties to involve the masses at any stage of the foreign policy making. For the political leadership, the external policy remained with the sole domain of government and beyond the reach of ordinary people in spite of the fact that Nehru government and its successors were euphoric about democratization of international politics during the heydays of liberal idealism. Therefore, the foreign policy of India has not been permeable to a mass debate. There was no attention to institutionalization of the democratic dialogue between the state and the masses.

The neglect of people's debates on foreign policy during the initial years of independence caused to its degeneration into the level of an intrigue between the ruling class and the state in the contemporary times. Interestingly, there were instances when political differences on foreign policy and objective academic comments were considered as tantamount to sedition. [33] The approach of the political parties and the 'think tanks' to the foreign policy debates has been overwhelmed by the spirit of national pride due to the lingering memories of national struggle for freedom. Its success largely depends on the efficacy of the establishment to disseminate a plethora of sentimental ideas like national interest, national security, political consensus and realism creating false consciousness.

Militarized Security Concerns and the Plight of Democracy in Foreign Policy

For a majority, military security is the quintessential of a country's foreign policy. It is a longstanding historical tradition in International Politics which regards national security as the foremost objective of foreign policy. National security as the key concern of foreign policy is crucial to conduct much of the external relations away from the masses. In fact, such a conception is undeniably related to the emergence and existence of the nation-state system also. In spite of the potentials of globalization to tremble the nation state system national security remains as a tedious rhetorical device in the foreign policy making. Recently, critics have raised concerns about the continuing centrality of military security in the foreign policy. Moreover, they demand for a comprehensive definition of security through liberating it from the straightjackets of military science. In this context, a look into the matter—cognizance of the foreign policy establishment of security—would be worth. M. Dubey rightly cautions about this:

"It is also seen that the state, in collusion with the elite, indulges in activities which create domestic threats to security, such as suppression of human rights and pursuing an elitist development paradigm in which the vast number of the poor do not participate and increasingly marginalized". [34]

Security concerns in the foreign policy naturally forces the state to be militarized. [35] It has two consequences as far as the domestic as well as the international politics is concerned. In the domestic arena, it inexorably enhances the coercive power of the state. At the international level, it leads to arms race and war. In plural societies the security concerns are abused to debilitate the social harmony. Illustration of the dissident communities having global presence, for instance Muslims as a threat to the national interest and security even in the official reports is an example. Hence, it is high time to redefine the concept of national security from a 'social constructivist' point of view in the foreign policy research. [36]

Globalization of security concerns has become an indispensable factor in the hogwash of the capitalist West to consolidate its dominance. Foreign policy and military policy are used to propagate the neo-liberal democratic ideology and its underlying economic order everywhere. [37] As a result, the capitalist states militarized the world to ensure the security of capital and the stability of state apparatus which safeguards the former. [38] They fine-tune the foreign policies of weaker states with a prior and massive penetration of their economic and political system.

Unsurprisingly, the policy perspective of India show better compliance with the security concerns of the dominant players of global politics. It has to subscribe to their world view and has to remain as either a supporter or a silent witness to the onslaught on democracy at the international level. The fallacy of the US intervention for democracy has been exposed before the public and proved to be counterproductive to democracy itself in more than a case.

However, the US-led realists fail to grasp (or ignore deliberately) the necessity of democratizing the process and the content of foreign policy before or simultaneous with setting democracy as the objective of the policy. In fact, the liberal idealistic school, which has been pushed to the margins in the policy research, is no longer capable of resisting the advance of realism in international politics. Moreover, both of them converge on the dominant economic ideology of the present world order, neo-liberalism in practice.

Neo-liberal Economics and Dependency in India's Foreign Policy

Separation of economy from politics is the characteristic feature of ordinary research in foreign policy. It prevents a critical political economy approach from emerging in the mainstream research. It is worth mentioning that public policies are formulated not in isolation from the socio-economic structure. This fact compels one to look into the influence of the New Economic Policy on India's foreign policy.

The ruling class, which has better access to the state

apparatus, has relatively stronger influence vis-à-vis the policy making bodies also. This is more so in the case of foreign policy. Since the foreign policy is regarded as solely shaped by the national interest and since it is always kept beyond the mundane political controversies for that reason, the ruling class could easily appropriate the policy to pursue their business interests. However, this crucial issue largely evades critical public attention.

With the end of the Cold War, the international economy rushed into neo-liberalism. It forced the developing countries like India to reorient their foreign policy. Even though during the initial years of independence India did not seek a complete break with world capitalism, it was able to exercise greater manoeuvrability and flexibility within the limitations imposed by the circumstances of the world economic system. India's experience had been deployed as and when necessary to join with other third world countries in analyzing problems, evolving new concepts, putting forward practical proposals, negotiating compromises and pressing for concrete action. [39]

The closed economic model provided the infant capitalist class adequate protection from the foreign players. This was in addition to the state patronage to them in many ways. Nehruvian foreign policy is also acknowledged for the unsuccessful efforts to cut into a balance between the masses and the ruling class. It is doubtful whether the Nehru government could follow such a policy if it did not have the tacit legitimacy of the ruling class.

By 1990s, India abandoned the economic path of 'self reliant growth' and the policies like 'import substitution' in favour of the export-led growth strategy partially under the pressure of international agencies and partially due to the inner-contradictions of the state-led development model. [40] The changing trends of India's foreign policy are related to the changing character and the newer ambitions of the Indian bourgeoisie. [41] The New Economic Policy heavily relies on the collaboration between foreign and domestic capital.

Currently, the government has to conduct the foreign policy paying utmost attention to the economic tie-up with the international economy. [42] In fact, the structural adjustment programme forced Indian economy to increasingly depend on the capitalist states. Therefore, the question, whether such a dependent economic policy could ensure independence of foreign policy, does provide food for thought.

The official stance of the government based on militarized security concerns and neo-liberalism points out that India pursues a kind of dependence through its foreign policy. In recent years, the formulation and conduct of India's foreign policy has singularly suffered from a holistic approach. It has become *ad hoc* and reactive rather than pro-active. [43] The foreign policy is over concerned with the legitimacy it seeks from the major powers [44] viz., the global economic players and their patron states; and the ruling class of India, rather than the Indian masses. India's increasing adherence to the capitalist bloc is a potential threat to the democratization of foreign policy since it enhances the class disparities, strengthens the national monopolies and facilitates the emergence of newer elite conglomerations in the domestic politics. However, the pro-capitalist foreign policy holds legitimacy of the ruling class. It is a matter of grave concern that the Indian state works in tandem with its western allies to suppress the suffering millions, for instance, environmental victims, refugees of neo-liberal development model and the working class who combat the neo-liberal policies in global, national and local politics.

Diminution of idealism is a reason for India playing a passive role in the UN system. Post-Cold War era also witnessed the erosion of the UN not only in security matters but also in development activities. Initiatives from the third world to the UN reforms became ineffective with the Indian establishment adopting vacillating stance. [45] India's affinity to neo-liberalism and its inability to resist the US-led imperialism precipitated the decline of multilateral mechanisms like the UN. Demise of multilateralism, on its part, also erodes the remaining possibilities of democratizing India's foreign policy under international compulsions.

Ruling Class Character of Foreign policy

Confrontations between the state and the populace characterize the national politics of all countries today. Failure of the state in domestic politics creates hiatus between the aspirations of the people and the official version of the governments. It quakes the democratic foundation of pluralistic societies and weakens the legitimacy of the nation-state. Cleavages based on class and ethnicity pose severe challenges to the claims of the government to represent the nation as a whole, which further deteriorate its international image to act as the spokesperson of the entire populace. Therefore, the declining legitimacy of the state in domestic politics makes its external policy partisan which, in turn, exacerbates the alienation of people.

Globalization is characterized by not only the expansion of imperialism and capitalism but also the emerging people's resistance at the global level. The overlapping character of many a contemporary issue of mass unrest in different quarters of the globe provides them a transnational outlook. Permeation of capital and presence of imperialist forces have contributed to the globalization of multifarious local issues and movements. Consequent to these developments, the foreign policy has to focus on the transnational movements of the working class, environmental victims, women, racial minorities, muslims and other ethnic/terrorist groups etc. But the Indian foreign policy remains cool minded about the newer dynamics, mainly the subaltern terrain of global politics. Interestingly, the Indian state disturbed by numerous intra-state conflicts and disruptions strive to interpret them as potential threats to national security and democracy. [46]

Like a majority of democratic states it is also very eager to push these issues onto the global security agenda which was prepared by the US to lead the 'War on Terror'. This becomes counterproductive since the foreign policy, which aims at the victimization of the dissidents, actually contributes to the alienation of people from the state in domestic politics.

While a few decades ago it was the development paradoxes of the state-led economic model which caused ethnic and intra-regional conflicts, now the pro-imperialist foreign policy and neo-liberal economic policies of the nation states become a crucial reason to augment the antagonism of different sections of the society against the state. In the context of globalization, though the resentments of the masses are economic to the root, they are manoeuvred by the ethnic fundamentalists. [47]

Indian foreign policy establishment has an infamous track record in combating the human rights violations through international cooperation. Most of the acts of its omission and commission were justified on the basis of the benign principles of 'right to national self determination' and 'non-interference of external agencies in the domestic affairs'. It may be noted that unlike the Latin American countries, for instance, Venezuela Indian government has not declared solidarity with the global social movements. At the same time, India's foreign policy establishment is enthusiastic to cooperate with the pro-capitalist non-state actors of the global politics, for instance, multinational corporations. Increasing presence of business magnets in the diplomatic parleys also points out the vulnerability of our policy towards the ruling class.

It is also true that the foreign policy makers are wary of international attention on the pathetic conditions of dalits, working class, tribal population and women partially due to the false pride of national glory and partially due to the fear about a possible exposure of India as a 'failed state' before the global public. Definitely, a failed state would like to hide its inner contradictions because if revealed, they would unleash divisive forces and give another blow to its declining legitimacy. It would be worth mentioning that the defiance of our foreign policy establishment against internationalization of the domestic issues of the masses through democratic means aborts the possibility of substantive solutions. India's ambivalence towards internationalization at the initiative of the masses rather than the government and the ruling class is an obstacle to democratize our foreign policy.

Three critical questions are of great relevance to analyze the foreign policy of India from a democratic perspective: (a) How far our foreign policy represents different sections of the domestic population, especially working class, muslim minority, dalits, indigenous communities, etc., and what is its reaction to the diverse aspirations of them?; (b) How far the foreign policy of India is responsive to the demand of a new world order based on substantive democracy?; and (c) Is the failure of Indian state to play a crucial role in restructuring the present world order related to its class character?

At the outset, it could be stated that among the various government policies the least democratized are defence and foreign policies. Always matters related to them are never disclosed in name of national interest and official secrecy. It is similar to the wariness of the government about public attention and its defiance against people's control over the matters relating to the neo-liberal economic policy. While it causes massive corruption in defence, it leads to underdevelopment of the masses in the economy. As far as the foreign policy is concerned, lack of transparency and democracy makes it elitist in character. It is a mystery, why the policy, which is supposed to preserve the national interest, is so secret.

Debates in the mainstream, especially among the educated people, about foreign policy are monotonous rather than pluralistic. Pathetically, they are uncritical of the establishment in the name of national interest. Besides this, the foreign policy analyses are not a serious item in the vernacular press of India. [48] It indicates the existence of a shared consensus among the upper class, urban upper-middle class, English media, higher bureaucracy, top brass of bureaucrat-turned-politicians, military heads and diplomats. [49] Therefore, the discussions about foreign policy are misconceived as an exclusive arena of specialists and experts possessing the same values and ideology of the establishment. This contributes to evolve manufactured public opinion based on the myopic vision.

Domestic Political Changes and Foreign Policy

Over the last few decades, the domestic realm of India has been witnessing socio-political changes which rightly reflected in the configuration of the party system. Even though the political spectrum of both the centre and the states was pluralized due to the formation of caste parties and their efforts to mobilize the middle caste groupings into the higher echelons of political power, its reflection is yet to be visible in the foreign policy. In fact, the demands of the other backward caste (OBC) parties were limited to the national politics. In the foreign policy making, the OBCs have failed to ascertain as an influential social segment like a 'group for itself'. Their political alliances with national parties like BJP and the Congress were crucial to synthesize their class interest with the ruling class. However, these political alliances contributed to the evaporation of radicalism of the middle caste parties. Hence, the elites of the middle castes articulate the same voice of the ruling class at the international level.

In the context of globalization, the middle caste parties also adopt neo-liberal economic policies of the mainstream political forces and hold the same perspectives of the upper class sections of the upper caste groupings. In fact, the political economy interest of the upper stratum of all caste groupings converges on globalization. The similarities in their economic aspirations have become an important reason for the lack of democracy in the foreign policy of India. It again proves that the OBC parties failed to resist the class character of the foreign policy, though they accomplished to change the caste character of Indian politics in the domestic arena.

The role of regional parties in foreign policy making is an emerging area of research. In India, the regional parties' view is scarcely different from the national parties' foreign policy. Even though they are vocal if the foreign policy has a negative implication on the regional population, for instance Kashmir issue and Tamil nationalism, they are not capable of systematic restructuring of the broader policy framework. Importantly, on issues of foreign policy having relevance to India's emerging capitalist class, for example pro-US relations they are true followers of the national parties. The indifference of the Samajwadi Party of Mulayam Singh to back the decision of the Left to withdraw support from the UPA government is the recent example.

On the other hand, the domestic concerns of the regional parties rarely become a global issue unless it involves some transnational aspects. This observation is true in the case of caste based politics in India. The caste system is truly Indian, which prevents its transnational importance. Except the tribes, and Dalits to a certain extent, no other caste groupings shall find interest in the transnational movements of resistance to neo-liberal globalisation. Recent demand by the caste parties for reservation in private sector jobs is a line of hope. But the perception of its advocates about neo-liberal globalisation is more important to make it a politically strong movement. On the other hand, the identity movement of Muslims which may have much global significance, but their presence in the mainstream Indian politics is very marginal. The recent endeavours of Muslim community in this regard are marred by state repression and public fear about terrorism.

India's parliamentary democracy is also not effective to stir up a debate among the masses about the unpopular foreign policy since the political parties consider it as an unimportant item on their electoral agenda. [50] It has been stated elsewhere that there exists a broad consensus among the political parties about the policy. Except the Left, no Indian political party thinks about a systematic change in the foreign policy so that it could echo the concerns of the Indian masses in the global arena. Pathetically, a majority of political parties is confused by the mysterious dichotomy of national and international politics and celebrating the myth of national interest.

It is clear that the collaboration of India's comprador ruling class with the world capitalist classes under the tutelage of free market economy is a supplementary reason to deprive the nation's foreign policy of a mass character. Neo-liberalism increases India's dependence on the dominant states in our policy options. Therefore, the efforts aiming at global solidarity between the Indian masses and the world poor to fight for their common cause have been foiled. It is important that while the neo-liberal state bridges the domestic rich classes with the foreign rich through its pro-imperialist foreign policy and economic policy, it denies opportunity for the Indian poor to associate with their brethren outside. The support to imperialism in India's foreign policy is hidden, while the neo-liberal pledge of its economic policies is the most visible. India is pro-imperialist if one looks at the intertwined relationship of its foreign and economic policies. It precisely explains the class character of Indian state in the foreign policy in the neo-liberal time.

Micro movements at the grassroots, which are called otherwise as civil society groups, NGOs and new social movements in India constitute the low profile politics of the process. Many sociologists and political scientists focused attention on this relatively new dimension of domestic politics. [51] However they have very little influence in the process of policy making. The policy making is still dominated by political parties and the pressure politics of the dominant classes.

Though it has many drawbacks, the undiluted enthusiasm of the masses about electoral democracy, which is visible from the increasing percentage of votes polled in the post-reform elections, forced the academics to rethink their optimism about the waning out of the state and the emergence of civil society as active participant in the domestic politics. [52]

Really these movements are of immense potentials to democratize the foreign policy and security. But they fail to influence the establishment because of the following reasons:

1. They are geographically scattered.
2. Little faith in state and formal democratic politics.
3. They are not becoming the constituents of political parties.
4. They hold diverging perspectives among themselves.
5. Unlike the caste/communal groupings they have not created any crisis of governance. Their depoliticized activities actually contribute to the success of Indian democracy.
6. Indian state which is no longer liberal to these movements prevents their trans-nationalisation.

Indian Left and Foreign Policy

Compared to their counterparts Left political parties still hold strong critical perspectives about the foreign policy of Indian state. More than an appraisal of Left, we focus on the challenges of the Indian Left to become a critical corrective to the neo-liberal-imperialist syndrome in India's economic and foreign policy. Left is attempting to legitimate its views before the public and among regional and caste political parties, which are sharing the ideas of sovereignty and national interest while discussing foreign policy.

The conceptual frame of criticism of the government's foreign policy is not convenient bases of argument for the Left since Marxian theory is widely noted for a critical framework giving little space to these utopian terms. But in Indian politics, the Left parties too have to raise their criticism against foreign policy based on the concepts alien to their ideological foundations. Press reports show that in the recent event of Indo-US nuclear deal, the Left party leadership was citing national interest at stake as a reason to oppose it. It shows an example to prove that the strong critics having a revolutionary world view has to come in tune with certain irrational perspectives to gain acceptance of the public in Indian democracy.

Anti-Left intelligentsia—both the critics and the cohorts of the pro-US foreign policy— may argue that it was a failure of the Left, but the former seldom promote critical intervention in the public mind to inspire broader and logical way of understanding about nationalism, national interest and sovereignty. Another challenge before the Left is to find out justification for the actions of their state governments which are cooperating with the capitalist investors and seeking aid and assistance from the imperialist states while the Left as the national opposition is fighting the foreign policy's bias to US-led imperialist bloc and neo-liberal policies. Moreover, such events cause disenchantment from civil society groups in domestic politics. Nandigram issue in West Bengal proves this point. The damages to their political criticism negatively affect the possibilities of organized political opposition to the foreign policies of the establishment. In spite of best efforts the Left finds it difficult to coordinate non-Congress and non-BJP alliances in the form of a third front on the basis of the ideological principles of the Left parties.

The Left is also facing difficulties to find out a suitable ally from the non-Congress and non-BJP parties in domestic politics. Though the Left envisages the third front as a coalition suggesting alternatives to the policy perceptions of the Congress and BJP the motivations of regional parties and several splinter groups have little compliance with that of the Left. It was a reason to suggest that the Left should revisit the idea of third front through forming an alliance of the civil society groups and new social movements on the basis of a more interactive relationship. This is a distant possibility, though a democratic option. The party leadership agreed with this occasionally. For example, Prakash Karat observed in the World Social Forum (2004) about the limitations of the political Left, and indicated the possibilities of cooperation with new social movements. He said:

"The Left parties on their part have still to catch up with some of the new realities and challenges. Their struggle for alternative policies, their conception of a Left and democratic platform to challenge the imperialist-liberalization-communalization is mainly centred on the daily economic struggles and the electoral-political battles. There is an insufficiency in both the conceptualization of and the struggles in the social and cultural spheres. Neither has the Left been able to fully deal with the complexities of technology-driven social trends and the social impact of the new economics. This gap, apart from other organizational constraints, makes it difficult for the Left to respond in a timely fashion to the issues raised by some of the social movements" [53]

But this is a programme yet to evolve by the CPI (M) in concrete terms in Indian politics. It raises several questions. What is the actual gap between the political Left and the civil society groups in their criticism of neo-liberalism and pro-imperialist foreign policy is spite of the fact that the establishment is their common enemy? How the opposition of civil society groups to Left political parties, mainly CPI (M), be justified since actually it paved the way for the Congress to come to power in recent election, 2009? Is globalization a hindrance to the Left to sharpen their agitations against the establishment with the help of New Social Movements? Why a mutual understanding is lacking between the critics of neo-liberalism and imperialism in domestic politics?

Civil society has equal responsibility of this quagmire. For example, the attempts of the Left to seek alliance of certain sections of the Muslim community on the basis of anti-imperialist and anti-Hindutva principles in Kerala provoked strong criticism from the civil society for appeasement of minority communalism in the 2009 election. On the other hand, the same Left in West Bengal faced criticism from civil society including the Muslim sections because of the government's attempts to keep in tune with the neo-liberal compulsions by means of forceful industrialization and eviction of rural people. The decision of the Left to withdraw support to a government that indirectly tilted the policy in favour of the US was concealed in the civil society discussions. The Left faced a failure not because of the emptiness of its policies and the humidity in its ideological battery, but due to the multiple obstacles that prevent ideological debates and policy-wise estimation of the contesting political parties in Indian elections.

Class-wise evaluation of the public opinion for or against the anti-imperialist posture of the Left is a matter of concern. Prabhat Patnaik rightly observes in his article the comparative cost of anti-imperialism for the Left in Indian politics. He remarks the predicament of the Left (read CPI (M)) in the following lines:

"All over the world, in countries where the urban middle class has escaped as yet the adverse consequences of globalization, anti-imperialism among the students, the educated youth, and the literati is at low ebb. On the contrary there is even a desire to welcome closer integration with the imperialist world as a means of ushering in a secular and progressive modernity, and of countering phenomena like feudal patriarchy, religious authoritarianism and communal fascism...Left movement gathers momentum in situations where the urban middle class has also suffered from globalization and hence makes common cause with the workers and peasants. But it faces problems in situations (in India) where the urban middle class is a beneficiary of the globalization. In such cases, the resistance to imperialism and globalization often gets championed by the forces other than Left political parties; or, if the Left remains committed to the interests of the 'basic classes' and resist globalization, it often suffers through isolation from the intellectual strata and the urban youth and students." [54]

In the analysis of the problems faced by the Left political parties to combat imperialism, Prabhat Patnaik greatly differs in tone and tenor from many spokespersons of civil society who are explaining the failure of Left (including its debacle in 2009 election) as the failure of certain party organizations, mainly the CPI (M), rather than taking it as part of the general failure or the predicament of the Left.

This paper is of the view that the critical minds of the civil society that presents highly fragmented individual explanations do not properly understand the limitations of the Left and they do not recognize the differences of the Left in Indian politics from other political parties. Therefore, the civil society's critical reactions to the Left political parties lead to apathy of the masses about politics. It has a dangerous consequence. It leads to further weakening of the organized critical opinion within the political society. In most of the cases the civil society's criticisms based on idealist images of revolution and apolitical solutions caused to the decline of the Left political parties' ideas [read CPI (M)] in practical politics.

As mentioned earlier, the foreign policy is not an important theme for debates in Indian elections, especially among the masses. Yet defenders of national pride in rhetoric and the hate campaigners (Congress and BJP respectively) were able to share the popular mandate to continue more or less same policies—both economic and foreign—as a result of the decline of the Left. It compels us to find out other arenas of social lives, than the elections and parliamentary politics to democratize government policies. But here also the nationalist and consumerist middle class consciousness is a hindrance.

History of the Congress shows that it was also a victim during the Nehru period of its idealist and 'democratic' foreign policy behaviour in relations with China. It raised public criticisms in 1960s against the Congress since the wide belief was that the government sacrificed national interest before China. The negative public reaction against a government that sacrifices the national interest need not be the same on all occasions. For example, the pro-US foreign policy of BJP and Congress since 1990s evaded strong criticism from the public.

[55] Especially they do not create any anti-incumbency factor in the general elections. It shows that Indian public is much worried about the directly negative consequences of foreign policy more than the hidden and indirect consequences of today's policy compatibility with the dominant states.

The definition of security based on perceived challenges to India's military and energy requirements given by the UPA government to justify the Indo-US nuclear deal was more convincing to the public. Public are more reactive to the direct consequences of the foreign policy than to the indirect and gradual ones. Most of India's foreign policy in the contemporary time belongs to the second category in which the consequences are indirect and gradual. However, empirical evidences are absent to prove/disprove the public support to foreign policy, except election results and related surveys and media reports.

Conclusion

Aforesaid said analysis points out that democratization of foreign policy requires a multiple intervention from the part of the progressive minds. Firstly, the utopian concepts that we regularly use in foreign policy debates needs critical scrutiny because most of the terms we use in foreign policy talks, for instance national interest and democracy (procedural definition) are meaningless and unscientific from a critical social science perspective and thus prevents democratization of the policy. Usual foreign policy discussions ignore very important concepts like ruling class character of the state since they seldom approach foreign policy from the political economy perspective. Similarly, majority of the popular media usually popularize the myths rather than the facts about external relations.

The propagandists gloss over the contradiction, whether India could speak to the world outside unanimously since most of the domestic policies of the government has divided the socio-economic structure helter-skelter. Therefore, the relationship between the domestic socio-political structure of the country and its interactions with the world outside through the medium of foreign policy is to be thoroughly investigated. This would be helpful to bring out the impacts of foreign policy on the domestic society and its consequences on the already imbalanced relations of power for public evaluation.

The debased idealistic position of many contemporary admirers of Nehru (mainly the veteran mainstream critics) is not sufficient to democratize the foreign policy of India. The idealistic position of the old generation foreign policy experts is lacking in objective understanding of the contemporary dynamics of global politics. This is more so, since we have to strive for futuristic suggestions as well. Idealism of Nehru was significant only while the principles of nationalism and modernity were sound in international relations. Now, the foundational principles of nation state, not the state's coercive power, have been ravaged due to globalization. Modernity also faced setbacks due to the emergence of innumerable questions of underdevelopment and cultural conflicts.

Therefore, there is no question of resorting to Nation State and nationalism to democratize the foreign policy. It is worth remembering that liberal humanism which is the basis of idealism is pliant before realism since it is devoid of theoretical criticism. The viable alternative is, therefore, to seek for critical paradigms through incorporating Marxian tools to recapitulate the present world order giving adequate stress to the problem of destabilization of the nation-state and the emerging state-society divide—both open and concealed forms—and the social struggles.

Secondly, on the political front two processes are imperative: (i) Diversifying the mainstream debates on foreign policy through filling up the gap between different criticisms; (ii) Percolation of such debates to the grassroots and initiating a debate on an alternative order from below. The difference between '*democracy as the objective of foreign policy*' and '*the democratization of foreign policy*' should be specified in critical studies. The former is based on a false assumption which seldom apprehends the paucity of democratic substance in the foreign policy making, but the latter brings this issue for critical scrutiny.

Definitely, only a democratized foreign policy can take democracy as its objective. It can only assure a comprehensive view of security. It requires restructuring of the elitist foreign policy establishment, radicalization of the content of the policy and democratization of the process of policy formulation through enlarging the membership that takes part in decision making. In the Indian context, a synergistic relationship between the political Left and the progressive sections of the civil society is more desirable to fruitfully reorder the foreign policy to secure substantive democracy and security in both internal and external dimensions in times of globalization.

End Notes

1. It seems that we are inspired by the advice of Machiavelli to Prince about the distinctive standard of morality in domestic politics and foreign relations.
2. Morton Halperin, *Bureaucratic Politics and Foreign Policy*, The Brooking Institution, Washington DC, 1974, p. 101.
3. J.D. Hagan, 'Domestic Political Conflict, Issue Areas, and Some Dimensions of FP Behaviour other than Conflict', *International Interactions*, Vol. 12, No. 4, pp. 291-313.
4. The question of sovereignty in foreign policy is similar one in international politics. Sovereignty centred explanation of foreign policy is outmoded since most of the states have become part of either form of the multilateral system and accepted the existence of international community as a reality in their policy making. Thus democracy became a parameter to evaluate foreign policy and an objective of the same in the post-world war and in the contemporary times. Certainly, it has the potentials to promote open ended discussion compared to the opaque argument based on sovereignty. In the view of this paper, democracy provides a chance for raising questions against those who introduced this in international relations and foreign policy making, though they aimed at producing consent to their coercive actions under the safe cover of this benign term.
5. Peter Gourevitch, 'The Second Image Revisited: The

International Sources of Domestic Politics', *International Organisation*, Vol. 32, No. 4, 1978, pp. 881-912.

6. "At a less dramatic but equally basic level, the classical view about national interest ignores the question: whose national interest are we talking about? Is it not possible that given the vagueness of the concept, each government or elite group may interpret a country's national interest to promote its own national interest?" See: N.K. Jha, 'Coalition Governments and India's Foreign Policy' in M.P. Singh and Anil Sharma (eds.): *Coalition Politics in India; Problems and Prospects*, New Delhi: Manohar, 2004, p. 294.
7. Robert D. Putnam, 'Diplomacy and Domestic Politics: The Logic of Two-Level Games', *International Organisation*, Vol. 42, No. 3, 1988, pp. 427-460.
8. No critical mind would agree with this, but this is a fashion in our discussions, both mundane talks and media debates about foreign policy. For a similar observation, See: A. K. Ramakrishnan, 'Neo-liberal Globalisation and India's Foreign Policy: Towards a Critical Rethinking', in Rajan Harshe and K. M. Seethi (eds.), Engaging with the World: Critical Reflections on India's Foreign Policy, New Delhi: Orient Longman, 2005
9. Andrew Moravscik, 'Introduction: Integrating International and Domestic Theories in International Bargaining' in Peter B Evans, HK Jacobson and RD Putnam (eds.), *Double Edged Diplomacy: International Bargaining and Domestic Politics*, University of California Press, Berkely, London, 1993.
10. It is a fact that while examining the trajectory of world history based on the dialectical process Marx would not foresee a situation of world politics in which the class war was conducted by the nation states. Therefore, the modern state system of international politics was largely beyond the comprehension of Marxists on conservative lines. Truly the nation state, not simply as a class instrument but as a cultural unit and benefactor of national interest, was an unexpected element in the course of human history against the prediction of Marx and his orthodox followers.
11. The communist bloc also subsumed to the liberal definition of democracy by setting up international security regimes in the international politics.
12. The communists failed to make much intervention in the

domestic politics with their notion of democracy towards the end of the Cold War. Therefore, the Cold War terminated in creating more relevance to the notions of democracy upheld by the capitalist bloc than its rival communists.

13. Sebastian Huluban, 'Domestic Sources of Post-Communist Foreign Policy: Institutional Analysis of Hungary and Romania 1999-2000', *Centro Argentino de Estudios Internacionales*, www.caei.com.ar.
14. The contentious debate over the preponderance of liberty and equality in democracy was unresolved in the Cold War. It is continuing in the policy prescriptions that propose freedom as the more important objective for human emancipation than equality by the neo-liberal intelligentsia.
15. Unlike the old cold war rivals of the US, in the post-Cold War the authoritarian regimes and the ideologues of medieval authoritarianism have lesser influence on the debates on democracy. Normally in a clash between market fundamentalism and medieval feudal order and associated religious dogma the democracy of the former supersede the latter in ideological battle.
16. David Harvey, *A Brief History of Neo-liberalism*, New York: OUP, p. 19.
17. Jarrod Weiner and Jessica Young, 'Globalisation and After? Continuity and Change in the Politics of Securitization and Responsibility', in Samir Dasgupta and Ray Kiely, *Globalization and* After, Sage Publications, New Delhi, 2006, p. 267.
18. While there was evidence of the securitisation of economic globalisation in US policy from day one of the Bush administration, it was 9/11 that firmed up this trend. For the key members of the Bush foreign policy team, globalisation is now seen not simply in neo-liberal economic terms, but also through the lenses of the national security agenda of the United States. See: Richard Higgott,' American Unilateralism, Foreign Economic Policy and the Securitization of Globalization', *CSGS Working Paper*, No. 124, 2003.
19. 'Constitutional deficiency' at the international level is the only point which the globalists see as a negative of the emerging global democracy. See: Ruth Zimmerling, 'Globalisation and Democracy: A Framework for Discussion'.

20. Sven Bislev, 'Globalization, State Transformation and Public Security', *International Political Science Review*, 25(3), 2004, p. 281.
21. Mark F. Plattner, 'Globalization and Self-Government', *Journal of Democracy*, 13(3), (July), 2002, pp. 54-67.
22. Some of the liberal economists have crossed all boundaries to place markets above democracy. For instance, WH Riker says, "market can do better choices than the ballot boxes can do". See WH. Riker.
23. Ibid, p. 10.
24. Though there is a difference of opinion among the critics of neo-liberalism to identify globalization with the US dominance its imperial project is qualifying the argument that neo-liberalism is under the aegis of the US. This point is always highlighted by those who criticize the Latin American governments' attempts to counter globalization with a country-cantered perspective.
25. Liz Fikate, 'People's Security vs. National Security', *Race and Class*, 44(78), 2003.
26. Ray Kiely, 'Business as Usual or Radical Shift? Theorizing the Relationship between US Hegemony and Globalization' in Samir Dasgupta and Ray Kiely (eds.), *Globalization and After*, Sage Publication, New Delhi, 2006, p. 99.
27. Higgott, op. cit, p. 1.
28. "Methodologically we have made a difference between globalization as an objective present-day reality, a value-free phenomenon that has its positive and negative elements and characteristics, and globalization as neo-liberal oriented policy directed from leading world centres and powers. This sort of pro-globalization policy is usually labelled as globalism." See: Mislav Kukoč, 'Democracy and Neo-liberal Globalisation'.
29. Immanuel Wallerstein, "Globalization or the Age of Transition?: A Long-term View of the Trajectory of the World-System."
30. Foreign relations are traditionally bureaucratic than democratic. EU and UN are more bureaucratic than democratic institutions. See for this argument, Mislav Kukoč, op. cit.
31. M.S. Rajan, 'India's Foreign Policy: The Continuing Relevance of Non-Alignment', *International Studies,* Vol. 30, No. 2, April-June 1993, pp. 141-150.
32. For an informed discussion about the influence of the western ideas on India's political leadership, see: E. Malcolm Hause,

'India under the Impact of Western Political Ideas and Institutions', *The Western Political Quarterly*, Vol. 14, No. 4, December 1961, pp. 879-895.

33. When the Communists raised few critical questions regarding the policy of India towards China at the time of Sino-India war of 1962 the establishment pounced upon them. The description of *Aksai Chin* and NEFA as disputed territories by E.M.S Namboodiripad based on relevant historical facts became prey to the rage of nationalist intellectuals. Ironically, our foreign policy establishment indirectly recognized the post-War status quo in the India-China border as part of normalizing the bilateral relations in recent times.
34. M. Dubey, 'India's Foreign Policy: Aims and Strategies', in Nancey Jetly (ed.), *India's Foreign Policy: Challenges and Prospects*, New Delhi: Vikas Publications Pvt. Ltd., 1999, p. 11.
35. In India the highest military expenditure, state-sponsored communal fascism and violence, alliance with the hawkish states at the international level in name of realism and incredible sufferings to the depressed classes from the elitist economic policies were recorded while the country was ruled by the BJP led coalition (NDA). It shows that militarization of the state in external affairs is rightly a reflection of the undemocratic domestic policies of the government.
36. For analysis of 'social construction of national interest', see: Martha Finnermore, *National Interest and International Society*, Cornell university Press, Ithaca and London, 1996.
37. Democracy is the pretentious objective of American intervention all over the world because the US administration requires the sanction of the American public who bear its financial cost and wants to justify its unilateralism among the global community. See: Morton H. Halperin, 'Guaranteeing Democracy', *Foreign Policy*, No. 91, Summer, 1993, pp. 105-122.
38. The author contends that the capitalist West pardoned India for its nuclear tests mainly because of the willingness of India to become an economic partner of these countries by adopting neo-liberal policies. It shows that nuclearization of India is no longer a threat to their international hegemony so long as India remains with the capitalist bloc.
39. K.M. Seethi and P. Vijayan, 'Political Economy of India's Third World Policy', in Rajan Harshe and K. M. Seethi (eds.), *Op. cit.*,

p. 49.

40. Indian state failed to mobilize sufficient resources for development through radical nationalization of private property. Its failure to implement land reforms and procrastination of decentralization of power precluded the mass from achieving political mobility. The state also siphoned huge sum of public money into the hands of Indian bourgeoisie through the public sector banks and financial institutions. The philanthropic endeavours to satisfy the developmental demands of the masses without disturbing the economic interest of the ruling class actually forced the state to borrow from foreign agencies. The balance of payment crisis in the 1990s is related to the problematic trajectory of development path of Indian state. For similar arguments, see: Pranab Bardhan, *The Political Economy and Development in India*, New Delhi: Oxford University Press, 1984.
41. Prabhat Patnaik, 'Inaugural Address', *National Seminar on India's Foreign Policy: Emerging Trends in the New Century*, Organized by V.K. Krishna Menon Study Centre for International Relations, Thiruvananthapuram, 2-3 April, 2007.
42. It is argued that domestic political and social demands for sustained higher GDP growth rates have forced India to join the march to globalization, which has increasingly shaped its foreign policy. For details, see: Walter Andersen, 'Recent Trends in Indian Foreign Policy', *Asian Survey*, Vol. 41, No. 5, September -October, 2001, pp. 765-776.
43. Dubey, *op.cit.*
44. Ramakrishnan, *op.cit.*, p. 34.
45. Today, India has very limited ambitions as far as the UN system is concerned. The permanent seat in Security Council is perhaps the only demand of India vis-à-vis the UN. Besides, India is more concerned about getting membership in the G-8 club and other forums of the rich countries.
46. Infamous description of Naxaism as the most dangerous domestic threat to security by Prime Minister Manmohan Singh is the best example.
47. Therefore, the ethnic movements are deprived of the revolutionary potential to restructure the world capitalist economy.
48. Since the beginning of 'open diplomacy' after the First World

War diplomacy lost its secrecy. Therefore, the foreign policy establishments adopted more congenial attitude towards the media to avert scathing criticism. The transformation of the mainstream media into an industry has brought it closer to the ruling class and the state at their disposal.

49. David Harvey explains the consent factor to explain the neo-liberalism's attempts to forge a political consent for the theoretical utopia in the following words: "So how, then, was sufficient popular consent generated to legitimise the neo-liberal turn? The channels through which this was done were diverse. Powerful ideological influences circulated through the corporations, the media, and numerous institutions that constitute the civil society–such as the universities, schools, churches, and professional associations. The 'long march' of neo-liberal ideas through these institutions that Hayek had envisaged back in 1947, the organisation of think-tanks (with corporate backing and funding), the capture of certain segments of the media, and the conversion of many intellectuals to neo-liberal ways of thinking, created a climate of opinion in support of neo-liberalism as the exclusive guarantee of freedom. These movements were later consolidated through the capture of political parties and, ultimately state power.
50. Partha S. Ghosh, 'Foreign Policy and Electoral Politics in India: Inconsequential Connection', *Asian Survey*, Vol. 34, No. 9, September 1994, pp. 807-817.
51. Raka Ray, Shelth and Katzenstien.
52. Chandhoke.
53. Prakash Karat.
54. Prabhat Patnaik, 'Reflections on the Left', *Monthly Review.*
55. BJP and Congress used different strategies to gain legitimacy to their same pro-US policies. The BJP fostered the support of its cadres and the public by means of propaganda of antagonistic nationalism presenting China and Pakistan as the national enemies. On the contrary the Congress, which partially depends on the antagonistic nationalism to gain public support, primarily received moral legitimacy in the middle class evaluation of which the benefits of globalization and cooperation with a powerful US are the key determinants of India's development and international status.

Index

Index

A
A.N. Prasad, 259
A.P.J. Abdul Kalam, 203
A.Q. Khan, 29
Abu Sayyaf Group, 157
Abu Sayyaff, 158
Achille Laura, 48
Admiral Gorshkov, 97
Al-Qaeda, 78, 133
Al-Qalqashandi, 224
Andaman and Nicobar Islands (AN), 9
Anglo-Saxon race, 145
Angola, 18
Anti-Money Laundering Act of 2009, 44
Arabian Sea, 5, 11, 68, 73, 180
Arab-Israeli War of 1973-74, 108
Arun Prakash, 119
ASEAN Regional Forum (ARF), 12, 154
Asghar Khan, 155
Asia-Pacific Economic Co-operation (APEC), 128
Association of Southeast Asian Nations (ASEAN), 129
Atal Behari Vajpayee, 35, 91
Australia, 18, 67

B
Bab el-Mandeb Strait, 37
Bahrain, 199
Bangladesh, 20
Barbary Coast, 19
Bay of Bengal, 11, 13, 64, 68, 95, 129
Bhabha Atomic Research Centre (BARC), 259
Bharatiya Janata Party (BJP), 35
Buddhism, 152

C
Cape of Good Hope, 70
Caspian basin, 108
Central Asia, 1, 18
Central Industrial Security Force (CISF), 50
China, 32, 67
Chinese People's Liberation Army-Navy, 10
Civilian Nuclear Agreement of 2008, 137
Coast Guard Act of 1978, 46, 47
Coja Mehmed Markar, 226
Cold War, 8, 89, 117, 154, 283
Communist Party, 35
Congress Party, 35

Conservation of Foreign Exchange and Prevention of Smuggling Activities Act (COFEPSA) of 1974, 44
Contact Group on Piracy off the Coast of Somalia (CGPCS), 22
Convention for the Suppression of Unlawful Acts against the Safety of Maritime Navigation,
Customs Auxiliary Craft, 55

D
Defence Framework Agreement, 137
Defence Policy Group, 79
Department of Atomic Energy (DAE), 257
Diego Garcia, 12, 73
Djibouti, 101

E
Egypt, 18
Egyptian Queen Hatshepsut, 212
European Union, 67
Exclusive Economic Zones (EEZs), 70
Extended Neighbourhood, 1

F
Far Eastern Naval Command, 159
First World War, 208

G
Geoffery Till, 8
Gerakan Aceh Merdeka, 157, 158
Gulf Co-operation Council, 199
Gulf of Aden, 22, 73, 79, 101
Gulf of Suez, 227
G.V.C. Naidu, 9

H
Hainan Island, 113
Hassan El Zayyat, 213
Hillary Clinton, 79
Hinduism, 152
Hormuz dilemma, 18
Hormuz Strait, 109
Horn of Africa, 18, 70
Hu Jintao, 72
Humayun, 230

I
India's Look East Policy, 8, 11
Indian Customs (Marine Organization), 41
Indian Maritime Doctrine 2, 27, 37
Indian Nuclear Doctrine, 6
Indian Ocean Littorals, 18

Indian Ocean Naval Symposium (IONS), 22, 69
Indian Ocean Region (IOR), 1, 3, 67
Indian Ocean Rim-Association for Regional Co-operation (IOR-ARC), 85
Indian Ocean, 20, 21, 67, 73
Indian Penal Code (IPC), 44
Indigenous Aircraft Carrier (IAC), 97
Indonesia, 9 18, 20, 67
Indo-US Civil Nuclear Deal, 203
Indus Valley, 15, 207
INS Khukri, 168
INS Nirupak, 168
Inter-governmental Panel on Climate Change (IPCC), 80
International Energy Agency (IEA), 189
International Fleet Review (IFR), 9
International Maritime Boundary Line (IMBL), 162
International Maritime Bureau, 79
Iran, 67
Iranian Islamic Revolution of 1979, 200

J

Japan Maritime Self-Defence Force, 37
Japan, 67
Jawaharlal Nehru Port, 56
Jawaharlal Nehru, 16, 93
Jemmah Islamiah (JI), 78, 158
Joint Declaration for Co-operation in Combating International Terrorism, 168
Joint Declaration on Security Co-operation between Australia and India, 141
Jusuf Kalla, 168

K

K.M. Panikkar, 68, 92
K.N. Chaudhri, 220
Korea, 67
Kumpulan Militant Malaysia, 158
Kumpulan Mujahideen Malaysian, 157
Kurt M. Campbell, 138
Kuwait, 199

L

Laskar Jihad, 158
Latin America, 71
Liberation Tigers of Tamil Eelam (LTTE), 41
Lombok Strait, 70

Look East Policy, 152, 177

M
Madagascar, 72
Mahabharata, 153
Maharashtra Control of Organized Crime Act (MCOCA), 45
Malabar Exercises, 11, 95
Malacca dilemma, 18
Malacca Strait, 68, 69, 70, 71, 109
Malaysia, 8, 18
Maldives, 9, 13, 20, 72
Malik Ayyaz, 230
Mamluk rulers, 223
Manmohan Singh, 35, 91, 154
Marine Police, 56
Maritime Dimensions of Foreign Policy, 19
Maritime Doctrine, 6, 82
Maritime Domain Awareness System (MDAS), 63
Maritime Low Intensity Conflict (MLIC), 49
Mauritius, 20, 69, 72
Middle East, 67, 71, 107
Ministry of Defence (MoD), 2
Ministry of Finance, 55
Ministry of Home Affairs, 58
Ministry of New and Renewable Energy, 193
Mir Abdul Rahman, 236
Mir Iyantullah, 236
Mount Sinai, 226
Mozambique, 9, 18, 20, 72
Multilateral Fissile Material Cut-off Treaty (FMCT), 257
MV Alondra Rainbow, 49
Myanmar, 20, 197

N
Nag Chaudhury Committee, 54
National Commission on Sea Governance (NCSG), 62
National Committee on Maritime Security (NCMS), 63
National Democratic Alliance (NDA), 256
NATO, 19, 143
Naval Diplomacy, 7
Navy Act, 1957, 46
New Global Order, 255
Nine Degree Channel, 70
Nirupama Rao, 71
Nizam of Hyderabad, 240
Non-aligned Movement (NAM), 154
Non-Proliferation Treaty, 36
Non-tate actors (NSA), 41
North Arabian Sea, 64

North Korea, 32

O
Oman, 20, 101, 199
Operation Active Endeavour, 39
Operation Desert Storm, 74
Operations Enduring Freedom, 74
Organization of Arab Petroleum Exporting Countries (OAPEC), 108
Organization of Petroleum Exporting Countries (OPEC), 108

P
Pacific Ocean, 73, 156
Pacific Shield, 83
Pakistan, 73
Panch Shila, 154
People's Liberation Army (PLA), 79
Persian Gulf, 5, 68, 82
Planning Commission of India, 187
Port Blair, 95
Prevention of Terrorism Act (POTA), 45
Proliferation Security Initiative (PSI), 24

Q
Qatar, 18, 199
Qing Dynasty, 118

R
Rajiv Gandhi, 41
Ramayana, 153
Red Sea, 5, 70
Regional Co-operation Agreement on Combating Piracy and Armed Robbery against Ships in Asia (ReCAAP), 22
Robert Kaplan, 23, 73
Royal Thai Navy, 163
Russia, 67

S
Sagar Prahari Bal (SPB), 51
Sakhalin Islands, 93
Samajvadi Party, 293
Saudi Arabia, 107, 199
Sea Lines of Communications (SLOCs), 2, 67
Sethsamudram, 186
Seychelles, 13, 20, 72
Shared Awareness and De-confliction, 22
Sheriff Hussein, 208
Ship Building Programme, 5
Singapore, 8, 21, 69
Singapore-India Maritime Bilateral Exercises (SIMBEX), 161

Six Degree Channel, 70
Somalia, 73
South Africa, 18, 20, 67
South Arabian Sea zone, 64
South Arabian Sea, 64
South China Sea, 5, 100, 113
Southeast Asian Treaty Organisation, 154
Soviet Union, 8, 89, 108
Sri Lanka, 9, 13, 20, 57, 69
Sri Vijaya, 152
Strait of Bab-el-Mandeb, 70
Strait of Hormuz, 70, 71, 93
Strait of Malacca, 37, 93
Sudan, 18, 197
Suez Canal, 37, 68, 70
Sunda Strait, 70
Suppression of Unlawful Acts against Safety of Maritime Navigation and Fixed Platform on Continental-shelf (SUA) Act, 2002, 45
Suresh Mehta, 3

T

Terrorist and Disruptive Activities Act (TADA) of 1987, 45
Thailand, 8
Tipu Sultan, 234
Treaty of Amity and Co-operation in Southeast Asia (TAC), 168
Tsunami, 78

U

US Pacific Command, 74
UN Security Council, 32
United Nations Convention on the Law of the Sea, 112
United Progressive Alliance (UPA), 255
United States Navy (USN), 10
United States, 67
Unlawful Activities (Prevention) Act (UAPA) of 1967, 45
US Maritime Strategy, 2007, 11

V

Vasco da Gamma, 208, 224
Venezuela, 197
Vietnam, 8, 21
Vikramaditya, 6
Vikrant, 6
Violent Non-state Actors (VSNAs), 159

W

Wayang Kulit, 153
Weapons of Mass Destruction (WMD), 243

Wen Jiabao's, 73
White Australia Policy,
145
World Bank, 109, 110
World War II, 107
WTO, 140

Y
Yemen, 69, 73, 101
Yudhoyono, 168